THE GREAT WOMAN SINGER

Refiguring American Music

A series edited by
Ronald Radano
and Josh Kun

Charles McGovern,
contributing editor

Licia Fiol-Matta

THE GREAT WOMAN SINGER

Gender and

Voice in

Puerto Rican

Music

Duke University Press   Durham and London   2017

© 2017 Duke University Press

All rights reserved

Printed in the United States of America on acid-free paper ∞

Designed by Mindy Basinger Hill

Typeset in Minion Pro by Westchester Book group

Library of Congress Cataloging-in-Publication Data

Names: Fiol-Matta, Licia, author.

Title: The great woman singer : gender and voice in Puerto Rican music / Licia Fiol-Matta.

Other titles: Refiguring American music.

Description: Durham : Duke University Press, 2016. | Series: Refiguring American music | Includes bibliographical references and index.

Identifiers: LCCN 2016031212 (print)

LCCN 2016034944 (ebook)

ISBN 9780822362821 (hardcover : alk. paper)

ISBN 9780822362937 (pbk. : alk. paper)

ISBN 9780822373469 (e-book)

Subjects: LCSH: Women singers—Puerto Rico. | Music—Social aspects—Puerto Rico. | Music—Political aspects—Puerto Rico.

Classification: LCC ML3917.P9 F56 2016 (print) | LCC ML3917.P9 (ebook) | DDC 782.0092/52097295—dc23

LC record available at https://lccn.loc.gov/2016031212

Cover art: Portrait of Lucecita Benítez for the LP *Soy de una raza pura*, original in woodcut by Antonio Martorell, 1973.

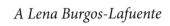

A Lena Burgos-Lafuente

La música (lo supe entre una y otra tienda)
era el perfume de un país, el recurso que quedaba
a ese cuerpo emputrecido para hacerse presente
de algún modo. Podía convertirse en anodina.
Adelgazar hasta no ser notada. Coquetearía con
su desgastamiento y, en determinado momento,
se alzaría prístina, metería el punzonazo.

ANTONIO JOSÉ PONTE

CONTENTS

ACKNOWLEDGMENTS

I feel very fortunate to have had the opportunity to engage with so many individuals and institutions that helped me out of sheer love for Puerto Rican music and the absolute certainty of its importance. My first thank you must go to maestro Antonio Martorell, for allowing me to use his beautiful image of Lucecita Benítez as the book's cover.

I honor the memory of Roxana Pagés Rangel and Marvette Pérez, staunch supporters of this book. Meeting up with them was always glorious. Thanks to Jossianna Arroyo, María Mercedes Carrión, Javier Guerrero, Lawrence La Fountain-Stokes, Fred Moten, Juan Carlos Quintero-Herencia, Julio Ramos, Milagros Ricourt, Raquel Z. Rivera, Rafael Rojas, Xavier Totti, and Alexandra Vazquez, who, at one time or another, lent concrete support to this project. I owe much to Ana María Ochoa Gautier, who enthusiastically backed my foray into music studies. Thank you to my dear friends Ivette Hernández-Torres and Luis Avilés for their incredible generosity in lending me their lovely home in San Juan, Puerto Rico. Over the years, their support truly amounted to the equivalent of a year's fellowship. Similarly, Yolanda Martínez-San Miguel and Eugenio Frías-Pardo have shared their pied-à-terre in San Juan, Puerto Rico, with me multiple times during the book's last stages, making it possible to conclude my work in a relaxed and welcoming environment.

My bud José Quiroga is always on my intellectual horizon. I thank him for his endless acuity and unwavering friendship. He is family. Thanks to another queer brother, Arnaldo Cruz-Malavé, for his constancy as much as his discerning capacity. Deborah Vargas and Yolanda Martínez-San Miguel have been great colleagues in the profession, important interlocutors, and fun, loyal friends. I have shared a steadfast personal and intellectual friendship with Ana María Dopico since we began our careers, back in the heady 1990s.

Rubén Ríos Ávila has influenced my thinking for years. First I admired him from afar, for impossibly lucid lectures on baroque and neobaroque poetics; then I had the honor of participating in Latin American queer studies panels in the 1990s with him. He has been an intellectual rock for me. Arcadio Díaz

Quiñones is my first mentor, all the way back to my undergraduate years. He taught me how to look at creative works historically, without sacrificing their aesthetic heart or enlisting any artist in the service of dogma. I have purposefully tried to emulate Sylvia Molloy's limpid-yet-hip scholarly style and her centering of the reader. Since her decisive engagement with gender studies in the 1980s, Sylvia has been the touchstone of an entire critical generation, to which I belong.

Three dear friends were deeply engaged with this work and remain present after their untimely passing. Leticia Stella Serra listened countless times to my ideas about this book and life in general in her lovely home at East 12th Street, not far from my own, in our beloved Manhattan. She faced a battle with ovarian cancer with great courage, teaching her "Fiolita" so much. José Esteban Muñoz was an absolutely unique person as well as luminous thinker. I will always expect to receive a text or e-mail with his witty nuggets, his gentle jabs, and his "You know I adore you." Thank you, my dear Mara Negrón, for your brilliance, grace, and affection. I had looked forward to many more years of meeting in San Juan, New York, and Paris *con Ernesto, Lena, y los muchachos, Rubén y Javier* . . . I miss you so very much.

I am happy to finally be able to thank the generous individuals who assisted me in all manner of archival inquiries and helped me in obtaining primary material. At the Archivo General de Puerto Rico, I thank María Isabel Rodríguez Matos and Marcos Nieves. Thanks to Tamara Yantín Ayala, Alfonso Giménez Porrata, and Pedro Malavet Vega for assisting me with Ponce-related queries. Thanks to John Pennino of the Metropolitan Opera Archives, Rob Hudson of the Carnegie Hall Archives, Yvonne Rivera Piccorelli of the Biblioteca Legislativa del Senado de Puerto Rico, Carlos Rivera of the Library of Universidad del Sagrado Corazón, Miguel Vega of the Colección Puertorriqueña, Luis Rosario Albert of the Archivos TuTV de Puerto Rico, David Morales of the Cuatro Project, and Pedro Juan Hernández of the Center for Puerto Rican Studies. For timely consults or assistance with archival materials, thanks to Eliseo Colón Zayas, Edgardo Huertas, David Marrero, Talía Rivera, Tristana Rivera, Yeidy Rivero, and Rafael Viera. I wish to render a tribute to the now-defunct Casa Viera in Santurce, Puerto Rico, where I regularly spent time perusing CDs and talking to collectors. Thanks to two dear friends in Havana, Cuba, Sigfredo Ariel and Norge Espinosa, and my close friends Gabriela Cano and Patricia Vega for welcoming me in their home at the Colonia del Valle, Mexico City, while I pursued research queries in Mexico.

There is no way to overstate the importance of archival collections to this work. My most important archival research sites were the Díaz-Ayala Cuban and Latin American Popular Music Collection, Florida International University, and the Colección Puertorriqueña of the University of Puerto Rico, Recinto de Río Piedras. I spent a charmed week at FIU and wish to thank the great librarians, especially Verónica González, for their assistance. I spent a couple of years, in the aggregate, at the Colección Puertorriqueña, a treasure trove for all Puerto Rican studies researchers. Its existence made this research affordable and it is my hope the Colección will be supported so other researchers can take as much advantage of its wonderful resources. I also thank the Archivo del Municipio de Arecibo, the Archivos TuTV de Puerto Rico, the Archivo General de Puerto Rico, the Fundación Nacional para la Cultura Popular, and the Ateneo Puertorriqueño. Warm thanks to the wonderful staff at the Archivo Histórico de Caguas.

Pride of place goes to the people I interviewed over the course of ten years or with whom I spoke on the phone to fill out my knowledge about the four singers covered. These conversations were both crucial and immensely rewarding. While grateful acknowledgments appear throughout the book, up front I must name the following: for chapter 1, heartfelt thanks to Velda González de Modestti, Helen Monroig, and Mariano Artau, who have since passed on; and to Glenn Monroig, Awilda Silva, and Miguel Angel Hernández. For chapter 2, I thank Silvia Álvarez Curbelo for an importantly clarifying conversation, and for her interest in this book; I also cherish the memory of interviewing Ruth Fernández herself. For chapter 3, effusive thanks to Carmen Ortiz, Joaquín Mouliert "El Pitirre de Fajardo," Luis Miranda "El Pico de Oro," and Egberto Almenas. For chapter 4, warm thanks to Ida de Jesús, Edna Rivera, Pedro Rivera Toledo, Javier Santiago, Gabriel Suau, and Roberto Tirado.

A group of individuals stand out in my gratitude. I truly struck gold when I found two ideal collaborators, Arturo Butler and Grego Marcano. Mr. Butler is a diehard fan of La Calandria and recalls taping her singing live in the bodega of his block in the Bronx while a young boy. I cannot thank him enough for letting me have copies of his personal collection of Calandria 78-rpm recordings. Marcano is the son of Piquito Marcano and steward of his father's legacy. Aside from obtaining important records and CDs, which were out of print and very difficult to find, I am very grateful to Grego for allowing me to use much of the visual material in chapter 3. Roberto Silva, who continues the art of *decimar* in Puerto Rico and mentors dozens of young *decimistas*, did not hesitate to share his contacts and thanks to him I was able to talk to several of the greats of jíbaro music. Osvaldo Rivera, archivist extraordinaire of the Radio Universidad de Puerto Rico, had just received the bulk of the Tommy

Muñiz Collection and was in the middle of processing the entire deposit when I contacted him. He shared his wonderful space with me for several days, a small office with two computers and various audiovisual machines where I could view items in older formats. Finally, an extended interview with Mita Torres proved to be one of the highlights of my research and a turning point in my thinking for chapter 4. I thank Mita for her time as well as for sharing invaluable archival materials that together helped me understand an entire artistic group of signal importance.

I wish to acknowledge the support I received in the form of grants from the Professional Staff Congress of the City University of New York (PSC-CUNY), through their Faculty Research Awards program; the CUNY-Caribbean Exchange Program, Centro de Estudios Puertorriqueños, Hunter College, City University of New York, through their Puerto Rican Diaspora Grants; the CUNY Diversity Projects Development Fund, City University of New York; and the Díaz-Ayala Travel Grant of the Cuban Research Institute and the Libraries at Florida International University. José Quiroga, Juana María Rodríguez, Arlene Dávila, and Arnaldo Cruz-Malavé read early portions of the manuscript and provided their typically lucid suggestions. Thanks as well to the anonymous readers for their invaluable feedback. Much gratitude goes to the Refiguring American Music series editors, Ronald Radano and Josh Kun. I greatly benefited from the legendary editorial acumen of my editor at Duke, Ken Wissoker. Yvette Nevares, my good friend, helped me immensely with the preparation of camera-ready artwork for the book. I am deeply grateful to the audiences that attended talks at various universities and conferences while I was researching and writing this book, and the colleagues who invited me. During the very final stage of production, I enjoyed the gracious assistance of Wilfredo José Burgos Matos.

My amazing sister-in-law Louise Murray has been not only family but also one of my closest friends for over two decades now, and a source of support through some very trying times. I also wish to acknowledge the sustaining presence of my adored nieces Najda Galib-Fiol and Zaimar Galib-Fiol, my brother-in-law Hamid Galib, and all my nephews and nieces over a couple of generations.

My music education began in my childhood home. My father, Juan Fiol Bigas, had a large record collection; he loved Caruso, Belafonte, marching band music, and opera. My mother, Emma Matta Méndez, loved all music, from classical to popular. She took me to the Festival Casals, my first live operas (*Aida* and *Carmen*, when I was about six years old), and numerous concerts and open-air events, including the unforgettable open-air, free concert Lucecita Benítez gave in La Puntilla in 1975. My sister Liana played the accordion; from her twenties on, she sang with the choir (her passion to this day). As a little kid I received letters from my sister Liza recounting her college visits to the opera in Washington, DC. Later I could not wait for Saturday to arrive, so I could spend the afternoon in her apartment in Hato Rey, where I would listen, wide-eyed, to her myriad tales about music and musicians. A gifted guitarist and singer, a wondrous musical storehouse and erudite, Liza is without a doubt the single most important influence on my experience of, and thinking about, music. My brother Juan played the trombone and brought late-1960s and early-1970s rock to my ears, including some of my perennial favorites (like the Moody Blues, *A Question of Balance*), played in his snazzy hi-fi stereo that he carted with him from college a few precious summer months a year. My sister Lynn never left the house without her guitar. I heard her sing with her guitar every single day of my childhood. She played her favorite records like any true fan, over and over. Thanks to her I listened to La Calandria and learned to respect jíbaro music. My brother Antonio played the trumpet and was a huge fan of Chicago; I know "Only the Beginning," "25 or 6 to 4," and "Does Anyone Really Know What Time It Is?" by heart. My sister Lía phoned Radio Uno every day to vote for her favorite artists and ask the DJ to play her favorite songs. Our family owned a record player that we children had to share among so many budding audiophiles, and I remember how Lía and I discussed which songs we were going to play in "our" turn. Since I idolized her, I always agreed with her selection. I still idolize her. My brother Carlos and I shared all our childhood years and music was a common language. We were religious in our weekly listening to the American Top 40 with Casey Kasem. Carlos bought progressive and punk records for his collection, although I had no idea as a kid that that's what the bands were called. He also gave me my first vinyls (I didn't own many more, being an '80s-cassette fiend): Donna Summer's *Bad Girls* and *Live and More*. *A la familia Fiol-Matta, gracias por el regalo de toda la música.*

As I began to write this book, I met Lena Burgos-Lafuente, whose musical knowledge is astonishingly capacious and who also comes from a music-loving family. She captivated me from the moment I heard her voice. She exponentially increased my listening with her loving playlists and huge MP3 collection. Thanks to her, I became more conversant about bolero, salsa, flamenco, décima, jazz, post-punk . . . She is the most perceptive and original thinker I know. I'm hooked. This book is for her.

INTRODUCTION
I AM NOTHING

In 1969, at the height of the Cold War, the Puerto Rican singer Lucecita Benítez won the First Festival of Latin Song in the World with her performance of "Génesis":

Cuando nada en la tierra quede que tibie el sol
Cuando nadie en la tierra quede que evoque a Dios
Cuando sobre la tierra no haya ya ni dolor
Solo habrá una lumbre y esa será el amor
¡El amor, el amor! ¡Para empezar!

When nothing is left on Earth to feel the warmth of the sun
When no one is left on Earth to invoke God
When not even pain will be felt on Earth
There will only be a flame and that flame will be love
Love, Love! To begin again!

Considering its lugubrious content, it seems odd, more than forty years later, that the music industry and listening public frantically celebrated "nothingness" in this very melodramatic way. The muscular symphonic orchestra rushed to keep pace with the singer who had appeared, seemingly, out of nowhere and literally came out of the nowhere that was Puerto Rico to Latin America, the United States, and the world.

Ironically, the singer's name means little light, akin to the flame of love that rises after the apocalypse's destruction in the last, triumphant bars of the song. It is not the name her friends and family use to address her: She is Luz, Luz Esther, or Lucy. Lucecita is a stage name, a diminutive that always has seemed not quite right for this mercurial singer, and yet also on the mark in Latin American Spanish as a signifier for the enormous affection she has evoked in generations of Puerto Ricans. "Lucecita" incorporates the love that the song names as the world's salvation — resonating with the adoration the singer easily provoked — but it also contains a kernel of societal diminution, mockery, and domestication: women as marginal, minor, and suspect.

The song attempted to re-create beginning and end, alpha and omega, genesis and dissolution. It was a response to both the terrifying prospect of global, nuclear annihilation, and the colonial condition of Puerto Rico that diminished social life. It stands as a testament to the increasing paranoia of the small colony, its anguish expressed as an anxiety over its smallness and presumptive incapacity to affect its destiny or the world's. "Génesis" also entailed a subliminal protest of the topsy-turvy gender and sexual world which the star, paradoxically enough, embodied in her dashing tuxedo and grippingly loud vocal volume. Its author, fellow Puerto Rican Guillermo Venegas Lloveras, found himself suddenly owing his major triumph to a masculine woman, one the public did not know how to read. At the dawn of her career, she was often described as "boyish" or "androgynous." In 1969, she disconcerted all of Latin America by presenting as mannish.

Venegas Lloveras could not have foreseen the artist's eruption onto the world stage with his song, since she had been a wondrous but inoffensive and "feminine" youth star up until that moment. He probably never imagined that his status as the songwriter of "Génesis" would become subordinate to the performer's. In a music industry practice that is not yet quite extinct, singers functioned as the placeholders for someone else's genius. Furthermore, that genius was invariably male, whether the songwriter's, musician's, or bandleader's.

Lucecita had transformed Venegas Lloveras's predictable song into a watershed sonic and visual event. She had single-handedly put Puerto Rico on the map. She was the one the adoring public rushed to see when the winning cohort returned to Puerto Rico. She was the figure that admiring singers and musicians came to respect. It is telling that in his 1992 memoir, Venegas Lloveras wrote, "Total genius is men's priority. A true man is he who can penetrate everything. Women were born for flirting, not for knowledge; to be dominated, not to dominate; to give children, not ideas. Do you know of a single woman who has attained the status of Thinker? A single woman who has shaken or altered the intellectual conscience of the world? Do you know of a single woman possessing an unparalleled probing capacity [*inigualable penetración*]?"[1] "Génesis" expressed extreme male melancholy, yet a masculine woman unexpectedly delivered this affect home. The songwriter's lament for women and men who did not conform to the expected roles of a misogynistic

and homophobic society, who dared usurp the masculine dor
among them — throws into the sharpest of relief just how ve:
cursion into pop music can be.

In Lucecita's case, no scripts were available to subordi
eruption. She was not feminine. She did not sing softly ω
erosexual love. She claimed the masculine prerogatives of expreω
and political ideas outside of marriage and motherhood, eschewing the ιω
that her managers sought to implant in her earliest persona. When it came to
representing difference, decked in her stage costume that night in Mexico and
armed with her mind-blowing delivery, she proved she had no intention of
merely supplying a commercial hook to sell songs.

Lucecita Benítez would become an international icon in only a couple of
years; would survive attempts to erase her career and silence her magnificent
voice; would claim her right to speak and not merely to sing; and would refuse
all imperatives to civility, moralism, and even proper nationalist performance. In
her later career, all the way forward to the 1990s, she would be baptized the
National Voice of Puerto Rico in the simulacrum of late colonial society, when
difference did become a commodity and nationalism coexisted with — indeed fueled — Banco Popular television specials honoring the people, selling
brands and financial products more than songs and music.

Lucecita's career arc is like a crash course in history combined with an embodiment of the crucible voice can throw us into. The absolute nothing of
dissolution, of ceasing to be, which "Génesis" evoked, gave way to the relative
nothing that the singer claimed for herself, when she informed the public
that it could not dictate what she was. "I am nothing," she said in 1974, furi-
ously and presciently. She was not legibility, but potentiality. She could not
be generalized: She was singular. That's what she meant when she said, "I am
nothing."

Lucecita troubled several paradigms that have dictated matters when it comes
to women's careers as pop singers, in Puerto Rico and elsewhere in Latin
America. Almost all women who entered pop when the pop music business
began did so under some kind of pressure to perform values — whether of the
moral kind, nationalism, the home and reproduction, or liberationist politics.
Lucecita was not the only singer in Puerto Rico who had troubled morality,
class-defined participation in music, or politics. In this book, I discuss three
other women who, each in their own way, did so too. And there are others.
However, Lucecita was, decidedly, one of the first women singers who broke

of any possibility of being described as a "great woman singer." The quali-
er did not make any sense after her triumph with "Génesis"; she became a
great singer, period.

This meteoric rise did not solve problems for the artist so much as it created an excruciating existence where she found herself increasingly dissatisfied with the content of her repertoire, to the point of asking herself, "Why
am I singing this nonsense?"[2] The answer is more complex than resorting
to a straightforward repressive paradigm, to recall Foucault's critique of how
power operates.[3] The "great woman singer" reveals the procedures of the
pop music singing career established as an arc, a feat of determination and
stamina, a fight to the death with oversignification, a zealous, successful stew-
ardship of persona, and the ultimately successful defense of the voice. It also
reveals the toils of the biopolitical uses of voice within a collectivity, and the
"distribution of the sensible" that makes plain an inside/outside partition.[4]
The book aims squarely at a critique of the logic of the exceptional — still the
critical rule in dominant accounts, despite commonsense knowledge about
marquee artists who were women since the nascent days of the pop music
industry in the region, back in the 1930s or so.

The Great Woman Singer refuses to espouse a predetermined idea of what
is feminist in music, nor does it seek to theorize what this standard of feminism in music might be. It is not a survey of women in music or a tracing of
resistance by women to the strictures of dominant music making. My interest
in the female pop music star is about querying instances where singularity
erupts despite heterosexism and misogyny, through the vehicle of voice. My
goal is to disrupt the normative business of scholarly studies on women artists. Overall, I aim to really listen to women's voices, in the sense of paying
attention to their conceptual dimension, away from notions of natural or intuitive performance.

I detail how four paradigmatically iconic artists elaborated their concept,
troubling the gaze on their figures as simple manifestations of artistic serendip-
ity or, alternatively, as creations made possible by male insufflations of spirit.
The book narrates their histories and analyzes their work outside the poverty
of critical tools and the near-universal gesture of dismissing women artists
as merely women singers.[5] Yet, it's not as easy as merely rejecting or ironiz-
ing the epithet, however much we may wish it gone from our consciousness.
The ideology we seek to disrupt influences our apprehension of these voices,
inescapably. If we do not critically isolate this problem of the collectivity — this
imposition of acritical listening — we won't be able to dispel it.[6] The grouping,

then, of these four artists qua women is a function of the hermeneutic: a move to unsettle matters, not to reaffirm them. Speaking of the voice as if it were not in actuality covered by gender (riffing on Hortense Spillers, who spoke of a subject "covered by race")[7] is simply to contribute to the further buttressing of the status quo we see verified in books on Latin popular music, which to this day only name Celia Cruz and La Lupe, usually in passing, in their surveys; or in university courses on Latin American popular music that can run for years without studying any women artists; or in the record store, however vanishing, that includes a section on women, which women are expected to browse and men should not approach lest they be taken for members of "the gender vanquished for all time, women."[8]

Politically speaking, the Cold War had crossed Lucecita's performance of "Génesis" in a chilling way. The prospect of nuclear war lent a hair-raising quality to the last verse of the song, "Sólo habrá una lumbre" (there will only be a flame). Regardless of whether the flame represented love, listeners were clearly preoccupied with extinction, with war. Several great women singers had labored within the protocols of the Good Neighbor policy and the Cold War, becoming either goodwill ambassadors performing the folklore of Latin America, like Libertad Lamarque; steamy sex symbols, like Carmen Miranda; or maternal stalwarts in Mexican movies, like Rita Montaner (although this great star was burdened with problematic "black" roles, such as the "mammy" figure of the 1948 *Angelitos negros* [Little black angels]). In this book, I refrain from making value judgments on any decisions to represent, preferring to investigate matters in terms of their historicity: what was allowed or possible, individual temperaments, and voice operating in the realm of the future perfect. The future perfect is the time of the *arkhé*, according to Giorgio Agamben:

> The *arkhé* towards which archaeology regresses must not be
> understood in any way as an element that can be situated in chronology
> (not even one with a large grid, of the sort used in pre-history); it is,
> rather, a force that operates in history — much in the same way in
> which Indoeuropean words express a system of connections among
> historically accessible languages; in which the child in psychoanalysis
> expresses an active force in the psychic life of the adult; in which the
> big bang, which is supposed to have originated the universe, continues
> to send towards us its fossil radiation. But the *arkhé* is not a datum or
> a substance — different from the big bang, to which the astrophysicists

try to assign a date, even if it is in terms of millions of years. It is much rather a field of bipolar historical currents within the tension of anthropogenesis and history, between the point of emergence and becoming, between arch-past and present. And as such — that is to say, to the extent to which it is, as anthropogenesis itself, something that is necessarily supposed to have factually happened, and which yet cannot be hypostatized in any chronologically identifiable event — it is solely capable of guaranteeing the intelligibility of historical phenomena, of "saving" them archeologically within a future perfect, yet not grasping its (in any case unverifiable) origin, but rather its history, at once finite and untotalizable.[9]

When it came to war and pop music, Lucecita troubled paradigms too. In early interviews, when she was a youth star, she had spoken out against the Vietnam War: "What's happening in Puerto Rican music is happening all over the world. We love independence and have a rebellious spirit. For instance, we are against the draft and we can make that part of our music. Why should we fight for something that does not concern us? Some people are looking for adventure but, there are so many dead Puerto Ricans and for what? For nothing, it is not our quarrel. I for one am against all these impositions."[10] Here we have an example of a disquieting, societal "nothingness" that is not the same artistic and political "nothing" she later claimed.

In "Génesis," Lucecita eschewed the edifice of goodwill. She presented as anything but folkloric in sartorial terms. Musically, she unleashed a powerful *balada* that departed from the esteemed Pan-Americanist *bolero*. Lucecita's performance of "Génesis" did not offer the "Latin American" sound, or the "American" sound of her youthful LPs. Even the theme of the song — planetary trauma — hardly corresponded to the usual fare women sang all over the hemisphere. Most women's pop hits were about failed heterosexual romances; hardly any were about the state of the world. That discourse was reserved for political song, which knew one "great woman singer" of its own by 1969, the Chilean Violeta Parra. Yet Parra became encased in the well-worn, gendered narratives of doomed love affairs and an unspecified depressive personality.

I am resolutely not interested in indicting any singer's political stances, or in interpreting any career as a reflection of personal woes. Critical biography is a mode of analysis in this book because, from a Benjaminian perspective, the "biographical historicity of an individual" contains what is allegorical in their life and therefore is an avenue to grasping the arkhé, what in history is "untimely, sorrowful, unsuccessful . . . expressed in a face, or rather in a skull."[11] Keying into the career of women singers must entail this approach to history for three reasons: Their histories have not been written, nor a general history of a collective subject; it is hard to piece together the actual sources of these histories, necessitating a method that will privilege the question over the answer; although associated with freedom and play, music careers in given contexts are very tough and often unsuccessful, notwithstanding the existence of talent. If we add to this women's dominant treatment as all nature, as body, animal, and so forth, the Benjaminian allegory emerges as not only suitable but also urgent.

In reconstructing an archive of voice, I do address and in certain cases re-dress the problems of omission, politics of memory, and, last but not least, plainly sexist approaches to popular music that still hold sway in popular culture. Yet my purpose is to examine embodied existences within the very dense grid of significations in which multiple subjectivities circulate, which includes music producers, arrangers, entrepreneurs, politicians, fans, and citizens who are not especially attracted to music. Women singers labor along the twin poles of adoration and derision. With the complexity of such affects in mind, I cite singers from Puerto Rico as paradigmatic for Latin American and American Studies. Adoration is presumptively benign, but the widely regarded positive aspects of music performance require critical attention, in order to detect their "patterning" effects.[12] We associate derision with disciplinary power. Examining contempt, aside from charting its obvious negative impact on careers, also affords insights into collective fantasy, which pop women singers symbolize in an easily consumable and shareable way. In this book, I examine the reining in, ordering, correcting, or training of women's vocal performances, but also the lines of flight opened up in these performances, their *écarts* and silences.

All the women I named in the preceding section, from the more straightforwardly political to the more conservative, were "great women singers" because a thinking voice took up residence in their careers, unleashing questions and providing answers — consciously or not — in response to the cultural moment of their times. In this book, a narrative toward elucidating how voice calls to thought unfolds, until the thinking voice appears fully formed in chapter 4. I mimic the qualities of "future perfect" that the voice in music performance must have, presenting the reader with a problem that takes its time in becoming graspable or knowable. Sidestepping dominant notions of voice, particularly notation (as in the highbrow musical pedagogy that recognizes voice solely as a musical instrument) and intuition (the widespread notion that a singer trades not in conceptual thinking, but only in spontaneous execution), I come to isolate the performing voice as an object (thinking voice in performance), while advancing the study of voice as thought producer (presenting the voice as it thinks, riffing on Martin Heidegger's treatise *What Is Called Thinking?*).

Chapter 1 details Jacques Lacan's treatment of the voice as part object or *objet a*. In a nutshell, the part object exists as both an illusion and its foil. I employ the part object to indicate the breach between associations of voice with plenitude and the reality that voice, in the last instance, represents lack or, to put it more colloquially, a puzzling absence that must be reckoned with and is not pacified by enjoyment (which musical voice represents for most listeners). Applied to the voice, the part object entails separating from accounts of the voice as always already knowable, as certain, and focusing on its status as having "no specular image, no alterity."[13]

The rest of the book follows this template, establishing a relationship to the archive but not allowing it to dictate interpretation. I have had in mind, among others, Sylvia Molloy, who pithily stated,

It is true that archival work is absolutely necessary as a starting point for any reflection on gender. But I would like to think that those of us who work on this unstable category of gender do it *from* gender more than *in* gender; that we are attempting to articulate, not just a reflection on gender, but a *re-flexion* (if I can be allowed the word game here), that is to say, a new *flexion* in the Latin American cultural text (in that text's totality, not in select parts) that will allow us to read otherwise, in many different "otherwises."[14]

While the book is, in a certain sense, an archive, bringing into painstaking play both sonorous and nonsonorous items from the past (and as such thinks from an archive), it is, above all, a critical theorization of voice and gender, with an anchor in psychoanalytic thought without being exclusively psychoanalytic. In "Recommendations to Physicians Practicing Psychoanalysis" (1912), Sigmund Freud explained the nature of psychoanalytic listening, which specialists often refer to as "distracted" or "wavering" listening: "[It] consists simply in not directing one's notice to anything in particular and in maintaining the same 'evenly suspended attention' . . . in the face of all that one hears. . . . To put it in a formula: [The analyst] must turn his own unconscious like a receptive organ toward the transmitting unconscious of the patient. He must adjust himself to the patient as a telephone receiver is adjusted to the transmitting microphone."[15] Peter Szendy usefully paraphrases Freud, closer to our purposes: "If I summon here the expression 'wavering listening,' it is of course because I am thinking of Freud's famous phrase, a phrase that might basically be saying this: the sense of a discourse is not a *given* to be deciphered, but must be *constructed conjointly* by the one who utters it and by the one who listens to it. It obviously does not go without saying that this *psychoanalytic* listening can be translated into the vocabulary and practice of *musical* listening."[16]

As in Freud's technological metaphors, this book's method imitates "the telephone adjusted to the microphone" and listens distractedly to all available objects in the sound archive. Needless to say, some sounds are distorted or missing. Others are too loud. Singers don't always speak into the microphone. And so it goes. An archive might give a sense of plenitude and illusion of mastery, but I have worked with its incompleteness and contingency in mind. I could also not include everything I encountered: A process of selection and indeed forgetting had to take place. Without the latter, I would have encountered a disquieting "nothing to say."

Relatively ignored, local music had been of passing interest to the Spanish imperial state. At the dawn of Puerto Rico's second colonial period, in the early twentieth century, professional ethnologists bolstered their credentials in managing imperial subjects through ethnographic recordings. Photojournalists trained in the American Works Progress Administration (WPA) presented the occasional portrait of the native musician. Columbia and RCA Victor pressed 78s according to the racist conception of ethnic music that Ruth Glasser encapsulates in her classic, *My Music Is My Flag*: "The record companies persisted through the years in treating Puerto Ricans and other ethnic audiences as dumb animals with an unreasonable instinct for music, or at best as mere sale ciphers."[17]

The *prócer* (founding father), the Spanish-born Manuel Fernández Juncos, cleaned up the lyrics of the revolutionary anthem into the official version of "La Borinqueña" in 1903. He simultaneously churned out wholesome children's ditties to be sung by rote by schoolchildren suffering from Spanish being intermittently, yet consistently, banned in instruction. The peasant figure, the *jíbaro*, was characterized as having only one talent — music — while Afro–Puerto Ricans were tasked with the entertainment of elites. Both were folklorized. Musical pedagogy evolved around European classical music and for decades was taught as the only music worth studying in a formal setting. Women in Puerto Rican music occupied a decidedly minoritarian place in the sounded world, being, in discourse and in the aggregate, representative of the qualities that made up the presumed secondariness of pop — capable, at best, of incidental music in the classical vein.

The state invested popular music with a degree of power and prestige upon the establishment of the Estado Libre Asociado (ELA, Commonwealth of Puerto Rico) in 1952. Controlling pedagogical channels from primary school to higher education, shaping markets after the ELA, creating the country's Institute for Puerto Rican Culture and other cultural institutions to advance its agenda, the state largely succeeded in its quest to employ music as palliative; revenue-generating arm of tourism to provide the needed "local color"; and card to assure investors that Puerto Rico was "peaceful" and, as such, represented a safe haven for investors. The climax of the state's success in controlling the musical happened in the 1950s and 1960s, captured in the 1957 David Ogilvy advertising campaign for the Festival Casals de Puerto Rico, "Pablo Casals is coming home — to Puerto Rico," paid for by the Commonwealth of Puerto Rico (figure I.1).

Naturally, the state could never control all of the arenas that affect touches, even if that is its sustaining fiction. The performance space is one arena where the designs of mandated enjoyment might falter. In this book, I trace both mandated enjoyment and when its designs fail. I unpack enjoyment's dependency on the performing, female body and detail when, how, and why various forms of control short-circuit, despite their certainty of managing women. I examine, in equal measure, the advantages of music as a profession where some women could craft a space of artistic expression, and the limitations of their careers in music.

With the ELA, song opened up to female stars, who were still regarded as exceptions. What was thought of as feminine subjectivity was barely considered a locus for creativity. As to women singers specifically, they entertained. They did not think. The lives and works I have selected came to exceed power's advantages as well as the limits power imposes. Hence their singularity. They also became uncannily aligned with standardized music genres, immediately putting them in touch with larger cultural scripts. As women who persevered in the face of a world that denied them the hallowed space of the artist, women who succeeded as professionals but also became icons, the four artists studied in this book give the lie to normative functions of music, showing the

FIGURE I.1 Ad, "Pablo Casals is coming home — to Puerto Rico," *New Yorker*, February 2, 1957. The government of Puerto Rico sought to advertise the island to foreign investors and tourists by promoting a festival of classical music, signifying refinement and civilization. Reputedly this single ad helped to boost tourist expenditures by the millions. Removing the cellist from the picture avoided the risk of "visual bromide."

parallel ability of music to disrupt and reorder a variety of injunctions, among them how enjoyment should proceed and where, how patriotic allegiances should be expressed, how obscenity should appear in the repertoire, how politics should enter music lyrics, and how consumption should become the main activity of subjects in capitalism.

As elsewhere, the Puerto Rican musical constellation has many more women singers than I can study here, many excellent in their own right, many beginning full-fledged careers around the founding of the ELA in 1952. They have loyal fans and successful records, despite the industry's prejudiced practice of limiting the number of women recording artists because they felt that women did not sell records since women did not buy records. However, the

resent four careers that are singular within this context, which
rouping to consider voice, gender, power, and thought.

Off . . . the Nation," reviews Myrta Silva's (1927–1987) stel-
ail how the artist was able to wrest the dominant percep-
female performing body and create a highly autonomous
ptual intervention, which I theorize as a cynical ethics. This meet-
ng ground of Jacques Lacan's ethics and Michel Foucault's parrhesia focuses
on the relationship between speech and song. Contra Jacques Derrida's famous critique of the autoaffectivity of voice in *Voice and Phenomenon*, which
assigned voice a metaphysical burden that it simply could not shake off, Myrta
Silva as figure and her simultaneous practices of *parlando* and self-reference
mock the very idea of autoaffectivity and provide a template from which to
examine similar uses of speech-song and self-referential lyrics. This chapter
sets up an extended meditation on the obscene as the obverse of a cleaned-up
repertoire, as the stage from which to construct an approach to the symbolic
capacities of voice. The star female body veers from being apprehended as a
beautiful object visually to becoming a visual disturbance in multiple ways,
while her vocal capacity to enthrall through play with voice's role in the symbolic order dispenses with notions of the beautiful as the needed identity of
presumptively female pop music. Voice is installed in thought instead. Silva
proved that an exceptional pop voice is one that knows how to foreground
listening. I examine Silva's voice also as a television producer, host, gossip
columnist, and social chronicler, which together comprise the totality of her
figure and represent the multifaceted aspects of voice. The chapter rescues her
musicality from accounts that have buried it, examining her repertoire of self-
referential songs, many obscene, and articulated almost completely around
word play. Concomitant with a psychoanalytic understanding of voice as part
object, the treatment of words is not just semantic but sounded. Of all the
singers studied in this book, Silva comes closest to having carefully thought
her singing.

Chapter 2, "So What If She's Black?," discusses Ruth Fernández (1919–2012),
a black contralto working in pop genres whose nostalgic self-narrative of star
inception would point us to a linear account of progress from early U.S. empire to the modern Commonwealth of Puerto Rico. An unusual call, "So what
if I'm black?," is the center of a preoccupation over being, the classic analytic
quandary. This call is not a statement as much as a demand, for recognition
as much as reparation. It is difficult to decipher. The protestation indicates a

permanent suspension in which metaphysical and ontological questions are never settled. While race is an important analytic in chapter 1, it takes center stage in chapter 2, not primarily because the singer was black (although this is no small detail in a racist society) but because the singer's entire career is threaded around this cry and its attendant societal questions: What are you, and why are you? Are you a woman? Should you exist as a singer? Dialogical models are put to the test in a radically unequal structure of interlocution. I isolate intra- and intergroup interpellations figured in songs, together fissuring the oneness of the polity that "nationalist sonorousness" attempted to manufacture in the early days of developmentalism in Puerto Rico and through its heyday in the 1950s and 1960s (as elsewhere in Latin America).[18] Here the star female body is routinely derided as unsuitable visually and attractive sonically. The chapter's twist is this subject's entry into the certifiably political sphere, where she helped install a conservative mode of thinking via pop music, manipulating the listener as shrewdly as chapter 1's exemplar even if, ultimately, her decisions might have restricted the freedom of her music.

Chapter 3, "Techne and the Lady," pivots to migration and music. It seeks to prove the solidity and importance of more modest forms of the star female body, and their crucial role in the larger structure of which they are a part, refuting the general notion that huge sales numbers and big markets alone determine fame. Each Latin American nation has its own set of local stars, like Ernestina Reyes, La Calandria (1925–1994), who perhaps did not reach hemispheric fame but were critical to localized musical politics. These stars often found their reception in circuits excluded from today's archive of music, which mostly records middle-class practices of middlebrow culture and middlebrow attempts to enter musical culture considered high in the pedagogical imagination of music (classical music). In this scheme, country music mattered only as occasional spice or entertainment, or as values vessel. Country musicians often were forced to create personas that were buffoons or dim-witted. Some knowledge of their practices is available in manuals of folkloric music, anthropological investigations into instruments, preserved ditties, and folk songs, all studied within the matrix of the national popular. Focusing on local circuits of exchange that underwrite the star female body in Latin American country musics dislodges the primacy of lettered interpretations, and their moralizing injunction toward collective representation, in favor of an aesthetics of the moment favoring bricolage and invention. La Calandria mobilized a prototypical women's folk voice, similar in color and texture to those found in flamenco, *perico ripiao* merengue, or Mexican *rancheras* (the latter was a favorite genre of the singer's and her working-class audience). Calandria was fun loving and unconventional, embodying country music's class-defined aesthetics, which seemed garish and uncouth to elite listeners but were delightful to the working-class audiences of Puerto Rico and New York. She pursued her free-wheeling, party-going ethics in the jíbaro milieu, which was more permissive and elastic than middle-class, highly capitalized entertainment, thus putting an accent on the present and undercutting the state's tight conceptualization of temporality and women's role in its reproduction.

Chapter 4, "The Thinking Voice," grows out of the three preceding chapters, which lay out an argument for understanding the propitious moment when this voice emerges, showing how—along with the exhilaration it provokes—the voice carries with it the history of struggles, the reality of duress, and the relative triumph of endurance. Pure pop is not readily associated with thought, although female stars often evoke feelings precisely because they only come to being as creatures of thought. Usually propped up on spurious grounds that have little to do with their own conception of self (sometimes when they are too young to have one to begin with), they have to truly fight to the death in order to arrive at independence of concept — to formulate an alternative to heteropatriarchal ideas of what their art should be about and the form it should take. Otherwise they are simply mowed down, spit out by the machine when capital is done with them. If, on top of that, a singer becomes aligned with the arkhé, the expression of thought in voice reaches beyond the recording, concert hall, or TV screen into the very psychic structure of a collective. This I demonstrate by taking Lucecita Benítez (b. 1942) seriously as a musician. Identified with left-leaning politics, the artist's residence there and elsewhere was never entirely comfortable. Lucecita traversed successive stages when she changed personas very swiftly, going from being a youth star in the 1960s to her three iconic incarnations: the auteur of the late 1960s, the artiste of the early 1970s, and the diva of the 1980s. I examine these in turn.

In music, you have to play the cards you're dealt. Women artists know this from the get-go. Their lives as working musicians are complicated. Aside from all the labor that most musicians face, the years of debt if not poverty, the long hours playing and recording (often for a pittance), women singers must confront their intense symbolization, one whose decisive elements they have a tiny or no hand in shaping. The women portrayed here are remarkable for their intellect, iconic significance, and influence. All expressed ambivalence about the pedagogical imperative to represent what national music should: respectability, accomplishment, values, and triumph. In one way or another, all expressed, directly or subliminally, the philosophical protestation, "I am nothing." All have been subjected to an oblivion that, up to this day, remains as profoundly puzzling as it is disturbing, rendering them as the "nothing" in pop.

As in the Festival Casals ad, where the machinery of advertising evacuated the body of the world-famous cellist, absented any hint of the act of performance or any visual trace of listening to performance, and stated that the inclusion of Casals playing the instrument would be equivalent to a "visual bromide," the nothing is the center of this book, its key.[19] My approach to the nothing, though, proceeds to different ends from that of the ad, resolutely away from Latin America as paradise and Latin Americans as natural-born performers for someone else's pleasure and profit. I do not expel the visual from my archive. I do not make claims for the sonorous over the visual. I place them side by side as part objects, elements of a sensorium, while centering the sounded voice. I listen "distractedly." Not confined to the nation-state, or any regional understanding of the musical phenomenon, the inquiry that follows hopes to approximate what Lauren Berlant wrote of the "case": "When it doesn't work to change the conditions of exemplarity or explanation, something is deemed merely a case study, remanded to banal particularity. When it does, a personal or collective sensorium shifts."[20]

ONE
GETTING OFF . . . THE NATION

In a 1973 interview, the mercurial Puerto Rican singer, entertainer, and entrepreneur Myrta Silva stated, "*I'm a winner.* I only failed at the beginning of my career . . . ever since I became a public figure, I have never once failed."[1] Despite the singer's confident declaration, Silva was well aware of the entanglement between "figure" and "failure." She learned that failure was always around the corner when she set foot in New York City as a barely teenaged immigrant, circa 1938.[2] She emigrated, she said, to become an artist. Born in Arecibo, Puerto Rico, in 1923, Silva lived in poverty in the big city along with thousands of Puerto Rican and Latino immigrants, working an average of twenty-five revue shows a week as a means of support and a way to initiate her music career.

In a milieu Ruth Glasser lucidly describes as dominated by U.S. recording companies and their demand for "ethnic music," Silva advertised her talent to RCA Victor as a guaracha singer.[3] She staked her claim on her special affinity with the genre by describing herself as matching the genre's temperament in personality terms: "On my own initiative, I went to the RCA Victor offices, and asked to speak to the head of the Latin department, making it clear that if he did not see me they would lose out on the best guaracha singer there was, of this new Latin American genre."[4] Approximately three decades after Silva's daring stunt, in 1966, *TV Radio Mirror* would run a bilingual spread on Silva, "The Fat Golden One/La Gorda de Oro."

> In 1939, a young lady walked into radio station WARD in Brooklyn, said she was a great star and so impressed people that she was put to work singing and doing commercials. After her first show, for which she was paid one dollar, she sent herself one hundred fan letters. The young lady was Myrta Silva and she was thirteen years old. Today, Myrta doesn't have to send any fan letters to herself, since she has one

of the most devoted audiences in television. Myrta's show, *An Hour with You*, is aired live over Newark's WNJU-TV, the New York metropolitan area's first commercial UHF television. And that hour — Monday evening from 9 to 10 — is seen by over 90 per cent of the area's Spanish-speaking viewers.[5]

In 1967, Silva was awarded the *TV Radio Mirror* prize for producing TV's Top Variety Show in New York, and WNJU-TV received the award for Outstanding Programming in the Broadcasting Arts, for *The Myrta Silva Show*. Silva had become a beloved representative of the Puerto Rican community in New York of the 1960s. While hers was a Spanish-language show, the prize was for all New York–area television, not just Latino TV. Puerto Rican newspapers ran the news, citing the magazine's circulation of six million and the prize's standing as the oldest such prize at the time in the U.S. radio and TV industry. Silva is quoted as saying,

I accept this prize in the name of all us *hispanos* who live in New York City, so that it may serve as an incentive, so that you can see that your sacrifices and struggles have not been in vain. I am humbly grateful, because, above all things, this prize equals the recognition of Puerto Rican talent wherever we may find ourselves. Personally, I can say this is the greatest prize I have received in my twenty-seven years in show business. Most significant is the fact that this prize has been awarded to me in this city of New York, the greatest city on earth, and where I started my career going hungry and earning a miserable salary of fifteen dollars a month.[6]

From the beginning of her career, she had cared about Latinos in the city. She had been one of them. Silva debuted at the Atlantic Theater in Brooklyn in 1939, became a regular in New York venues like the Teatro Hispano, Teatro Puerto Rico, and Carnegie Hall, and kept a residence so she could maintain New York as the home base of her artistic operations. Among her many leadership actions in her crowning, 1960s years, she joined a protest against *Playboy* magazine for running a spread offensive to Cuban women and led a protest against Ed Sullivan in 1968 for derisive remarks about Puerto Rican women in one of his TV broadcasts.[7]

While she triumphed in New York City, and pioneered Latino television in the United States, her beloved Puerto Rico had become viciously split about its biggest star. Viewers were quick to question her national allegiances and harbored an uncomfortable-to-repulsed attitude toward her unmarried, yet sexual status. Silva's declaration of her greatest love — for her mother, Mamá Yeya — surfaced on occasion as palliative: "Es lesbiana, pero buena hija" [She's a lesbian, true, but she's a good daughter]. Other viewers simply went into panic mode, ordering their children to "turn off the TV; we don't watch that dyke in our house." The epithet of the Fat Golden One encapsulates the quandary of simultaneous hatred and adoration: Being called fat in Puerto Rico was completely insulting, and certainly desexualizing, but the adjectival phrase "de oro" conveyed feelings of appreciation and a statement about sterling character.

Even today, music critics and journalists use this soubriquet that Silva resented, in addition to the infantilizing diminutive *gordita* or *nuestra gordita*. Beyond these problematic appropriations and rejections, perusing music history books yields the conclusion that Silva, arguably the single most successful Puerto Rican twentieth-century pop star, appears as a footnote to a history narrated around male figures, a history written in lockstep with national-popular teleologies of cultural identity and progress. Figures like Silva have merited only a few lines or, at best, cursory mentions in brief articles devoted to women artists or composers. How can this narrative be written otherwise? What did Silva crystallize as an artist, and how did it happen? What are the stakes of this career and why has its illustriousness been all but forgotten? This chapter steps back in time to provide an archive-based genealogy to contextualize this shocking oblivion — an account based on music culture, not patriarchal and heteronormative fantasies.

Silva had a developed and conceptual understanding of her voice. At her most memorable, she used this vehicle against enforced strictures of sexual and gender behavior, targeting dominant bourgeois morality. She was never malleable and saleable. Silva believed completely in her artistic, individual, and social autonomy while refusing to be expelled from belonging and her right to have opinions, no matter how unpopular. Silva's triumph despite gender strictures (including her accomplishments in the business arena of the music industry) made the establishment very uncomfortable indeed. This discomfort was displaced onto insidious characterizations of her personality and artistic temperament. The few authoritative accounts of Myrta Silva's career have contributed to naturalize the dominant culture's construction of Silva. This gendered writing hampers Puerto Rican music criticism more generally and becomes onerous in the case of Latin American women artists of the twentieth century, who have received scant critical attention but many sexist interpretations.

Concretely, Silva was accepted into the guaracha and marginalized in the bolero. Incredibly, as a songwriter of intimate, reflective music, Silva was constantly under suspicion as a fake or, worse, a thief. She responded by consciously playing with an equivocation not of her making, namely, the inappropriate relationship the public established between her person and her persona, on the one hand, and music critics between her comedic singing and her bolero songwriting. From the start, she worked in two parallel voices. One was the party, ethnic, singing voice of guaracha (where Silva's own contributions were often erased in legal credits) and the other the Pan-Americanist, universalist voice of the bolero (a songwriting voice recognized legally but from which Silva was discouraged as a singer).

As an individual, Silva was certainly stung by the public reduction of her musicianship and musicality. Addressing negative comments about her vocal instrument decades after her first hits, Silva retorted, "I've done pretty well with my lousy voice." Referencing her desire to sing the famous bolero "Júrame" by the acclaimed Mexican songwriter María Grever, she quoted a conversation between the two. Silva reportedly told Grever, "Since I don't have much of a voice, I can't sing some of your songs," to which Grever responded, "You have what it takes to sing my songs, and that is heart, not a great voice."[8] Throughout her career, Silva called attention to voice as an entity that did not have to be only or primarily musically virtuosic in order to command an audience and own a song. Instead, she put into play a virtuosity that José Esteban Muñoz has linked to queer artistry: the brilliant, conceptual staging of negativity and failure.[9]

During her first decade of work, Silva developed a rich musical repertoire, covering guaracha, rumba, son, and bolero. She cut her chops as a percussionist and bandleader. She worked under contract to Victor on hundreds of recordings from 1938 to 1948. She later jokingly referred to her identity in most of them as "Vocal Refrain," indicating an unrecorded history of musical labor.[10] In the 1930s, she recorded several 78s with local bands in New York City until she met Rafael Hernández and he signed her to perform with his group, Cuarteto Victoria, in 1939. The standard tale is that Hernández "discovered" Silva, thus birthing her musical career.[11] The discovery narrative, a common trope in the writing of women's artistic careers, might unwittingly obscure Silva's initiative, ambition, talent, and musical labor prior to getting her first big break. It was Silva's parody of "Ahora seremos felices" (We shall be happy, at long last), her very first RCA recording (with the Julio Roqué Orchestra), that drew Hernández's attention. Upon meeting him at a Roqué dinner party, Silva told him on the spot that his music for "Ahora seremos felices" was "a piece of crap" and that he should be thankful that she had written new lyrics. (The adult Silva spoke of her parodic lyrics as "abominable" and expressed regret at having "assassinated" Hernández's song, an action she ascribed to her youth. Yet the parody works brilliantly.)

Hernández knew he had found a musical gem. He hired her as Cuarteto Victoria's female lead on a tour to Puerto Rico and Colombia, single-handedly raising the group's profile exponentially throughout the Americas. Even at such a young age, Silva had a canny understanding of what makes a music performance work and was an innate talent scout (for example, she discovered Bobby Capó singing in Old San Juan, and it was at her bidding that he became male lead for Victoria for a brief stint, launching his own, illustrious career in Latino pop). Hernández met Silva as an impossibly young female migrant who had become an artist against all odds. Silva earned ten dollars a record with RCA and five dollars a show with the Cuarteto Victoria. The older Silva vividly recalled these years:

> I'm an artist thanks to God's gift to me, namely, my stage presence, which I learned by working in theater. At age thirteen I became a presenter without ever having done it, simply because dire need forced me to. I was asked: do you know how to host a show? And I said: *Are you kidding? I'm the best!* But, have you hosted a show? *I'm telling you, since I was born!* In truth, I had never set foot on a stage. But I did then, and I was hired, and I spent three months as the MC of a show in the Teatro Hispano, on 116 and Fifth Avenue, yes, in the place where children were skinned alive. I was a child, and I survived; I'm still alive.[12]

The gritty, hypersexual, and harsh delivery that later listeners reflexively came to associate with Myrta Silva's personality grew out of an intersection between her naturally subversive temperament and the spaces she first worked in, where sentimentality and romanticism were completely out of place. Even at thirteen years old, Silva understood how critical persona was to success. She read the guaracha as framing especially well in the context of the rising recording industry, with its hunger for an ethnic Latino market along with dominant, predatory male fantasies of the woman singer.

Silva had gained fame by the time she began recording under sole billing around 1942. For decades, she maintained a unique and ultimately successful focus on building a whole enterprise aimed at financial and artistic independence. She achieved artistic independence in a few short years. RCA Victor paid tribute to Silva in Buenos Aires in 1950 as their best-selling artist for the Latino/Latin American market in 1947, 1948, and 1949. Financially speaking, however, things had been quite difficult throughout the 1940s, despite her fame. It was a time when the music industry extracted profit from underpaid artists and songwriters pretty much at its will.

Most specialists regard the 1940s as Silva's finest musically. She recorded dozens of 78 records during this time and had her greatest hits. When Silva started adding her cunning improvisations to song lyrics, her contributions to lewd songs went beyond simply acting the part of the Lolita that had been the basis of her early hits. As the 1940s wore on, she wrote elaborate recitative segments and provided song sketches to Cuban composers, most notably Ñico Saquito (Antonio Fernández). The child sex object figuration gave way to a fully developed, autonomous creation with no easy categorization, defying concepts of authorship confined to the legal songwriter.

In 1943 Silva became the first woman *timbalera* certified by the American Federation of Music, quite an achievement. She was a self-taught musician *que tenía la clave* (could follow the beat, usually 3/2). Silva's percussive approach to voice, particularly in her interpretations of guarachas, constitutes a breakthrough for female singing. She was an extraordinary *sonera* and, adding to her innate musical ear, understood the conceptual density of cadence (known by its various vernacular names, such as *el tumbaíto* and *mi cantao*). Playing the timbales, *soneando*, and bandleading: These musical capabilities inched her toward the masculine position in pop (and let's not forget that this was, decidedly, a man's world). Except for the occasional all-girl band, Silva's positioning was simply unheard of. Her genius lay in her uncanny and differently gendered ability to connect with the audience beyond passing entertainment value. She describes it as a capacity for improv: "I've always worked without a script. I am only great if the audience is. If the audience isn't into it, neither am I. . . . As we say in musical jargon, I work *ad lib*. The band can't keep time when I work, it can't bend me to its will, because I work *ad lib*."[13]

When Silva moved back to her native Puerto Rico around 1950, she achieved her goal of financial independence, becoming an influe   ' f ᵐᵒᵘˢ producer, TV host, and media personality. What is less kn
scores of artists in their careers. She unfailingly supɩ
featured all kinds of music and musicians in her sho\
Guillot, Eartha Kitt, and La Lupe to classical pianists Lᵢ
Sanromá. Silva's musical breadth is simply remarkabl

FIGURE 1.1 Album cover, Myrta Silva, *Por el norte
y por el sur: Recordando el pasado (Remembering
the past)*, Extra Records LL13, 1960s?. Compilation
of earlier hits. Silva is about sixteen years old in this
picture.

genius for the comedic in music performance, which she developed beyond
music performance into television and print journalism, expanding the reach
of her voice, a picture emerges of a figure far past her analytical due in Latin
American and Latino pop and gender studies of music and ethnicity.

Silva was always regarded as "all body," and her singing coded along this
presumptive excess. Initially the Lolita figure, she became the worldly sexual bombshell, and eventually and unwillingly morphed into the disgusting
object, bodily signified through the culture's scandalous reaction to an overweight woman past her thirties who continued to be sexually explicit and
outspoken. Figure 1.1 is an album cover featuring a very early, undated publicity photograph of Silva. Silva sports the tools of her trade, the maracas, and
stands in front of a prop (what appears to be a fake conga). Obviously, both
instruments immediately call forth consumption-driven *latinidad*, a spectacle
of ethnic identity. Silva is the image of party, excess, and fun, a visual portrayal
amplified by the inclusion of percussive instruments. The conga appears as

FIGURE 1.2 Myrta Silva with the Cuarteto Victoria, circa 1935. Courtesy of the Archivo General de Puerto Rico.

a phallic visual prop, not an instrument she played competently; a flimsy-looking column (a frequent item in contemporary portraits of women singers) visually underscores the patriarchal framing. Silva was an expert maraca player, but the photographer probably had in mind the parallel between the maracas and breasts, a common sexual pun in the contemporary imaginary to this day. The maracas join dance music, Silva's body, and Silva's given name to sex and good times. Her name is scribbled on the side of the conga drum, taking on a life of its own independently of how Silva's body is framed, decisively aligning Myrta Silva with percussion in a conceptual, musical manner. Although her voice's incorrigibility is inseparable from Silva's success since her earliest artistic work, it's de-emphasized in this shot. Silva's mouth is closed as she grins.[14]

Figure 1.2 is a portrait with the Cuarteto Victoria, slightly later than the publicity still in figure 1.1. This is one of several portraits that reflect the nascent Pan-Latino aesthetic dominating the music industry in New York in the 1930s and its representation of race as well as gender. Silva occupies the central position in the group of men. She is starting to resemble the mature artist but has not quite arrived at her visual autonomy. The wide grin and her bold, cross-legged stance were considered uncouth and unfeminine in photographs of Latin women singers. The maracas now sit right atop Silva's pubic area, reinforcing puerile puns about percussive instruments and women's bodies. Silva is dressed *a la guarachera*, representing the group's ethnic appeal through rising Latino genres.[15] The men are nattily dressed in suits and photographed without their instruments. In other portraits, they are seen with *rumbero* attire as part of their stage personas. The Victoria men were unable to separate themselves completely from racial and ethnic spectacle, but were not dependent on this costume or this persona more generally for success, and they were not associated with this iconography in the larger sense of discourse, as happened with Silva.

The musicians adopted Silva for contrast at more than one level. The group created a repertoire that played a pivotal role in shaping the ethnic Latino pop canon in the early twentieth century. Victoria built a dual repertoire, appealing to feelings of nationality and nostalgia that presented as pure and moral, on the one hand, while delighting audiences with another set of obscene songs with the woman singer as *punctum*, much like Silva in this photo, on the other. Beyond the superficial representation of the female body for merry consumption, Victoria capitalized on Silva's brilliant, thoroughly musical manipulation of the "other side" of codes of decent belonging. A series of visual cues indicates the moment when live performance joined the two repertoires onstage. Silva holds her instrument; simultaneously, the men exist as subjects above the materiality of instruments and the body, in a more abstract connection to music and culture. They hover over the woman lead singer in a vague gesture of ownership, while she is charged with materializing the ethnic sound.

Race is displaced onto Silva and away from the men. Stating the obvious, Silva was white skinned and the Cuarteto Victoria members were Afro–Puerto Rican. Just as with the guaracha's ambivalent racial character, the picture deposits unresolved meanings and struggles in her sexualized body, signified by her own body as well by as other signs, including the maracas, the folkloric, Afro-Cuban dress, and Silva's headscarf (derived from the *teatro bufo* and its *mulata* type). Like the *cabareteras* of famous Mexican movies of the 1940s and especially 1950s, Silva as artist, more generally speaking, recalls the culture's ambivalence toward its racial identity.[16] Its championing of its musical trove of genres during this period, many Afro-Caribbean, did not address antiblack

FIGURE 1.3 Myrta Silva performing "Nada" on the Banco
Popular special in tribute to an ailing Rafael Hernández,
1965. She is seen leading the band.

racism, much as the emergence of wildly popular women artists didn't resolve
the sexism of the music industry.

Figure 1.3 portrays Silva at the pinnacle of her career in television in the mid-
1960s, more than two decades later. This footage of a live performance shows
her performing her signature song, "Nada" (Nothing), in a TV special dedicated to an ailing Rafael Hernández in 1965.[17] To unbiased eyes, juxtaposing
the young and the middle-aged Silva may simply evoke the passing of time.
The first two photographs portray a precocious youngster; the third is the same
woman years later, well into a hugely successful career. To music-oriented
eyes, the older Silva occupies a different musical position from the two early
stills. Silva leads the band. She has musical authority. The microphone underscores her act of singing, making her voice indexically present and central as
she fronts the full orchestra. Yet to the sexist and homophobic eyes of dominant
culture, Silva's looks and actions in the third photo ranged from unsettling to
unacceptable. This, despite Silva's elegant clothes and plenty of bling, indicating her passage from working to upper-middle class and from working singer
to multifaceted musical force. From being the sexualized adolescent figure of
the late 1930s to the sexual bombshell of the 1940s, Silva turned into a desexualized figure upon which the public imposed its narrative: a loss of sexual appeal; a tragic love story to account for further disinterest in worldly pleasures;

and unspecified episodes of a derailed life. Yet Silva was not a victim of alcoholism or any substance abuse. She was firmly in control of her business. She evoked paroxysms of adoration and glee, evinced by the literally hundreds of photographs of, and extensive print articles about, Silva across the Americas. And she had, by all accounts of her personal friends, a very satisfactory personal life, including life partners.[18]

THE ABUNDANCE OF LACK

When music critics silence Silva by desexualizing her, they appeal to a simplistic definition of lack: Silva lost the capacity for sexuality and never got it back, thus her voice deteriorated and she turned to a pathetic existence as a bolero songwriter, in contrast to her glorious years as a guaracha singer. Silva wrote some of the quintessential boleros of the Latin Americanist repertoire, and her contribution should not be minimized. However, it is true that her genius at guaracha remains unparalleled; one could argue she is peerless. In the normative account, this guaracha success follows from her identity as sexual bombshell or prototypical nymphet of heteronormative fantasy. This is a notably shallow way to render Silva's performance of the obscene, hallmark of the guaracha. There may be a political move in obscuring the conceptual depth Silva gained with performance experience and as her fame and influence increased. She is still read as merely vulgar (in the sense of tasteless and low), yet her musical creation cannot be adequately described and theorized with this adjective. Silva's work must be understood historically as a carefully crafted, unique musical statement, whose treatment has ranged from taming to censoring, mirroring the battle with censorship she fought in her own career.

Silva's early repertoire almost exclusively featured songs with serial puns and double entendres taking full advantage of her nymphet status. For example, "Déjamelo ver" (Let me see it, 1939) posits the speaker's desires as polymorphously perverse, not Oedipally organized: "The other day, in La Marqueta / without wanting to / I noticed a pair of pretty eyes / that a woman sported."[19] Silva sings of selling her wares to the highest bidder in "La bombonera" (The candywoman, 1940): "I am the candywoman from San Juan / my candy is unlike any other you've tasted." In "Mami" (Mommy, 1941) she is the hysteric: "Mommy, mommy, mommy, it's so bad to be pretty, I feel a desire to not be what I am / Mommy, mommy, mommy, I feel so strange, I don't know what's gotten over me / Mommy, mommy, mommy, these dizzy spells are driving me crazy." She offers to be men's sexual guide in "Por el norte y por el sur" (North by south, 1941). In all of these examples, Silva stood for the oversexed girl of heteronormative male fantasy.

Silva was quite young when she recorded the sexually explicit song "Mis tres novios" (My three boyfriends) with the Cuarteto Victoria in 1940. (She rerecorded it later in her career, in a version today's fans can listen to via Spotify. The newer album artwork is not to be missed, featuring a brown-skinned "homeboy" figure and two white-skinned male figures, one tossing a dress jacket over his shoulder and the other one proffering a glass of champagne.) Silva's original performance of "Mis tres novios" brilliantly re-created the deceptive nature of romantic and sexual talk. Silva amplified the fantasy of the lyrics with her chunks in *parlando*, which I render here in italics:

Qué novios más chulos tengo
Me dan gusto, demasiado
Y solo porque los tengo
Locos con este cantao
Y yo le digo, papito, tú sabes que te quiero, te toco el clarinete, la trompeta,
  el saxófon, lo que tú quieras te lo toco, te poso boca arriba, boca abajo,
  de perfil, como tú quieras me retrato mi papi, ay

I have such nice boyfriends
They really please me, maybe too much
It's probably because I drive them
Crazy with my tune
And I tell them, Daddy, you know I love you, I'll play [touch] your
  clarinet, your trumpet, your saxophone, I'll play [touch] whatever you
  want, I'll strike a pose, face down, face up, in profile, sideways, which-
  ever way you want I'll spread my legs for you, oh yeah

Silva is backed by a small *conjunto* (ensemble), with horns, guitars, and a conga drum, and is probably playing the maracas in the recording. She affects innocence by cooing and babbling so words are blurred or lost, progressively substituting semantics for the materiality of sound. The sonic elements of Silva's voice, her modulations, choice of words, incorporation of spoken word, and sonic engagement of a complicit listener cannot be captured by the written lyrics or the song's sheet music, only by listening to the recording. One can imagine what a ruckus she must have stirred live. The young Silva played the male fantasy to perfection, cleverly performing traditional signs of female vulnerability and enticement: little girl voice, giggle, and nervous flounce.

Silva did not write any of the double entendre songs she initially became famous for. In a posthumous tribute to Rafael Hernández in the 1970s, a decade or so before she herself died, Silva was dead serious when she stated, "The first time I sang songs with double entendre it was because Rafael wrote them for me. I swear."[20] Instead of remembering Silva as a bombshell who lost her sex appeal, we should remember her sonic licentiousness, the way she was the first Latino star to transform the culturally inflicted passive position of the woman into a putative bottom power. In the same manner Silva spoke of herself as being dominant on stage, "Mis tres novios" speaks of a woman who is playing at submissiveness but is really the top, as do "Por el norte y por el sur" and many other humorous songs enacting male fantasies. The cantao — defined by tempo, rhythm, measure, intonation, modulation, and tone — became Silva's preferred way of tackling the heteronormativity and outright sexism of the songs. The cantao made her the top.

Silva's work began in the age of the circus, with its recourse to freakishness and outlandishness and its peculiar, cruel sense of humor. The song "Mis tres novios," in Silva's voice, probably this very recording, was a staple of the circus tour.[21] We should keep in mind that her voice at this point and until the advent of television was primarily an acousmatic voice, with the overtones of incantation and dominance that ensue when the source of the voice cannot be located or visually figured (as Michel Chion famously discussed in *The Voice in Cinema*). Silva was surely acquainted with vaudeville and burlesque and incorporated comedy theater's signature gestures and overall attitude when performing live. The circus, cabaret, vaudeville, and revue produced their own brands of normality and the acceptable in their enclosed realms; Silva adapted these formulations to the mass forms of Latino radio, recording, and, later, television. The first manifestation of the Silva voice, imprinted on the groove and heard over radio, recorded and live, respectively, set the tone for Silva's reception over decades. This first voice imbued Silva with an acousmatic presence that at once fascinated and unnerved the listener. She emerges as our first example of a thinking voice, given the encounter between natural talent, skillful deployment of shifting codes governing performing female bodies, and the larger-context game changer of the ascent of the music industry in unequal hemispheric development.

Through spoken singing or parlando, which emphasized this acousmatic quality by dissolving nearness and distance, Silva consistently played with the boundary between speech and singing to mine the illusory intimacy of persona.[22] This aided her in developing the stage creation much more than the average artist in Latino early pop, toying with the sexist imposition that assumed the coincidence of her person with the content of her repertoire. Her earliest performances utilized the scopic regime of necessity to satisfy simple, heteronormative male fantasies. But it was Silva's project to anchor the performance vocally, rebutting the scopic regime's primacy in musical listening to women and insisting on her rightful place as a singer and musician. It is no accident that her early repertoire, written by men, would revolve around fantasies where the woman as doll merely ventriloquizes heteronormative, male desire. Such fantasies depended on the scopic and its illusion of desire's mastery, a hand Silva expertly dealt. In what follows, I trace how Silva went beyond and intuited the symbolic quality of voice — its capacity to rearrange signifiers and therefore desire — and how she implemented this insight through her percussive performance.

It would be foolhardy to simply recur to a normative, feminist account of Silva as a successfully resistant subject because she wielded voice's symbolic capacities. While she emerged as a winner, Silva paid a price, one that I will delineate by reconstructing the trajectory of the original signifier/persona of Myrta across the decades in parallel with an eerie double, known by the signifier/persona of Chencha. Myrta and Chencha emerged from Silva's successful yet financially precarious 1940s career. Myrta was her artistic persona from the beginning. Chencha developed more slowly. Both personas established a relationship to truth as it is posited in lyrics.

Silva exploited lyrics, exposing their fixity in legalese as a fiction and cleverly playing off their notated existence to gesture toward the improvisatory and spoken, which lay outside of legal authorship, in the resonance of a song as it is performed (following Jean-Luc Nancy's remarks on resonance: "Resonance is at once that of a body that is sonorous for itself and resonance of sonority in a listening body that, itself, resounds as it listens").[23] Signifiers and speech are inextricably linked. Speech is likewise inextricable from notions of voice as interiority or conscience, which have very deep roots in Western philosophy and influence our understanding of singers, particularly of women who have been taken to be too close to their speech, less desiring or perhaps less capable of acquiring a distance from their artistic creations.

Most listeners knew Silva's records, not her live performance, but they were able to share in her performative speech because she so extraordinarily imprinted liveness and the inside/outside symbolic quality of voice into her recordings.[24] Parlando became a virtuosic performance of negativity, fitting in well with Muñoz's suggestion of queer virtuosity as a perspicacious staging of presumptive artistic failure. Myrta and Chencha became akin to Lacanian quilting points in the artist's own discourse and acquired an uncanny power or hold on the shared psychic space between performer and audience.[25] This quilting subjectified the artist in ways we may theorize from a careful analysis of her body of work, filling in her critical biography as production (that is, inserted in an entire political economy that depended on the symbolic and specifically on women's role in this symbolic domain) and teasing out the cultural import of Silva's subjectification as part of a larger discourse on women and music and not simply a product of her temperament, talent, or pathology.

SIGNATURE SONG

Upon recording "Nada" (Nothing) in New York City in 1942, Silva moved away decisively from the purely playful nature of her songs. "Nada" became her lifelong signature song. While Rafael Hernández has songwriting credits, the song does not make any sense without the phenomenological force that was Myrta Silva. Even if Silva did not directly pen the song, "Nada" reflects Silva's intentions as she began to inhabit the space of the figure: an artist whose meaning was born in music but who exceeded music's domain to become historically significant as a cultural phenomenon. This projection distinguishes Silva from other artists who worked with double entendre and the obscene.

"Nada," in spoken Spanish, is a colloquial interjection, similar to the English phrase. It can mean "I'm ready to wrap this up" as much as "I don't know how to wrap this up." It can be a conclusion to a series of statements, indicating completion, or an acknowledgment that resolution or completion is not possible. In this latter sense, it inevitably indicates a linguistic postponement of that which speech is trying to grasp. It alludes to the dialogic but not to a balanced state in which dialogue is reconciled. It is not antagonistic, necessarily, either. It is a point of suspension.

Just as in "My Three Boyfriends," in "Nada" Silva employs the plaintive girl-next-door voice, with its petulant tone and hints of babbling and cooing in the refrain. This aspect is in sync with her 1930s repertoire. There is, however, an important difference between these repertoires. Silva resignifies her persona, bringing it under her own purview and wresting it definitely away from her extramusical existence:

Nada, no quiero que me miren
No quiero que me digan, que me toquen, que me hablen, que me
   inviten a cantar
Nada, ya no me llamo Myrta
Así es que ya lo saben, que mi nombre ya no existe ni por tierra ni por
   mar

Nothing, I do not want to be looked at,
I don't want to be told what to do, be touched, spoken to, or be invited
   to sing
Nothing, I will no longer be called Myrta
So now you know that my name doesn't exist, not by land, not by sea

On the surface, Silva sings about a woman with an ill temper and foul character who wants a divorce. Taking the work of signifiers into account changes the
song's meaning completely, however. "My name does not exist" is the equivalent to saying, "My name from this moment on is a signifier." Silva's classic
singing of the refrain — "ay cara cara carambita, ay cara cara carambamba,
esta rumba ya me trae loquita, esta rumba ya me trae cansá" — is the song's
sonic key.[26] The syllables are nonsensically arranged, representing rhythm,
and the words also indicate cadence (esta rumba) and its physical effects (it's
driving me crazy, I'm totally fed up with the rumba). "Rumba" also alludes to
"the tales about my life." Silva decisively articulated a different entity from the
fantasy figure of her first two or three star years. This persona proposed an
ethical positioning in the face of life, including music; it proposed a cynical
position, targeting collective listening.[27]

Silva's performance of "Nada" is a direct response to her subjectification in
the music industry. "Nada" does more than play up a stereotype: It inaugu-
rates the period when Silva yoked listeners' laughter to the affect of disgust,
making music an "acoustic mirror" and Silva a "speaking body." The acoustic
mirror is Kaja Silverman's classic term for the female voice in cinema, which,
Silverman found, exhibited a lack of synchronicity with the paternal gaze that
classic Hollywood film fed upon, despite being, on the surface, completely at
its scopic mercy. The first Silva operated along the lines of the acoustic mirror,
escaping the scopic law through a parodic, vocal ventriloquizing. The speaking body is Shoshana Felman's classic treatment of the body that erupts upon
the surefire use of the performative utterance, linguistically birthing a simultaneous body of scandal and seduction, neatly describing Silva's emergence in
the 1940s as a sonic tour de force.[28]

For Felman, Don Juan is the epitome of the speaking body. The felicity or in-felicity of utterances is the goal and not their falsity or truth. When I think of the Don Juan situation as a linguistic seduction, happening through speech and sound, I recall Silva's sleight of hand with lyrics and the illusion of speech in her performance. I also cannot help but recall a couple of anecdotes I heard in Havana about Silva's seductive power. These recollections correspond in time to Silva's first Cuban visits and the 1942 recording of "Nada." One woman artist, Silva's contemporary, described Silva as "muy declarada" [completely out] and recounted how she "wooed women right there, in the CMQ cafeteria."[29] The artist did not want to be identified; she made it clear that any association with Silva entailed an automatic association with lesbianism and, therefore, disgust.

An interview with Manuel Villar of the Instituto Cubano de Radio y Tele-visión circles around Silva's sexual exploits in Havana. Villar said that speaking of Myrta Silva's love life was like speaking of Chano Pozo's.[30] He did not explain exactly what he meant by the comparison, but made it clear that the associa-tion with Pozo conveyed trouble and violence, linking Silva with inassimilable and genius figures — the "Saint Genets" of pop music.[31] René Espí, the son of Roberto Espí of the legendary Conjunto Casino, told me of Silva's bohemian escapades with his father. With a wide grin, he recalled his father boasting that he had had an affair with Silva. René wondered if his father was gleefully partaking in myth making because, as he said, "Yo sé que ella le descargaba a la otra onda" (I know she played with the other team).[32] René's anecdote sug-gested parallels between Espí's macho and Silva's butch seductiveness.

As far as I could gauge the matter from memory scraps, always tricky to navigate, Silva's queerness augmented the phantasmatic power of her perfor-mance. She exerted a fascination that ensued from a combination of musical talent, masterly interaction with the audience, and the discursive mystery of her sexual life. The audience was in on the cultural joke, knew about it, after the psychoanalytic knowing that Sigmund Freud named disavowal: "I know that she is, but . . ." Ascertaining whether Silva was a Don Juan or simply just having fun living as a relatively emancipated young woman is not critical to the analysis of the acoustic mirror and speaking body she astutely employed. I mention the anecdotes insofar as they shed light on the construction of Silva as a bodily phenom of sex and voice.

Later in life Silva boasted of having had "many loves" but deciding to remain "married to her career." She also spoke for the first time about a miscarriage. She employed mythical terms to relate fatal losses to account for her unmar-ried life, including a lurid tale about a suicide attempt in New York. She alleged

that she had always been "in love with love itself," a very typical public a'
of queer women who did not wish to self-disclose but cannot acc
thought of as closeted. Silva kept her private life out of the public ʹ
fully, without having to sacrifice leading a full life or conditionir.ͺ
work to preconceptions of women's lives. To protect her privacy as well aͺ
career, she had little choice but to resort to conventional discourse to elude reporters' questions and the public fixation with the details of her personal life.[33]

Silva has been written into discourse as androgynous or desexualized, even
in sympathetic quarters.[34] A tame androgyny, one that does not unsettle or
provoke, like the one that has sometimes been assigned to Silva, can be summarily dismissed. It is only slightly preferable to the more violent move of
desexualization. Both characterizations either overlook or refuse to theorize
Silva's vocal play, her lyrics to listen to, which confront the listener with the
socially disgusting in a precise and thorough way. Disgust is one of the "ugly
feelings" Sianne Ngai brilliantly analyzes in her book *Ugly Feelings*. She writes,
"There is a sense in which [disgust] seeks to draw others *into* its exclusion of
its object, enabling a strange kind of sociability."[35] Ngai's approach provides
another route to understanding the peculiar variant of seduction performed
by the acoustic mirror and the speaking body. Silva consciously launched an
attack against society's inhibitions, prohibitions, and hypocrisies by thematizing and theorizing her own performance in her humorous repertoire through
a complex negativity, therefore having, as it were, the last laugh: "Who's disgusting now?" The inability to preserve a comfortable distance from the object
(in "Nada," the singing, performing woman and later, the Chencha character)
came to define the success of any Myrta Silva performance.

The inclusion of the proper noun "Myrta" in the song "Nada" could well
have been Silva's idea, breaching the distance between signifier and signified
and between persona and person. Even if she did not directly collaborate on
the lyrics, the song was written for her, and the signifier can only do its work
due to Silva's prior labor and act of self-creation. The signifier "Myrta" gained
in importance as the years went on, thanks to Silva's musical intelligence and
artistic development of negativity. "Nada" 's title, "nothing," is what Silva is of-
fering her desiring audience onstage and in records, a negative of everything
that the male fantasies of other songs were based on. Structurally, this negative occupies the same position as the fullness of the presumptively available
woman.

As mentioned at this chapter's opening, Silva knew that the overlapping
of failure and figure never ended, that an artist was a target because a good

artist put desire itself in circulation. The artist creates a peculiar, public intimacy or Lacanian "extimacy." Mladen Dolar defines extimacy as "the simultaneous inclusion/exclusion, which retains the excluded at its core."[36] When in 1973 Silva said, "I'm a winner," she suggested that as a career, music had been a dangerous game. She knew she had flirted with the danger of failure for decades and had always come out just on this side of winning. She also knew she had multiple battle scars. Silva was able to disrupt musical laws of meaningfulness with her percussive voice, especially those governing women's normative performance. Past a certain point, more or less coinciding with "Nada," this capacity to annihilate the machine of meaningfulness and replace it with "signifierness," hovering on the very boundary, was regarded as increasingly threatening.[37]

Myrta and Chencha, Silva's two personas, became "letters," peculiar master signifiers related and unrelated to Silva.[38] She was their producer and she performed the labor to bring them about and maintain them. She extracted, eventually, profit from them. But since their significance depended as much on her as it did on larger social discourse, she could not control their displacement. Indeed, what happened to Silva is inseparable from gender discourse and the positioning of women in the social field as it is refracted in culture. Following Jacques Lacan in *Seminar XX, Encore*, women are charged with the burden of "signifierness," precluded from exchange in the sexual relationship because they are the ones exchanged between men. Indeed, one way to interpret both "Mis tres novios" and "Nada" echoes Lacan's playful, negative axiom: "There is no such thing as a sexual relationship." Lacan goes beyond literal exchange between men to elucidate symbolic circulation between various subjectivities, of which the feminine in patriarchal societies is a prototype. Women do bear the brunt of the letter as the vehicle of a particular nothing, similar to the mathematical zero: "Nothing is something."

I present the reader with the first nothing of several in this book. The nothing, obviously, is the overwhelming signifier in Silva's signature song. Upon recording "Nada," Silva circulated from 1942 to 1972 as she traveled to perform live and through records and radio and TV broadcasts, never quite being able to shake off her public identification with that particular song. Further, Silva's voice in the halcyon decades of Latin music exhibited the letter's displacement; hence through the nothing lies one way to theorize Silva's extraordinary success as a vocal performer of this and similar genres in which soneo, percussion, and improv articulated her evolving ethics of performance.

The weight of Silva's contemporary audience in completing the meaning of her musical persona and sustaining the displacement that solidified meaning can be gleaned in an extant live recording of "Por algo será" (Something in me, 1947), a brilliant example of Silva's performative use of innuendo and spoken word, asides, jokes, laughter, and other vocal elements such as sneering and moaning to create a mesmerizing and sexualized effect.[39] It puts into play the two signifiers of Myrta and Chencha, similarly to multiple songs of Silva's 1940s repertoire, and it deploys the signifier "nada" (nothing) as did other hits of the period, also broadcast live over the radio.

Silva worked as the hugely popular lead singer for La Sonora Matancera during 1949–1950; thanks to this stint, she was voted Best Foreign Artist of Cuba in 1950 (beating, as she proudly pointed out, the Mexicans María Félix, Los Panchos, and Jorge Negrete, all superstars).[40] Silva recorded this song with the Sonora live in the studios of CMQ Radio, and was the songwriter. Silva's *soneo* is half-sung, half-spoken, in response to the refrain, *por algo será* (there must be something in me):

Será que yo tengo un truquito que nadie lo sabe, yo tengo un tumbaíto
    pa' lavar la ropa
La mojo y la seco, la seco y la mojo, la vuelvo a mojar, la vuelvo a secar
Que tú me dices mami
Que tú me dices mimi
Que tú me dices mimita (por algo será)
Aunque tú camines como Chencha, te quiero, mamita (por algo será)
Nada, yo no soy más bonita que las otras, pero tampoco más fea . . . (ja,
    ja)
Que tú me quieres . . .
Que tú me lloras . . .
Que tú me buscas . . .

It must be I have a trick up my sleeve. I have a little rhythm when it
    comes to washing clothes
I dry them, I wet them, I wet them and dry them, I wet them again, I
    dry them again
Something in me makes you want to call me mami
Call me mimi
Call me little mimi (there must be something in me) [*sneer*]
"Even if you walk like Chencha, I love you, darling" [*with moan*]
There must be something in me
Okay, so, nothing, I may not be prettier than the others, but I'm not any
    uglier, either [*scoffs*]

[*Audience laughter*]

[*Moaning*]

Something makes you want me . . .

Something makes you long for me . . .

Something makes you seek me out . . . [*audience laughter*]

Silva quotes Cuban songs in her recitative and talks directly to the live audience present in the studio, seeking their complicity in the game. The audience is definitely giving her free rein, and she is able to be great, just as she explained when she said, "I work ad lib." The recording re-creates a double, simultaneous live audience: those who were present during the recording (preserved in the record grooves) and the fans who were listening to the radio (implied in the recording's location). We hear the audience responding to Silva with laughter and bursts of applause. And, of course, there is a third layering in the present, new fans created by the circulation of these recordings for commercial purposes as CD records and, more recently, in portable formats and streaming services, attesting to voice's "contemporaneity of the audible."[41] Today, part of the delight of the record is its retro appeal, but I believe the performance shines on its own and is now not simply a recycled curiosity.

The radio audience saw Silva gesticulating in a way that censors found highly troubling. Silva cut her chops, as she said, in live venues and often staged her songs, pointing to her body, using arm and leg gestures, and contorting her face. The listeners through the radio waves were not privy to this staging, but the inclusion of the studio audience in the broadcast engaged them in the live moment, allowing them to experience Silva's interaction with the live audience and her brilliant use of humor. These audiences were perhaps more savvy than more recent ones, which persist in a damaging forgetting. Back then, listeners knew that Chencha was a character clearly separated from Silva, that Myrta was an artistic persona and not a document of Silva's private life. They responded to her vocal, queer, negative virtuosity.

"Nada" is a reference to her own hit, more specifically to negativity in its productive aspect. The rest of the verse, "I am not prettier than other women, but I'm not any uglier, either," which elicits burst of laughter from the audience, is a cipher. At first it sounds like she is stating she is average looking and not the prettiest. Upon critical examination, the statement emerges as a negation of a negation. What is the artist really saying? There is no absolutely settled meaning for this and other phrases, like the "Nada" verse, "I will no longer be called Myrta." The import here is Silva's conscious deployment of the utterance in its "nothingness" or signifierness, in its paradoxically "full emptiness."[42]

Silva's given name, Myrta, does not appear in this live "Por algo será." She refers to herself indirectly as Chencha (she re-creates a dialogue with an addressee of unspecified gender, who, she claims, desires her in spite of her gait, which is like Chencha's). Silva had inaugurated this process of substitution and linking with the gesture of erasure of her given name ("I will no longer be called Myrta"). As with the earlier "Mis tres novios" and "Nada," in "Por algo será" Silva underscores cadence ("Será que . . . yo tengo un tumbaíto" [Must be . . . I have a little rhythm]). It is worth noting, for those unfamiliar with the Cuban repertoire, that Silva is quoting a Cuban song about cadence in her soneo ("El tumbaíto"), which she herself had recorded in 1946 with the Pérez Prado Orchestra; she quotes the song and her recording of the song, a kind of metonymy squared. The point is that the content of the "full emptiness" of voice is musical, not personal. Her signifiers' meanings relate to these objects that are at once immaterial (like music) and material (in all senses of the word: They are sensory objects and also commodities in the chain of production).

I DON'T DENY IT

Notions of middle-class normalcy and morality threatened to derail Silva's career in Cuba when she started running into trouble with that country's censorship board in 1947. As *Bohemia*, Cuba's premier entertainment magazine of the time, reported, "Dr. Alberto Cruz, Minister of Communications, signed the dense tangle of papers, and he summarized his findings thus: Radio 1010 could not keep airing its program, 'Radio Coctel Musical,' because Myrta Silva, one of the program's regulars, had performed two guarachas, 'Camina como Chencha la gambá' and 'El bombón de Myrta,' the lyrics of which were completely pornographic."[43] The article mentions that there were rumors that the show was censored because Radio 1010 was a Communist station. The minister is quoted as replying, "No, there is nothing political behind it. What happened was that Myrta Silva had performed two songs that had been banned by the Radio Bureau. And on top of that, when she says 'por aquí no ha pasado un tranvía' [a streetcar hasn't run between my legs], she makes a very provocative gesture."[44]

The Communist Party owned Radio 1010, but it was a purely commercial venture. It's probable that Silva's sexualized performance was the reason for the censorship. In fact, the nascent Radio Ethics Commission banned several Myrta Silva guaracha performances: "Adiós Comay Gata" (Goodbye, Comay Gata), "Camina como Chencha la gambá" (She walks like Chencha, the pigeon-toed woman), "Déjamelo ver" (Let me see it), and "Échale tierra y tápalo" (Cover it with a little dirt).[45] Censorship in the music industry was a common practice.[46] What was not common was a single artist with so many songs banned from the airwaves. A few years later, Silva would have to submit to censors in Puerto Rico too, possibly marked as an always already obscene singer.

Of these banned songs, "Camina como Chencha la gambá" deserves detailed scrutiny. It birthed the Chencha signifier in Silva's career. The folk Chencha originated earlier, possibly in Spain; it was Silva's idea to create a song based on the folk pun, "camina como Chencha la gambá" (she walks like Chencha, who is pigeon-toed). On more than one occasion, Silva explained that she created characters or situations and presented them to songwriters who created guarachas based on her ideas. The songwriter for "Chencha," Ñico Saquito, had Silva to thank for making several of his songs into hits.[47]

The original recording of "Chencha" in 1946 is historically significant. It was Silva's most successful recording and Fernández's most popular guaracha, out of dozens he penned.[48] Silva performed "Chencha" in social spaces as diverse as the Tropicana of Havana, the Escambrón Beach Club in Puerto Rico, and New York's Teatro Hispano. The song capitalized on the meanings the Myrta signifier had by then accrued as an oversexed woman, a simultaneously disgusting and desirable object. The mulata type of the teatro bufo, nineteenth-century Cuban comedic theater, must have been the songwriter's model (this would explain a verse in the song: "ahora dicen los malos mulatos" [the evil mulatos are now saying]).[49] "Chencha" is a *tango-congo* with a slow tempo, a genre associated with blackness in Cuban and Caribbean popular music of the early twentieth century, evoking what Robin Moore describes as a "generic primitivism."[50] As with the portrait a la guarachera with the Cuarteto Victoria, Silva again functioned as the nothing or empty space into which various gender and racial meanings were deposited, but not elucidated or examined. Nor were they, properly speaking, sutured. Their "display in nondisplay" is their salient characteristic; they are neither affirmed nor denied. Silva was regarded as a sexual bombshell, but was white skinned, at a remove from blackness; she was regarded as licentious, but everyone knew she "played with the other team," as René Espí jokingly recounted. Possibly Silva herself disidentified with the tango-congo rhythm for two reasons: It did not suit her improvisational style and it was coded black.

"Chencha" presents a knowing speaker, aware that she is squarely on public display. The song's hook concerns the subject's overexamination by the listeners, who are visually engaged in "figuring her out" (or more precisely, her gait: "camina como" [she walks like]). The gait is supposed to reveal sexual behavior, solving the societal riddle of what must be figured out. The scopic should install mastery on the part of the subject who fixes the object with the gaze; it should provide a reassurance regarding the viewer's supremacy in the "knowing game."

Despite being her best-selling record ever (more than half a million copies, an astronomical number for the time), Silva hated the original recording. She stated the arrangement was "horrible."[51] Perhaps her retrospective disgust had to do with the fact that she became indelibly associated with this song. As in negation in psychoanalysis, she may not have owned up fully to her resentment, especially because it aided her career, helped her in her goal of financial independence, and provided the persona for her TV character years later.

Peter Szendy has written about the arrangement as a very specialized act of listening.[52] Following Szendy's insight, and factoring in Silva's disgust at the first recording, we can theorize that she could not inscribe her own listening in the first period of Chencha's performance life, something she achieved in Chencha's second period. The second recording of 1961 testifies to this change. Silva arranged the song, led the band, and produced the recording. With this in mind, let's examine what unfolds in the performance, starting with the opening stanza:

Que yo nací con mi pata gambá
Igualita, igualita que Chencha
Y qué tengo que ver yo con Chencha
Si nací con mi pata gambá

So I was born pigeon-toed
Exactly like Chencha
Why in the world does that make me like Chencha
I'm pigeon-toed from birth

There are significant differences between the second recording of 1961 and the first of 1946. Tone is salient, an element that can't be notated with accuracy but is present from the very first verses. It's not simply more comical than the first recording; it is cynical. Additionally, Silva engages percussive voice much more than in the first version by playing with the beat at various moments. For example, she slows the tempo in minute 1:19 ("La ge-e-ente me gri-ita Chencha") to then accelerate it in the next verse, when she belts out a soneo ("Camina camina camina camina camina camina Chencha"). Silva also changed the arrangement. The ostinato rhythm is gone, replaced by a cha cha cha. Silva used brass completely differently from the first version, with full blares and comedic embellishments slightly reminiscent of circus music (like "Mis tres novios"). She stopped the orchestra before each repetition of the song's refrain, as in the first version. However, in employing trumpets in minor chords, the refrain's musical phrase turns ominous. Silva repurposed the playful key of the cha cha cha, bringing a slight hint of the uncanny into the recording. The orchestra goes from festive to retributive in few seconds. We hear a new cultural doll, created by the ugly intersection of music performance and a nakedly profit-driven entertainment industry in the postwar years, which disregarded the boundaries between public and private and capitalized on this blurring. This doll sings like she is refusing to comply with the scopic fantasy of dominance, like the dolls of horror movies.

[Orchestra full stop]
Pero camina como Chencha [trumpet blare in minor key] ([Chorus:] la
    gambá)
Camina como Chencha [trumpet blare in minor key] (la gambá)
Ay camina como Chencha [trumpet blare in minor key] (la gambá)
Camina como Chencha [trumpet blare in minor key] (la gambá)
[Orchestra full stop]

These changes opened up musical space for Silva to elaborate on the song via her virtuosic use of voice and masterly command of cadence. Silva achieved a memorable performance of Chencha in her 1946 recording, one attuned to the listening public's desire. Yet by changing the song's arrangement and irreverently altering its lyrics in the 1960s, by superbly injecting her comedic asides in order to mortally puncture the fantasy of self-reference, Silva "rewrote" the song to conform to her artistic desire: to embody the psychoanalytic nothing she put into play with "Nada" in 1942, the signifier's full emptiness. Inserting these asides into the written bars of the music of "Chencha" had the effect of a sonic infiltration of meaning.

This second recording largely transformed the reception of this song. Silva's reperformance suggests that listeners' engagement with the visual leaves the dominant subject open to the scopic illusion of mastery and therefore ripe for the symbolic reordering the voice as part-object can achieve. Hence, Chencha's gait, a would-be visual clue, is overpowered and disarmed by vocality.

The running commentary Silva offers at the end of the verses, switching from sung lyrics to spoken interjections while keeping her timing intact, elaborates a parallel narrative based on negation (in the psychoanalytic sense). "Que yo nací con mi pata gambá (yo no lo niego)" (So I was born pigeon-toed [I don't deny it]), becomes the battle cry. What is the meaning of an affirmation tendered as a negation? It is signifierness, a particular nothing developed across two decades since the original nothing of "Nada."[53] "Nada, ya no me llamo Myrta" (Nothing, I will no longer be called Myrta) is reformulated when Silva changes the song's lyrics: "Ya me cambiaron el nombre, ahora me llaman Chencha Silva" (They have gone so far as to change my name; now they call me Chencha Silva), presenting the monstrous hybrid of Chencha Silva in the place where Myrta once was.

Silva responds in the negative, to negative statements that were only expressed in fleeting gossip and chilling anonymous hate mail received in her TV offices by the time of her second recording of "Chencha." "Chencha" is not equal to Silva herself; the song explicitly refers in a first-person singing voice to a character in the third person. The lyrics had made this evident since the first recording, but the performance, including Silva's improvisations in 1961, amplify the distance between the flesh-and-blood Silva and her character, in the spirit of commentary about such equivocations.

By the beginning of the 1960s, "Chencha la gambá" had become a party staple, part of the collective archive of "ugly feelings." Silva effected an ironic distancing at the very moment of the recording, so that every time we listen to the performance inscribed in the record, we can witness Silva practicing an ethics, returning the listener to the problematic societal characterization of Silva and, by extension, any social subject placed in the dangerous position of scapegoat. The pun of Chencha's gait entailed the knowledge that Silva herself was queer and that, according to the song's heteronormative logic, she would be hard pressed to be a gambá. Silva's reperformance underscores the symbolic violence of the original guaracha. She emphasizes taunts on the street and the societal occlusion inherent in the name change, from the empty set of Myrta (her given name is not included in the song) to Chencha Silva, an entity based on the shared investment in gossip about the actual Silva's sexual activity. Purely sonorous and nonlinguistic interjections such as tone, sneers, and scoffs powerfully launch a cynical reaction to the public identification between artist and character, implied in the first version through an abject

FIGURE 1.4 Album cover, Myrta Silva, *Camina como Chencha*, Ansonia 1286, 1961. It portrays the streetcar passing between Silva's legs, mentioned in the title song. Notice the gold left ankle bracelet with the singer's name, "Myrta."

treatment of voice imposed by the arrangement. In 1961, Silva proffers a reading simultaneous with the performance of the song, creating a doubleness that registers as more than simply funny or possibly not that funny. The final verse is a resounding, potentially painful assumption of the persona and name of Chencha: "¡Que yo camino como Chencha!" (So I walk like Chencha!), Silva shouts, in a manner quite distinct from the original recording's fade-out, which featured Silva's hushed singing reflecting the extimate (simultaneously inside and outside) nature of gossip.[54]

Figure 1.4 is the cover for the long-playing record that included the second "Camina como Chencha," *Myrta Silva con Orquesta: Camina como Chencha*. Ansonia Records, a U.S.-based company, released this LP recorded in Mexico. Ansonia had targeted the nostalgia market since its beginnings, with a particular investment in the Latino migrant communities of the United States. Silva complied, to an extent, with the mandate for nostalgia. This LP is a compilation of earlier Myrta Silva material, which had been released as 78s, by then obsolete. Unlike other LPs of the time, these are not the original 78 tracks converted to 33-1/3 rpm, however. They are new tracks Silva recorded and combined to create a musical document of her global, musical personality. At this time, the song "Camina como Chencha" was the fan favorite Myrta Silva song; thus it is the album's title track and inspiration for the cover art.

Silva is shown as fetish. Her lower legs stand in for the total body, photographed from behind. The cover shows a carefully cut shaft of light emanating from Silva's legs, very visible against the dark background of the rest of the cover, which simulates a stage floor. The shaft of light leads the eye directly to the streetcar that is "passing between her legs." This image was created to echo the stanza where Silva is responding to accusations that she can accommodate "un tranvía" (a streetcar), a pun for a very large male sexual organ coming at full force, also referred to at points in the song as a "camión" (truck) and the "telón" (curtain) of the stately Teatro Nacional in Havana, all, obviously, hyperbolic renditions of the phallus.

Yet the artist corrected the fetish, so to speak, and figuratively stopped the tranvía in its tracks. The ankle bracelet with the name Myrta on her left leg merits some discussion. I have heard that this bracelet was a Nuyorican style touch; in other quarters, I have heard it said that city lesbians wore ankle bracelets as a code. I have not been able to verify either claim, but I find the possibilities interesting since, to my knowledge, women artists *de la farándula* (in show business) did not wear ankle bracelets. To be sure, they did not display them in public. Nor did they wear jewelry with their names. After 1960, Silva had bracelets, rings, necklaces, and brooches made saying either Myrta or Myrta Silva in gold and diamonds. This display is different from the bourgeois ostentation of society ladies, with which some viewers have confused it.

The gesture is not reduced to an individual desire to boast of wealth. When Silva alluded to her own riches, she spoke in terms of financial security and artistic freedom, not of having increased her value as a social being defined by class belonging. Silva embossed her name in gold as the only woman to do so in a milieu that thought of itself according to the symbolics of class stratification. Elites and haute bourgeois wore their wealth in spaces designated for interaction only between members, who collectively turned their nose up at everyone else, usually out of public earshot. Their code of propriety or, to use Bourdieu's term, their distinction depended on their withdrawal of ostentation from the larger societal gaze. Silva didn't care much for this distinction. She returned to circulating the quilting point of Myrta as a signifier.

DODGEBALL

The two "Chencha" recordings bookend a period that saw Silva finishing her contract with Victor, dealing with charges of obscenity, relocating to her homeland, and launching her broader entertainment career, which was very successful by the time of the Ansonia LP release of *Camina como Chencha*. It hadn't been easy. Silva appeared on the radio, including in her own program, *Una hora con nosotros* (An hour with us), and freelanced on TV shows beginning in 1954. She stated, "The newly born Puerto Rican television did not want me; they thought I was too vulgar."[55] The nationalist underpinnings that popular music acquired around this time, and the imperative to formulate a clean national repertoire, corresponded to the hegemonic project of the Popular Democratic Party, first established in 1948 and which rose to power in 1952. The party dictated the course of Puerto Rican politics for decades, specifically working the cultural realm as a plan for governmentality. Silva had no choice but to adapt to the commercial and tourist vision of Puerto Rico that became prevalent. Given the clash between her own ethics and the mandated program of culture as a stratified enterprise, where popular culture should represent a moral, national essence, Silva continued to deal on a daily basis with censors. Homosexuality, it goes without saying, was a taboo subject in all media and remained so for decades.

In 1956, WAPA-TV, one of Puerto Rico's and Latin America's first television stations, hired Silva to create the TV show *Una hora contigo* (An hour with you). It was a typical 1950s American-style variety show. First, Silva would sing the show's theme song, a bolero she wrote, "Una hora contigo." Segments included a fashion runway hosted by the actress Velda González, invited singers, Silva herself singing, and a humorous segment titled "Tira y tápate" (Dodgeball), which fast became notorious since it toyed with the discursively allowed and the not allowed, boundaries of taste, and class stratification. Silva had to procure advertising revenue, and she marketed products during this very segment.[56] She spoke directly to the camera while she was answering fan mail, bantering with television crews and gossiping about the colony's brand-new fantasy object, celebrities.

Silva's costume lampooned the working-class *comadre*, and she baptized her character Chencha, recurring to the signifier that she had deployed in multiple hits of the 1940s, in counterpoint to Myrta. The 1950s creation differed from her character, which, as we saw, corresponded to the mulata of the teatro bufo, a racist stereotype of an oversexed woman. Rapidly, Chencha became a second artistic persona of Silva's, following the quilting point the character had become in her repertoire. Chencha developed into a homegrown variant of the delirious subject, positioned at the bar of various repressions affecting discourse in Puerto Rico.[57] The negative virtuosity of Silva's Myrta persona started transferring into the Chencha character. This altered Silva's overall artistic existence; she borrowed Myrta's linguistic seductions to flesh out Chencha, but Myrta could not remain simply intact.

Although Silva continued to be piercingly cynical, dispensing a brand of wisdom attuned to the changes of developmentalism, she could not completely control the fate of the two signifiers she had brilliantly put into cultural play through vocal and musical performance. Voice can become a commodity as much as anything else, and its methexic quality as sound doesn't guarantee that it won't be put at the service of commodity capitalism.[58] Silva had embodied sexual desire through her performance, working its displacement through her voice as part-object. Now she ventriloquized a certain upsetting superego, a kind of comic Panopticon, and into this voice were grafted the paranoia of the small colony over its presumptive nothingness and the concomitant injunction to become something in the world. The force of Silva's musical voice as Lacan's part-object was not destroyed, but it's fair to say it changed aim, as we shall examine.

No extant footage remains of the television show. The LP *Myrta Silva presenta: Una hora contigo* is a wonderful material object that provides some sense of its visual and aural content (figures 1.5 and 1.6).[59] The album art portrays Silva in Chencha costume atop a TV camera; to her side Olga Guillot plays the piano, accompanied by other performers in conspicuous spotlighting. On the flip side, we see Chencha selling Lechoncito lard live. Lechoncito's makers paid for the record; we see the block of lard in a skillet in the lower-right corner. Since LP records were relatively cheap to produce, and artists often worked for a pittance or free, the records became a form of advertising. It was not a purely expedient use of LPs but could be in play generally as artists looked to the business sector to stay competitive in a cutthroat market.

Silva wrote a column titled "Tira y tápate" for the Cuban exile publication *Bohemia libre puertorriqueña*, from 1961 to 1965, a print companion to her television show. Although a silent medium, elements of Silva's complex television voice become audible. It is likely that Silva's television banter as Chencha was very similar or even identical to this print version, so we have a fairly good document of her spoken word performance and an aphonic facsimile of her mainly sonorous presence. We can imagine her sneers and scoffs as we read the segment "Échate p'acá" (Come over here) and "hear" her switch to

FIGURE 1.5 Album cover, *Myrta Silva presenta: Una hora contigo*, LPO 001. Empacadora del Caribe, San Juan, Puerto Rico, late 1950s or early 1960s. The album was created to advertise her TV show of the same name. The cartoon shows Silva atop a TV camera and portrays the show's guests: the Cuban singer Olga Guillot is at the piano.

another voice in the bulk of the column, typically divided into segments like "Noticias del patio" (Local music industry news) and "Noticias de afuera" (What's happening in the music world abroad), or their equivalents. The column features many photographs of her guests and of Silva with multiple celebrities from Puerto Rico, Latin America, the United States, and Europe. The key interplay between the scopic and the aural can be gleaned from the pages, even if the sound of the show is now lost.

The gossip segment was clearly the commercial hook, but Silva's main interest, just as clearly, lay in documenting music as it was played and listened to by Puerto Ricans. The bulk of the column concerns entertainment news and reviews and responses to fan mail, with a couple of paragraphs of show business gossip tossed in for good measure. The range of Silva's professional networks, her evident love of all music and musicians, and her belief in the importance of a native music industry have been, sadly, forgotten in today's memory of

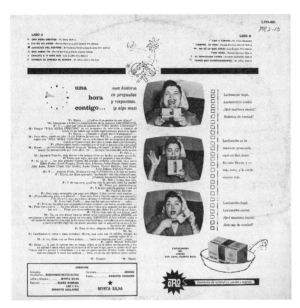

FIGURE 1.6   Flip side of album cover, *Myrta Silva presenta: Una hora contigo*, with images from TV show of Silva selling the sponsor's product, Lechoncito lard. The first tracks on both sides are the serious and jocular, eponymous theme songs of the show, respectively: "Una hora contigo" (An hour with you) for the opening, and "Tira y tápate" (Dodgeball) for the humor segment. Silva is shown in character as Chencha.

her. Silva's expressive qualities shine through in her columns, which feature her trademark, cynical stance toward life. She displayed an ethics similar to the Foucauldian care of the self and was hardly as superficial and banal as Chencha is remembered today. Rather, Chencha's intent was to speak truth to power.[60] Silva used gossip's profitability to aid her in undertaking her life commitment: the promotion of all art and all artists, in Puerto Rico and beyond. It can be said that one of her transgressions was to refuse the strict separation between autochthonous and foreign music in the rising tide of cultural nationalism and insularity.

Notwithstanding her success, instead of simply inspiring pride and affection (as she might have expected), Silva experienced an ambivalent reception in Puerto Rico. Silva forever remembered her years based in Cuba in an idealized way, probably because she had experienced a measure of musical belonging

Puerto Rican contemporaries went so far as to pejoratively label
ʃoricua cubana" (a Cuban Puerto Rican). Many Puerto Ricans still
 y take Silva for Cuban. Silva had sung what later came to be labeled
 ʃusic, had had success in Havana, and had acquired important business
 ɪs who made their way into 1950s Puerto Rican television and became
 upon the triumph of the Cuban Revolution. Yet we must not underesti-
mate Silva's labor to set up her successful career in Puerto Rico. We must also
remember that Silva wore many hats on her show. She produced the show,
procured the advertising, hosted, and performed as a singer and comedian,
filling the jobs of at least five people. Nothing was handed to her.

Adding to the hurtful rejection of Silva on such dubious, nativist grounds,
I have encountered several specialists who believe a technical diminishing of
Silva's singing voice happened around this period, thus justifying Silva's turn
to TV and her gossip character. Silva never lost her voice; she had the same instrument in the late 1950s as in the late 1930s. The conditions for artistic success
in Puerto Rico under the aegis of the newly founded Estado Libre Asociado
(ELA, Commonwealth of Puerto Rico) required of Silva to adopt a more normative repertoire, one that reflected immutable Puerto Rican values. These values,
it need not be said, were not intrinsic to Puerto Ricans but proceeded from a
narrative that was pedagogically instilled and vaunted in other arms, particularly tourism. The dominant narrative of music stressed the centrality of Puerto
Rico's great songwriter Rafael Hernández, and music pedagogy stressed classical training.[61] Silva is, arguably, the greatest interpreter of Hernández's comic
repertoire, so she was able to slot into the values discourse through this corpus.

Some songs of the nativist repertoire succeeded beyond their packaged call
to mass pedagogy. A still of Myrta Silva from the movie *Las canciones unidas* (The United Nations of song, 1960) shows Silva performing the standard
"Esos no son de aquí" (They are not Puerto Rican).[62] Silva is the best performer of this Rafael Hernández classic, recognizable to generations of Puerto
Ricans, with its catchy call and response:

Los que dicen "yes my dear," *esos no son de aquí*
Los que dicen "ba-bería," *esos no son de aquí*
Los que dicen guajirito, *esos no son de aquí*
Los que decimos jibarito, *¡esos sí, esos sí!*

The people who say, "Yes my dear," *they are not Puerto Rican*
The people who say "barbershop" [with a Havana accent], *they are not
 Puerto Rican*

The people who say, "guajirito" [Cuban word for peasant, country dweller], *they are not Puerto Rican*
Those of us who say "jibarito" [Puerto Rican word for peasant, country dweller] *are truly Puerto Rican, truly Puerto Rican!*

Silva was ideal for this song because she had worked negation so extraordinarily into her performance persona, as we have seen with a few examples of her extensive repertoire. "Esos no son de aquí" presents successive stanzas in which being Puerto Rican is first defined in three verses stating what being Puerto Rican is not, before the affirmation of what being Puerto Rican is in the last verse of each stanza. My paraphrase is less generic than the catchy original, which includes verses that can be easily transposed into other national contexts wishing to proclaim specificity by simply substituting terms, since "de aquí" would apply to any country. Perhaps this is why the song eventually became known unofficially in Puerto Rico as "Cuchifritos," since the word for Puerto Rican fried finger food is a more unique marker than the song's legal name.

Las canciones unidas is a loose amalgam of music clips from different parts of the world (not just Latin America), barely held together by the conceit of the United Nations calling for artistic representations to foster world peace and understanding. Silva was chosen to represent Puerto Rico, specifically the newly established ELA. This great clip is available via YouTube and has been viewed by thousands of Internet users. It opens with an aerial view of downtown San Juan, Puerto Rico's capital, undoubtedly chosen for its modernity (we see the snazzy Condado waterfront with its luxury hotels and images of the island as a tropical paradise). Silva and a chorus sing a few bars of "Preciosa" (Beautiful one), a Rafael Hernández anticolonial tribute to the island and Puerto Rico's unofficial anthem. After a minute, the movie switches to tropical music, to loud horns and swift percussion. The locale is probably very near or in the Escambrón Beach Club, which was an exclusive enclave between the Condado and Old San Juan sectors of San Juan (figure 1.7). A staple of period postcards, the Escambrón hosted many musicians from Puerto Rico and abroad, catering to affluent and middle-class Puerto Ricans and tourists (especially Americans) since the 1930s. Perhaps what is most striking about Silva's clip, in its Technicolor vision of Puerto Rico as an island paradise, is the visual separation of musicians and dancers. Racially, the divide is all too apparent. All the dancers are *blanquitos*, light or white skinned. The women dancers present an additional contrast to Silva. They are statuesque and dressed skimpily as they cavort about the beach. Yet, race and class differences

FIGURE 1.7 Myrta Silva performing the Rafael Hernández classic, "Esos no son de aquí," with Cortijo y su Combo, in the Mexican movie *Las canciones unidas*, 1959. The site is the Escambrón Beach Club in San Juan. Silva leads the band.

notwithstanding, musicians and dancers together exist for the foreign imagination as harbingers of both desire and investment possibilities.

Silva's band was none other than the groundbreaking Cortijo y su Combo, which completely revolutionized both the playing and the role of Afro–Puerto Rican music, particularly *bomba* and *plena*, in the 1950s and beyond. Rafael Cortijo can be seen playing the timbal set. While Silva's positioning against the musicians is slightly reminiscent of the early portrait with the Cuarteto Victoria dressed a la guarachera, she is a quite different punctum, to recall Roland Barthes, from that earlier image of the white-skinned singer surrounded by brown- and black-skinned musicians. Silva leads the band, orchestrates the breaks, indicates the tempo changes and the brass section entrances, and controls the volume. The clip amply demonstrates that Silva had lost none of her musical abilities or performative power; she still had her *cosa*, her thing, as she sang in "Yo tengo una cosa" (I have a thing) in *Myrta Silva y Daniel Santos en TV*, a later, mid-1960s LP.

When Silva's musical and social power exponentially increased with her flush years (from the late 1950s on), so did rejection and shaming. The game started to become nasty. Silva stopped producing her show on Puerto Rican television

in the 1960s. She later refuted the rumors that gave a network ratings $\dot{c}$
as the reason, mentioning specific trouble with censorship.[63] Cultural]
ing, there was a discernible move toward removing the so-called u'
elements of Puerto Rican society from media visibility, replacing t]
disgusting" with models of squeaky clean artists (presumed to be more m_
toward the middle of the decade. Undeniably, the ascendancy of youth culture
played a part, as the music industry sought newness to extract the most consumption from viewers and listeners and started to look down on older musicians,
relegating them to nostalgia formats. Silva began to speak of a split between two
selves in myriad interviews: "Who am I? The one who unveils herself in her
ballads and songs: a frustrated romantic. Everything else is a mask."[64]

It may seem odd that the same artist cultivated the cynical and conventional positions simultaneously. In one of her guises, she was uncompromising and unsentimental. In the other, she reclaimed the membership that
women's sentimentality afforded.[65] Silva's splitting certainly resonates with
queers and other socially disgusting subjects, who have for decades described
fielding multiple social identities at great personal cost, who have spoken
about cloaking a true or intimate being under the protection of a necessarily hardened social exterior. Yet it is still a conundrum that her identification
with the bolero became so strong at this point in her life. In the 1960s, Silva
became progressively more interested in songwriting, specifically of boleros,
than her much-lauded singing, especially of guarachas. In her later analysis,
she spoke as if the two always already stood for incompatible selves: "The
truth is that an intrinsically incompatible artistic reality lived in me. I was
first successful as a guaracha singer, which I popularized in mass taste. But
when it came to songwriting, my preference was for the romantic bolero. The
singer overshadowed [*opacó*] the composer. Several years passed, which saw
the rise and fall of other pop music genres. And then Myrta the composer
emerged and gained the upper hand, and the originary situation was reversed:
This time, the composer dethroned [*destronó*] the singer."[66] It could be that
Silva, consciously or unconsciously, anticipated that Puerto Ricans would
not memorialize a musician in her lifetime, whereas they definitely would a
songwriter. For decades, Puerto Ricans valued *compositores* as creators. At the
same time, they diminished musicianship expressed in performance, so Silva's
impression was completely on the mark.

Perhaps there is no better example of national nastiness than the insidious accusation that Silva stole two songs from her contemporary, the Puerto
Rican songwriter and show business personality Sylvia Rexach. The lurid

quality of the theft tale, the hagiographic narrative surrounding Rexach and her drinking problem as a personal weakness she could not overcome, and the consistent attacks on Silva in Puerto Rico leave its veracity open to question.[67] Was this accusation born out of gender panic and virulent homophobia? Dozens of musicians respected Silva, among them the towering stars of the Latin American constellation who recorded her boleros. It is not a coincidence that during the same time Silva acquired the epithet La Gorda de Oro, which, far from being an affectionate term, signaled loathing and disgust over an overweight woman past her thirties being unabashedly sexual, on the one hand, and hopelessly romantic, on the other, without parading a legible male object of desire for the public view.

It appears that the collective was willing to be entertained by Silva and benefit from her business genius, but not willing to extend to her the mantle that it happily bestowed on the suffering and abject Rexach (a common construction of the modern woman musician's life).[68] Ultimately, was Silva's queerness the source of her culturally mandated estrangement from the bolero? Facing the chokehold of censorship and realizing, in her prophetic way, that she would be trapped in dominant scripts excluding her from musical creation and renovation, we can surmise that her desire to avoid an artistic dead end was the one, chief reason for her move to the vibrant New York City. The artist still had one more round of the game in her.

THEY CALL IT *BUGALÚ*

In 1965, Silva went into what she later called "voluntary exile." She spent four years in New York City producing, hosting, and performing on the pioneering and critically acclaimed TV show, *The Myrta Silva Show*, for which (as we saw above) she won the prize for Best Variety Show in the New York Area in 1965. Silva's identity as a Latina precursor is an interesting and unexplored aspect of her life. While reading about her in old newspapers and the entertainment press, one finds mentions of her residence in New York and identification with the community. Her "Tira y tápate" column is evidence of her heartfelt attachment. She always included a segment discussing Puerto Rican artists in New York and the United States, giving fans a prominent role and speaking highly of Puerto Rican migrants, which ran counter to how migrants were regarded in Puerto Rico until the very recent historical past: as traitors or at best poor facsimiles of the national "original," as subjects irrevocably damaged by their displacement.

While a transnational market was being created to include the migrants and cater to a panethnic belonging, I do not doubt that Silva's allegiances ran much deeper than commercial gain. She felt that the audiences in New York had made her a star.[69] Silva clearly had a proto-Latino audience in mind when she relocated. In her show's first anniversary, she opened with the following monologue in Spanish: "My dear TV viewers: It seems like only yesterday that this jíbara from Arecibo arrived at Channel 47 to try and produce Hispanic [Latino] television for all of you. My show, your show, *Una hora contigo* . . . is now a year old. I would like to thank . . . not only all Puerto Ricans but also the legion of Latin Americans that live together in this metropolis of New York."[70] Silva was not merely an entrepreneur who exploited a market niche. She thought of the Latino community as held together by cultural needs and a shared economic existence in the wonderful but difficult new home of the city. Nevertheless, the diasporic community held on, sometimes too tightly, to the national-popular framework for pop music. Regarding the Chencha signifier, the queer negative virtuosity had fewer and fewer opportunities to come to the fore.

"Chencha," biting humor and social commentary notwithstanding, had transformed into a queerly normative formulation of women as consuming citizens. By the mid-1960s, Silva had become overly identified with her gossip queen persona in Puerto Rico, rendering her musical voices (as a singer and songwriter) secondary. The New York show remedied some of that. The identity of this show, of which some clips are available on YouTube, is illustrated in *Puerto Rico canta y baila* (Puerto Rico dances and sings), recorded in 1966 with musicians of the Tito Rodríguez Orchestra. Its title echoes a revue Silva presented in Puerto Rico's Tropicoro Hotel in May 1964, prior to her relocation. Pursuant to dominant formats catering to tourists in San Juan at the time, she included traditional, Puerto Rican folkloric genres of bomba and plena, which were not really her repertoire. In a closing bolero, she refers to herself as a daughter of the Puerto Rican nation, very differently from her bolero temperament, reflected in her own "Qué sabes tú" (What do you know) or "Tengo que acostumbrarme" (I have to get used to it). She incorporated a *chisme* (gossip) track, echoing her "Tira y tápate" TV show segment. In fact, the cover shows Silva dancing in her Chencha costume, sans partner or orchestra. The cover's back side features images of Silva on her Channel 47 TV show out of the Chencha costume, with luminaries such as Roberto Rohena, Tito Puente, and La Lupe. The liner notes are upbeat about Silva's Spanish-language TV shows for Latino consumers in the U.S. market, and Silva is shown in a

FIGURE 1.8 Album cover, Myrta Silva, *Canta canciones mi mamá no me enseñó* (Songs my mother never taught me), Tico LP 1171, 1968. This is the third of three in a series and the only one to feature a solo artist.

pretty picture as Chencha, beaming. The images and liner notes convey a vision of a woman entrepreneur who is creating community for her folks in the city.

One of the community's needs was humor. Away from Puerto Rico, Silva used humor and specifically the obscene to return to the ethics as well as the parlando that had made her a household name. The album *Songs My Mother Never Taught Me, Volume III*, was the third in a series of off-color records produced by Tico Records in 1960s New York (figure 1.8). The liner notes portray Silva as "la reina del doble sentido" (the queen of double entendre), reframing her earliest title, "la reina de la guaracha." On the album cover, Silva looks up to the presumably Catholic sky, clasping her hands in prayer, making the album's transgression both sonic and visual. Silva's return to obscene music is quite the statement, almost a pornographic *ars poetica*. While the eruption of the obscene in a relatively mainstream way in the Latino recording industry is an important fact, it's not my main interest here. The type of laughter it may elicit in the casual listener is not the type of laughter I'm pursuing in this analysis. Rather, I'm interested in the laughter that some listeners may key into if they tune into Silva's call to thinking.

Silva's record is different from the earlier ones in the series. Aside from being a solo record, it includes, like her earlier classics, a parallel commentary that initially may not be apprehended but is apparent once the listener has decided to look out for it, perhaps after becoming more knowledgeable about what the signifier Myrta stood for — what Silva's persona was — and what her tribulations as an artist under constant examination for deviance had been. Critical listening is now required to understand the comedic ramifications of this record, taken as innocuous because it is "merely" pornographic. What were the terms on which Silva invited the listener to enjoy her most obscene record? How did Silva negotiate this opportunity to articulate, once more, her principled cynicism?

For starters, the record was exported to many places, so Silva was not confined to island reception. She regarded New York as a metropolitan city, with a sophisticated audience. The album exists between the coalescing Latino and the more traditional Latin American music markets. This in-betweenness freed up performative space. It appealed to New York by adopting the bugalú, which was all the rage. It reformulated old classics from Silva's Cuban period, catering to nostalgic listeners, but Silva changed the terms of this nostalgia through her performance as much as her alterations to the original lyrics. The new versions refuted all sentimentalism and use of song as a surrogate for a lost home. The recording included elements that go beyond a normative rendition of comedy toward an opportunity for queering, such as the chorus of shrill backup singers in falsetto (all men), who humorously evoke the middlebrow records favored by upper-middle-class listeners. It was a patriarchal album in its original conception, to be sure, and can be regarded as sexist, but Silva made quick work of transforming that content into a tour-de-force, ferocious reply to her many detractors. She played with insults jabbed at her (as in "Chencha la gambá") and demolished any vision of Puerto Rican behavior as moral (as was preached at the time in all official outlets). *Canciones* is the evil twin of LPs like *Puerto Rico canta y baila* and the forcibly cleaned-up collective repertoire.

To add to the complexity of the album, *Canciones* was released with different covers for multiple markets. I offer two examples. In theory, there could have been a different cover for every Latin American country, responding to regional imaginaries regarding Silva and her creations. The first is from Mexico, where the album acquired a content warning, "Sólo para adultos" (For adults only). It featured a soft porn cover of a nearly nude woman outfitted in

FIGURE 1.9 Album cover, Myrta Silva, *Canciones que
mi mamá no me enseñó*, Tico R-2570, 1969. The album
acquired a content warning when it was published
in Mexico: "Sólo para adultos" (For adults only). The
cover shows a model in light bondage costume.

a highly stylized, light bondage costume (figure 1.9). The second cover, from
Peru, is also soft porn, but this time the woman is shot through a camera
filter to produce a diffuse, boudoir effect. Both are images of female sexual
availability and both are completely at odds with the actual content of Myrta
Silva's record and her persona. We don't know who decided what to put on
the covers for different national markets, but we can definitely notice that the
covers favor a white supremacist racial idea of beauty. Silva's own body and
pose, in what we presume to be the original cover, unmasks dominant fantasy as hypocritical, bourgeois, and false. The really scandalous gesture is
her insertion in the scopic regime: a rereading of the *Camina como Chencha*
cover of Silva as fetish, as oversexed. We witness the resurgence of the horror
movie doll, the speaking body, and the acoustic mirror, all wrapped into one
explosive, "disgusting" package.

Silva's positioning is difficult to adjudicate. These multiple covers lend
credence to the idea that the album was in collusion with the dominant

Latino ethos of the time. I will briefly outline how Silva was able to wrest her creation from this ethos and why she continued to compel critical listening and exhibit an understanding of what calls voice to thinking. To me, listening to the album without factoring in the Myrta Silva text is tantamount to having listened to a quarter of the record. (It's also important to point out that Silva stands for an entire, varied, hemispheric, and successful career, and that her late creations grapple with the fate of so many artists who have long careers. They are often required to perform old hits and respond to public expectations that they may have outgrown and no longer relate to. This was certainly the case with Silva. In a sense, she is locked in a battle with her own iconic status.)

"Dr. Bugalón" is the album's last out of ten tracks of nonstop, obscene humor. Throughout the record, Silva plays with calling herself *loca*, as in mentally ill, and also with clear overtones of sexual deviance. In this track, "loca" concretely refers to a drag queen. The song's pun is that the doctor who is treating the queens is a *bugarrón*, a man in the active position who has sex with men while being married or publicly heterosexual. The doctor's last name, the puerile pun "Bugalón," mixes bugalú with bugarrón. What Silva does with this bugalú, however, can hardly be considered puerile. This song is significant because Silva engages gossip concerning homosexuality and therefore her own sexuality (a hot topic for Puerto Ricans at the time) by centering attention on the figure of the queen, for whom the closet is not an option and who interacts constantly with a normative male subject because of her desire and economic need. "Dr. Bugalón" names a psychiatrist, vaguely American (Dr. John Bugalón), who "specializes in treating queens." In the other tracks, Silva's improvs mention psychiatry and taunts about her own mental state, accusations which I'm certain she received in anonymous hate mail, a fact she repeatedly mentions in her "Tira y tápate" columns. An entirely recitative song, the chorus pitches in the doctor's name at precise intervals as the refrain: "El doctor Bugalón . . . el doctor Bugalón."

Silva stages the song as a phone conversation between the receptionist, presumably a feminine woman ("señorita"), and herself. The receptionist asks Silva if she wants to be treated by the doctor, to which Silva responds, feigning amazement, that she doesn't have that "problem." This response provokes an extreme reaction in the receptionist, to the point that she gets cut off "inexplicably" after every parlando chunk of Silva's. The suggestion, not so hidden, is that finding out that Silva is not a loca but instead a "queer woman" has caused such sexual excitement in the receptionist that she has lost the line, amplified by the entrance of the big band in increased tempo and volume. When the receptionist picks up the phone, she cannot place Silva as a woman, mistaking her for a loca. The identification of Silva with the loca is clear. The other interpretation, of course, is that the receptionist is revolted at the revelation of Silva's gender nonconformity. The revulsion is erotically charged, tinged with sexual fascination: The receptionist keeps taking the call that fails after every long verse in parlando.

The final recitative is:

Óigame óigame óigame, ¿por qué se le cae tanto la comunicación? Haga algo porque aquí no se puede tener nada caído. . . . Estamos en un mundo que todo tiene que estar parado, señorita. . . . Bueno mire, déjele este mensajito a mi amiguita Rocío de la Noche. . . . Apunte apunte apunte apunte apunte. . . . Dígale que llamó *Myrrrta* para saber de su estado y que Pancho Tranca le manda recuerdos . . . y que Tato Machete ya salió con fianza por romperle lo que ella sabe a la Rata del Bronx . . . y que todas sus amiguitas, como la Pani, la Michelle, la Miroslava, la Godina, la Roy, la Lirio del Valle, la Tina, y la María René, y yo, todas la recordamos . . . y que nos alegramos que esté bajo los cuidados del Dr. Bugalón . . .

Excuse me, excuse me, excuse me, why do we keep getting cut off? Please do something about it because in this day and age we can't be walking around with anything down. . . . Everything has to be erect, miss. . . . Please give this message to my friend Evening Dew. . . . Write it down, write it down, write it down, write it down, write it down. . . . Tell her *Myrrrta* called to see how she was doing and that Big Stick Steve sends her his love . . . and Machete Tato was let go on bail after he was arrested for breaking the Bronx Rat's you-know-what . . . and that all her girlfriends, la Pani, la Michelle, la Miroslava, la Godina, la Roy, Lily of the Valley, la Tina, and la María René, and I, we all are thinking of her and are happy Dr. Bugalón is taking good care of her . . .

Silva returns to her given name, Myrta (as we have seen, a very powerful name charged with meaning, which she emphasizes sonically by stretching the rolling "r," much like "girrrrl") to identify herself as the caller, and expresses familiarity with a scene by listing a string of names belonging to various queens in New York City, with herself as the last name on the list. Her alignment happens because queens are in a position similar to hers: objects of ridicule, disparaged as being physically deformed, presumptively hypersexual and gender noncompliant, yet also feared because of their power to unmask normative subjects and the hypocrisy of society. Silva doesn't make them into martyred exemplars of the nothing. Instead, she posits them as walking negations. The tone is mocking; what is being mocked is not as clear-cut, however. Is it the queens, or the policemen who beat them up, or hypocritical men who sleep with them and disown their desire, or generally the society that diagnoses queens as abnormal and in need of gender correction? The song, as mentioned, is entirely in parlando; it exhibits Silva's intact swing, perfect musical timing, and eerie contemporaneity.

SPIT IT OUT

During her finest musical moments, Silva had embodied the void that Mladen Dolar refers to as the "third level" of the voice, as the "blind spot in the call of the other and a disturbance to aesthetic appreciation."[71] Silva resumed *El Show de Myrta Silva*, with its "Tira y tápate" segment, on Puerto Rico's Channel 11 for two years (1971–1973). Her original Chencha creation morphed into a drag queen persona, who sat in front of a crystal ball called Bola (Ball) and supposedly unmasked secrets about celebrity sex lives (in particular, tales of marital infidelity, perverse sexuality, and homosexuality). This is the only image of Silva that Puerto Ricans remember today. Often they simply confuse the character with the artist, as if they were interchangeable, to the point of occluding Silva's primary identity as an artist, whether singer or composer — forgetting she was also a producer, host, bandleader, and artist agent, among the many roles she took on during her career.

There is scant extant footage of the 1970s character. Here is an excerpt from a typical TV monologue. This section addresses sexuality and particularly homosexuality:

> Bola, ¿cómo fue, Bola? Espepítamelo. Ah, que una fiesta muy elegante que empezó con champán, caviar y paté de foie (paté de foie es hígado de ganso, saben). Ah, cuando las burbujas empezaron a hacer efecto empezó el calor y . . . la gente se empezó a quitar la ropa. Había un productor escondido de estos. Empezó a bailar con un tremendo pollo. Él estaba de lo más embullaíto y estaba así pegaíto, y cuando el productor le preguntó a la bella damisela y le dijo, "¿Cómo te llamas, mi amor?," la damisela le respondió: "Mi nombre es Jorge." ¡Eso es bueno que te pase, por no saber

adónde vas! Jorge o Georgie es lo mismo baby. . . . ¡Cómo, Bola! ¡Ay no,
Bola, si no me lo juras, no te lo creo!

Ball, what? What is it, Ball? Come on, spit it out. Oh, I see, there was a
very elegant party . . . with champagne, caviar and paté de foie [*to the
audience, with an air of contempt*] (paté de foie means goose liver, in
case you don't know). [*Sways back and forth, looking straight at Bola
and away to the side of the frame.*] Oh, when the bubbly started to have
an effect, [*mock sensual tone*] the heat was on . . . and people started
to take off their clothes. A closeted producer was there [*sneering*] and
he started dancing with this incredibly hot woman. [*Lowers voice*]
He was really into it, dancing cheek to cheek, you know, and when
the producer asked the beautiful damsel what her name was, the
damsel replied: [*exaggerates masculine baritone*] "My name is Jorge."
[*Chiding*] Well, you had it coming! Happens if you don't know where
you're headed! [*Chuckling*] Jorge, Georgie, it's the same thing, baby. . . .
[*Feigning surprise, as she moves on to the next piece of gossip*] Ball, what!
No Ball, swear, or I won't believe you!⁷²

The over-the-top, highly theatrical brutality is very similar to that of drag
queen discourse, which is scathing in its directness. Madame Chencha makes
fun of all the characters, not of queer people specifically, and not of anybody
as targeted, disgusting subjects. Madame Chencha had her pet peeves, but it
was certain behaviors, not entire groups, that set her off. Silva did not mince
words as Madame Chencha when she felt people were exploiting a situation
for their personal gain. The queer subjects she singles out in her comedy are
primarily those who parade around their normative life for all to see, not hesi-
tating to castigate others left and right, to then proceed to engage in so-called
illicit behavior out of the public eye while spared from the judgment and pun-
ishment they dispense.

Slavoj Žižek has addressed instances of the Lacanian real's eruption into
the social fabric. Silva, as master of voice's symbolic power, contained for her
listeners and viewers what he calls an "irreducible kernel of jouissance that
resists all symbolization."⁷³ Her extraordinary success as a singer had to do
with the "something" akin to the Freudian Das Ding, the "thing," which we
can playfully link to the cosa (thing) that all great soneros have. Recall Silva's
song, "Yo tengo una cosa" (I have a thing), which, in its 1960s recording, acquired directly autobiographical qualities relating her to this unsettling, cultural thing, and recall also her memorable recording of "Alcapurria" (Fritter)

from *Songs My Mother Never Taught Me*, in which she reminded listeners that "there is a very flavorful thing in Puerto Rico, what is it?" (En Puerto Rico hay una cosa muy sabrosa, ¿qué será?)

It's not known if the monologues were improvised on the spot or if she created scripts or sketches before going on the air. More likely than not, they were not completely extemporaneous. Silva's makeup and gestures clearly owe much to her loca figuration as it had been established in *Songs My Mother Never Taught Me*; instead of the working-class comadre that she had visually represented in her first incarnations, Silva's makeup is gaudy, exaggerated, and flamboyant. Figures 1.10–1.12 show Silva performing the monologue just quoted.

Estrellas, a celebrity pulp publication, reprinted the following monologue, "Tira y Tápate, by Chencha," in a commemorative issue published upon her death. This shows the difference between the 1970s Chencha and her incarnation in the original "Tira y tápate" columns. Like the performed monologue, above, it is exemplary of her engagement with queer subject matter:

— Vuélveme y cuéntame qué es lo que hay en el ambiente.

— ¿Que hay una actriz que está muy enamorada de un estilista?, por cierto muy bueno y polifacético.

— Bueno, pero en este negocio de "Show Business" hay cosas que parecen increíbles, pero no lo son y ésta es una de ellas.

— Sí, bola, yo doy fe, conozco a los dos . . .

— ¿Quién te lo dijo bola? No me metas paquetes, bola, que después soy yo la que quedo mal.

— ¿Que el galán no sabía de una discoteca donde ellos bailaban con ellos, y ellas bailaban con ellas? — ¡y bola, yo no entiendo eso! Vuelve, vuelve y explica eso más.

— Déjalo ahí, porque yo no quiero causar problemas, porque si causo problemas mejor me callo.

— Pero de verdad que él va ahí con todo y cámara . . .

— ¡Ay "visne," esta bola me va a buscar cada lío! Mira bola, hazme el favor de no decir cosas que no puedas probar, que nos pueden demandar.

— Okay, Ball, tell me what's happening in show biz.

— So an actress is madly in love with a stylist (by the way, he's very good and multitalented).

— Well, as you know, in this business of show business lots of things happen that seem incredible, but they aren't, and this is an example.

FIGURES 1.10, 1.11, 1.12 Myrta Silva performing as Madame Chencha on Puerto Rican television, Channel 11, early 1970s. She talked into a crystal ball called Bola. The staging recalls the white table ritual of espiritismo.

— Yes, Ball, I give you my word, I know both of them.

— Ball, who told you that? Don't lie to me, Ball, because I'm the one who will get blasted.

— That our Romeo can always be seen at a disco where guys dance with guys and gals with gals? Ball, I don't understand this! C'mon, c'mon, explain this a little more.

— Well, on second thought, let's leave it there, because I don't want to create any problems. Better to shut up.

— Really? He really goes there and brings his camera?

— Blessed Virgin Mary, this ball is gonna get me into trouble! Look Ball, don't bring up things you can't prove, because we'll get slapped with a lawsuit.

To my knowledge, no lawsuit was ever brought against Silva, but what was exacted was a steady proliferation of terrifying crank calls and anonymous letters. Silva had regularly mentioned these while she worked as a columnist for *Bohemia libre puertorriqueña*, in her first incarnation as Chencha. She exhibited righteous ire and on occasion challenged the author or perpetrator to identify himself or herself publicly, so the injurious speech could be adjudicated, mainly in the court of public opinion that journalism faintly still represented. In the 1970s, Silva continued to receive anonymous letters and threats. There was no longer a call on her part to match this hateful speech with its origin. Instead, Silva created Madame Chencha and her sidekick, Bola. No one could say who Silva referred to, even though many people were convinced that they knew the identities of the accused in Silva's discourse as Chencha. The shared nothing or constitutive emptiness of the monologue kept viewers hooked.

I met Bola while interviewing Silva's niece, Awilda Silva. I could not believe that I was seeing and touching the famed ball of my early childhood. Amazed, I realized it was simply a round vase turned upside down, catapulted into the sublime when amplified by the special effects available to TV at the time, when gazed at via much smaller screens than those available today. Transparent and very ordinary, Bola was completely clear, completely empty. It had been, once, a full emptiness endowed with an aphonic voice, like Silva's self-figuration in "Nada," her sexuality in guaracha interpretations, and the conventional love of her boleros; like Chencha's supposedly revealing gait, "Tira y tápate"'s jabs, and the ventriloquized drag queen's speech in *Songs My Mother Never Taught Me*.

Chencha mouthed ordinary discourse, reflecting back the obsession with so-called privacy and the morbid curiosity for what society's preferred scapegoats of the day did in their everyday life. Associates and friends of Silva's told me that she had a set number of stock monologues that varied little and that she never mentioned people by name. In their opinion, Silva was not really talking about anybody in particular, and she made things up for laughs.[74] It is true that the anecdotes resemble the ones mobilized in her recording of her theme song "Tira y tápate," from the LP *Myrta Silva presenta: Una hora contigo* (Myrta Silva presents "An Hour with You"), figures of a generalized critique of sexual hypocrisy in celebrity-driven culture and frenzied consumerism. Without discounting the problematic aspects of Silva's performance as Chencha, Silva always acted with an ethics in mind, what we might call a cynical ethics, fusing Foucault and Lacan.[75]

Silva's 1960s columns inserted themselves in a larger commentary about musical life in Puerto Rico and wherever Puerto Rican artists or fans were. They were performative, but in a dialogical way, continuing the initial dialogism of "Nada." Silva often responded to fans' queries and shared information about artist performances that she received in the mail or by phone. She talked about actual phone calls and visits from a dizzying array of artists, many of whom were very famous. Silva's intonation, her different tones, even her physical gestures jump off the page. Her 1970s re-creation of Chencha, by contrast, exists in a closed, claustrophobic discursive world, one could say severed from the artistic persona of Myrta.

I'm not proposing that Silva should have continued to sing beyond her interest so her Myrta persona could prevail. The public demanded the old Silva, the Silva of the past, particularly tied to "Nada" and other Rafael Hernández songs, in tune with the standard narrative of Puerto Rican music emphasizing male greatness and calling on women as surrogates, at best. What if Silva had been able to host a live music show in the 1970s? Who knows what Madame Chencha would have been like, and the opportunity rising artists would have had? An award-winning variety show, like Silva had just achieved in New York, was unthinkable in 1970s Puerto Rico because the entertainment industry was driven insanely to profit, capitalized as a side arm of other financial ventures, attracted to foreign pop stars more than Puerto Ricans because of the need to entertain tourists, and dangerously in alliance with the ever more repressive government bent on dividing artists into ideological camps. Thus, the drama of Madame Chencha goes far deeper than imagined.

Some viewers remember the general tone of Silva's monologues and are offended but ignore other aspects of the skits. The final iteration of the Chencha persona borrows heavily from the ritualistic practice known as *espiritismo* (spiritism) and its *mesa blanca* (white table), gesturing to the occult and proscribed religious practices of the same middle and upper classes that condemned Silva for her vulgarity. These subjects, one can surmise, might have felt exposed by Silva's skits in ways that they could not acknowledge to themselves or to the public. There are moments when Silva toes the line between effective sendup and cheap commercial hook, of course, but her positioning is more complex, embedded in what was allowable or possible. Silva had to run her shows through censors for years; a generalized climate of censorship and outright repression abounded. With this in mind, some of the key birthing elements of this new character, Madame Chencha, become more clear. Social repression and shaming went hand in hand with lifting the bar of discourse and producing the generalized phenomenon of scapegoating.[76]

One route to understanding the last Chencha appearances in Silva's career, and the perturbing fact that she is remembered only as Madame Chencha and as the performer of certain Rafael Hernández's songs ("Nada," "Esos no son de aquí," "Buchipluma no ma"), is the ascendancy of what Jean Baudrillard called "the desert of the real," a phenomenon actualized by the dominance of mass media and its particular code producing hyperreality. The cheating producer, the duped wife, the closeted homosexual, Madame Chencha, are all characters of the hyperreal.[77] Just as when Silva dissolved the presumptive separation between the listener and the singer in so many memorable performances, she dissolved the barrier between viewers and Madame Chencha, exposing everyone's partaking in the simulation of the real.

The last Silva, of the 1970s, dabbled here and there as an artist, without the heady drive of her decades-long career. She had occupied various laborious roles in her shows: She was producer, host, bandleader, singer, and comedian. She was exhausted. She devoted time to charity events and considered long-term projects for the care of elderly artists and the establishment of fellowships for young artists from disadvantaged backgrounds, with whom she identified the most. Her lens continued to be art, but as Puerto Rico was fast becoming a hyperreality, Chencha became a simulation.[78]

Silva performed "Camina como Chencha" (Chencha's Gait) in a rare 1973 live concert in Mayagüez, Puerto Rico. She once again altered the lyrics of the song, enacting yet another layer of readings.[79] Announcing her song, Silva says, "I'm going to sing the song that made me the most infamous in the hemisphere — I mean, famous — ladies and gentlemen, for all of you, 'She Walks Like Chencha'!" Later, she improvises: "Well, every one has a right to walk however they damn like. . . . In this day and age, everyone is doing the 'Chencha.'" This rendition of "Chencha's Gait" expresses an unmistakable defense of sexual freedom. The precious recording contains some segments of banter between Silva and her audience, much like the ones simulated in her original television show. At one point, Silva notices a couple of men who appear to be embracing or engaged in romantic or sexual affection. Silva quips, "What's that kid doing on the other guy's head? Hey, we all know Mayagüez has a queer reputation. . . . Get down, get down, get down from there. . . . Well look, if you like the position and he goes for it, well then, may you live happily ever after . . . celebrate!"[80]

Silva came to identify with her *sinthome*, a late, Lacanian reformulation of the more traditional idea of the symptom, when it's no longer culturally relevant or intellectually sensible to decode any message. There are various manifestations of this sinthome: her devotion to her mother, which from being a mask of normalcy to protect her from the accusations encircling her undisclosed (but not closeted) personal life took on an intense life of its own; her creation of a marriage to David Silva, the Mexican actor, which according to testimonies of friends never happened (for what cause we do not know, possibly as a cover, initially at least) and of a pregnancy with him, which apparently also never happened; the problematic jouissance of her later years as she became more virulent as Madame Chencha, even endangering her life as she received violent threats in her TV offices; and, finally, a more benign jouissance in her portrayal of her bolero songs as her children ("My songs are like my children, and I don't create quarrels between my children").[81] In the sinthome, Silva returned to the nothing.

She had created Myrta at a very early age (practically the very beginning of her career). Silva resolutely refused to signify anything other than this figure. She created another figure, Chencha, as a secondary character, but it exceeded her control and altered significantly Myrta's artistic trajectory. In part thanks to Chencha's success, collective memory has occluded Myrta. My reconstruction of Silva's brilliant career aims at a reparation for this forgetting. My analysis of voice as a Lacanian part-object aims to restore the performative power Silva commanded as Myrta and Chencha, and demonstrate how both of her memorable creations manifest a thinking voice.

TWO

SO WHAT IF SHE'S BLACK?

Afro–Puerto Rican musicians routinely entertained white-skinned Puerto Ricans and Americans in venues they were barred from as patrons in the first decades of the twentieth century. A female lead singer, however, was quite out of the ordinary, even this segregated ordinary. The Puerto Rican twentieth-century icon Ruth Fernández, like Myrta Silva, was a teenager when she began her career in live radio broadcasts of the early 1930s and as lead for Mingo and His Whoopee Kids. When she debuted in the posh Escambrón Beach Club in 1937 and started recording for RCA Victor, she was marketed as an authentic black voice, even characterized as a blues singer to translate her singing to the many Americans who frequented the club.[1] Fernández entered the star orbit of the music establishment as an exception: the first female lead of any orchestra in Puerto Rico, and also the first black star body in Puerto Rican culture.

Regarding her early start with Mingo and His Whoopee Kids, Puerto Rico's most successful band from the 1930s to the early 1950s, Fernández recounted, "At first, the band members didn't want me. They told Mingo: she's black. She's not pretty. But Mingo said: I'm not looking for a bombshell. . . . I need a singer who can come to this band with the class that this band is known for."[2] The facts of her gender and race do not tell the whole story. Considering the events happening at the time — three decades of U.S. colonialism with its mixed messages regarding the racial standing of colonial subjects, massive workers' demonstrations, endemic poverty, and routine repression culminating in the 1937 Ponce Massacre, right in her hometown — it's safe to say that Fernández accrued meaning because she became aligned with the evental shift from Spanish to U.S. colony in the context of the world wars, and was instrumental in the corresponding transition of racial regimes and how they were apprehended through music.

While Fernández was a pop music singer, she possessed a voice of great volume and color, was naturally virtuosic, and, although not trained, reflected a preference for classically inflected singing that she probably learned or was steered to in school. Fernández attended elementary school in the very first decades of the twentieth century. Thus she was schooled squarely in the framework of empire's civilizing mission. In this colonial context, her voice opened a gap in the available symbolics of music. This gap seemed to be filled with meaning from her very first appearances, but, in truth, it remained suspended as precisely that, a gap.

Aside from the strangeness of refinement in pop music, a steely cool the singer manifested from early on, listeners belonging to multiple publics regarded Fernández's voice as masculine, at a disjuncture or dissonance with her body. Fernández narrated how, when she was singing with Los Hijos del Arte (Art's offspring) on the radio, circa 1935, Domingo Colón, bandleader of Mingo and His Whoopee Kids, heard her on the street and asked, "Who's that? Is it a young man? Is it a woman?"[3] The newly hybrid colonial society naturalized her deep voice with its mighty volume as one appropriate for a black woman, establishing an insidious connection between vocal register, race, and beauty. Words like "dramatic," "grave," and "strong," which Fernández and others used to describe her vocal appeal, functioned as code for bodies and sounds that were admitted into performative spaces in vexed ways.

The code was not only of the commonsense variety; it found expression in high, musically literate culture too. The renowned Catalan cellist Pau (Pablo) Casals told Fernández that her voice reminded him of his cello, an anecdote she proudly recalled.[4] According to the Cuban critic and esteemed music collector Cristóbal Díaz-Ayala, Armando Oréfiche, the great Cuban bandleader, pianist, and composer of the 1940s also referred to Fernández's voice as a "violoncello."[5] An American, Glen Sauls, heard Fernández sing on the record *Ñáñigo*, reportedly called her "Lady Baritone," and invited her to join the Met roster of singers on behalf of Rudolf Bing (the Metropolitan Opera House general manager from 1950 to 1972).[6]

In interviews, Fernández gave her vocal difference as the reason for her success, studiously deflecting attention away from her musicianship or stage presence: "Tenía una voz grave, distinta" (I had a deep, different voice).[7] The late Marvette Pérez, then Latino history and culture curator at the National Museum of American History, conducted an extensive, groundbreaking oral history of Fernández in which she spoke of her voice as "a rare gift" and recalled how, when she began singing, people affirmed that "she resembled a man." Contralto voices were unrecognizable in the pop milieu as female voices; society did not have a name for them: "I had such a deep voice. Later I was told I was a contralto."[8]

It seems unlikely that Fernández was simply mouthing racist descriptions she heard. Rather, in her interviews she was performing and simultaneously reenacting a particular voice, one she adjusted and refined as her career unfolded, with the clear intention of intervening in Puerto Rico's cultural and political decolonization across the twentieth century. Fernández's understanding of the inescapable consequences of racially defined national music in early colonial life, and her decision to explicitly represent race for elites as Puerto Rico "progressed" to liberal modernity, distinguish her from the plethora of brilliant black women singers of the Greater Caribbean in the short twentieth century.[9] Today, her career provides a valuable launching pad to complicate standard accounts of the careers and vocal quandaries of black women singers in the Caribbean and Latin America.[10] This chapter is structured around instances of sonic interpellation at key moments of Fernández's musical career, which are explicitly articulated around race and led to Fernández's later, diva cry: "So what if I'm black?"

The eulogies delivered during three official days of mourning upon her passing in early 2012, at age ninety-two, continued the baffling and sometimes infuriating lack of depth in repeated paeans mostly limited to superficial biographical sketches heavily influenced by the artist's own account of her life. Notwithstanding the large number of primary documents, appreciations, and interviews extant in the archive, there are, to my knowledge, no critical considerations of Fernández's large musical output and her role in the intersection of culture and politics, so illustrative of other such figures in the Latin American constellation of the twentieth century.[11]

One of the most successful Puerto Rican artists from the 1940s to the 1960s, Fernández was a household name for decades in Puerto Rican homes on the island and in the United States, as well as famous throughout Latin America (especially in Cuba and Mexico, the two major musical markets of the time). Her career began in 1930s Puerto Rico, in radio and in local, live venues; in the 1940s she scored a huge triumph in the Cuban operetta *Cecilia Valdés* (recorded 1948); in the 1950s she hosted radio shows in Puerto Rico (some of which featured a gossip slant, such as *La chismosa* [The gossip queen] and *¿Te enteraste?* [Did you know that?]). Starting in the 1960s, by then installed as a symbol of Puerto Rico's modernity and adopted by the government as its official cultural ambassador, she shifted toward pedagogical television. She hosted programs with didactic names like *Almorzando con Ruth Fernández* (Lunchtime with Ruth Fernández, WKBM), *Del brazo con Ruth Fernández* (Guided by Ruth Fernández, WKAQ), and *Cantemos con Ruth Fernández* (Let's sing with Ruth Fernández, WIPR).[12] She was also featured in the musical interludes of the movies *Caña brava* (Indomitable sugar cane) and *Romance en Puerto Rico* (A romance in Puerto Rico), and appeared in an American cult film, *Fiend of Dope Island*, in a nonsinging, nonspeaking role as Tula, a "tropical" bartender. Her cinematic visuality corresponded to the imaginary of the tropical island inhabitant; it clashed with the image she painstakingly developed for her artistic persona, as we shall see.

Adding to her mystique, Fernández became revered by the thousands of Puerto Ricans who emigrated to New York and other U.S. cities from the 1950s on. She became an avuncular figure who addressed migrant affective wounds of deep loss and painful missing through music, earning the moniker of Titi Ruth (Auntie Ruth; she remained childless and repeatedly invoked her numerous, adoptive *sobrinos* [nephews and nieces]).[13] She performed live in well-established venues for Latino audiences in the city, like the Teatro Hispano, Teatro Puerto Rico, and Carnegie Hall, as well as local Latino clubs. She toured U.S. universities. She participated in a historic 1965 Metropolitan Opera House concert at the Lewisohn Stadium. And she was on TV in the tri-state area with WNJU's *The Ruth Fernández Show*, taped partially in Puerto Rico and rebroadcast in the States. In the 1980s and 1990s, her LPs were reissued as CDs sold in Puerto Rican and New York City stores under the rubrics *Música del ayer* (Yesterdays' music) or Puerto Rico. Now, as with so many artists of the past, she enjoys an afterlife on YouTube, iTunes (variously shelved under Latino and World), and Spotify.

After her most estimable recording and performing period, dating from the late 1930s to the early 1950s, Fernández turned to an intense symbolization of "local color" at the service of the Popular Democratic Party (Partido Popular Democrático, PPD). She lived a celebrity life, one she publicly presented as both moral and pedagogical. Her celebrity life culminated in her becoming a professional politician in 1972, past her personal, musical heyday but entirely as a consequence of national music's potential for political marketing. Promoting herself as "the singing senator" and as "La Negra de Ponce" (the black woman from Ponce), she served as senator at large for eight years and later became a special aide for cultural affairs to the governor of Puerto Rico from 1985 to 1993. Without a doubt, Fernández's willingness to represent racial uplift through music, her fit with the populist narrative of the PPD, and a societal investment in classical music as the measure of civilization and musical education (which Fernández's voice clearly substantiated, since to the "uneducated" ears of colonial subjects, she did sound like a virtuosic contralto rather than a pop singer), combined to make her the PPD's media darling for several decades.

Standard interpretations of Fernández's career thus far lack insight into the complexity of Fernández's musical personality. She becomes, simply, a heroic figure within a middle-class ethos, espoused by a heavily white and light-skinned, elite group and funneled to the rest of the population via the state's cultural arm. Fernández's repetition of her racial tale appeals to certain social sectors in Puerto Rico up to this day, indicating the existence of a "policy of the ostrich" in which race is the pure signifier passed along the intersubjective chain without, however, becoming a letter (see chapter 1).[14] Recalling the title of a groundbreaking Puerto Rican book on race, Isabelo Zenón Cruz's *Narciso descubre su trasero* (Narcissus discovers his derriere), as when the ostrich's head is buried in its backside so as not to see, race becomes a construct of benevolence whose pernicious role in the symbolic chain is not exposed; its logic of segregation ranging from condescension to brutal exclusion and degradation are disguised. In this light, it's important to reconsider Fernández's influential self-narrative, one she started telling once she became preoccupied with cementing her place in posterity as the twentieth century inched toward a close.

The travails of her virtuosic voice can be read as the actualization of an aspirational desire to belong to the sphere of those considered educated, those who presumably safeguarded the collective's highest values (a desire that resonates with the Spanish phrase *tener una voz educada*, possessing a trained voice). Legend has it Fernández would have preferred to sing jazz or opera. Whether this myth is true or not, there is certainly a distinct quality to this voice, an uneasy residing in Latin American pop music because of its operatic sound (which was not the norm in the *sabor* [soul] and *sentimiento* [feeling] genres that Fernández favored).[15] This did not stem from her timbre as an immanent fact. She chose to interpret pop music after what was thought of as highbrow singing. It didn't hurt that Fernández had a passionate investment in fashion since she was young and became known for her legendary collection of designer dresses. She knew that voice was not just heard; it was as much "seen" in performance. She cannily employed the scopic register to influence collective listening.

The Slovenian thinker Mladen Dolar wrote, in *A Voice and Nothing More*, "We are social beings by the voice and through the voice: it seems that the voice stands at the axis of our social bonds, and that voices are the very texture of the social, as well as the intimate kernel of subjectivity."[16] Fernández's "intimate kernel of subjectivity" manifested in voice is extremely hard to decipher, while the form she gave to the social via voice is comparatively easier to piece together. Her personal reserve ran deep, despite her constant display. She tunes us into another variant of overexamination of the woman singer, one whose key is race. Constantly scrutinized visually and vocally, she constructed a persona, literally a glittering surface to match the wonder her voice provoked. Like other women singers thrust into crucibles of voice, Fernández gave form to the extimate. As I discussed in chapter 1, Jacques Lacan theorized the extimate as the point of intermediacy and undecidability, resting just at the interior-exterior juncture of individual and social subjectivity. Fernández's extimacy, though, is of a decidedly different nature than Myrta Silva's. The Puerto Rican crucible Fernández embodied concerned the shape of its pop singing as it began to inhabit the world as a form of ambassadorship, breaking out of the insularity enforced by U.S. military rule. The crucible responds to changes in the colonial structure and world transformations regarding struggles for self-determination and freedom. Fernández's own narratives about her career can be regarded as both true and untrue, which is to say they are performative. Seen retrospectively, her strategies were hugely successful as both a shield for the singer and an active intervention into culture and politics.

THE SENSORIUM OF RACISM

Fernández's first hit was an "Afro" song, "Y tu abuela onde etá." Fortunato Vizcarrondo wrote the poem in the late-1930s context of Caribbean avant-garde poetry, specifically *poesía negrista* or *afroantillana* (Afro-Antillean poetry). In this literary movement, prominent in the 1930s and 1940s across the Spanish-speaking Caribbean, mostly white or light-skinned writers rendered "black speech" as inherently rhythmic and sonorous, assigning black bodies an immanent relationship with pure sonority. This poetry claimed to represent the orality and sound of the newfound (literarily speaking) black subject. Domingo Colón (bandleader, as mentioned, of Mingo and His Whoopee Kids; the English name of the group should not go unnoticed) set the poem to music with Fernández in mind. This is no small detail since the poem's speaker is masculine, resonating with his initial confusion as to whether Fernández's voice was masculine. Colón explicitly linked Fernández's voice to black sound, using the acoustic coordinates supplied by Afro-Caribbean poetry to implant this identification. Following Freud's treatment of identification, its misfires enhance its capacity to perform symbolic work. In the societal view, Fernández's gender made her contralto voice unnatural, and her race made it black, joining two signs to embody a perpetual dissonance and thus create a very productive series of misfires.[17]

Released in 1941 by RCA Victor, "Y tu abuela onde etá" is a slow-tempo tango-congo with an ostinato rhythm. Like the first version of "Camina como Chencha" examined in chapter 1, it evoked what Robin Moore has described as a "generic primitivism."[18] It is a performance of blackness following how elites and popular sectors were codifying racial alterity through literature. As one of the first sound reproductions of this codification, it is a prime example of an early "acousmatic blackness."[19] During the 1930s, an entire polemic around the appropriateness of including blackness as intrinsic to the Puerto Rican national character raged, especially around the publication of poet Luis Palés Matos's so-called black poems, collected in the pivotal *Tun tun de pasa y grifería* (1937). Closer to musical debates, the intellectual Tomás Blanco published "Elogio de la plena" (In praise of plena) in 1935, making a case for plena's inclusion in the canon of national music as a "miscegenating genre."

Setting needle to groove, we hear the singer attempting to embody the sonic blackness that the poem's linguistic apprehension of the black speaking subject proposes:

Ayé me dijite negra
Y hoy te boy a contejtá:
Mi mai se sienta en la sala.
¿Y tu agüela, aonde ejtá?

Yesterday, you said I was black
Today, I'm going to respond to you
My mother sits in the parlor
And your grandmother? Where is she?

In order to epitomize this black-black interlocution, as written by a white-skinned poet, Fernández employs her deep register, laughter, and conversational musical phrasing such as sung whispering and sung questioning. In this early recording, she seeks to match societal expectations about the comical nature of such conversations, yet also manages to introduce a supplement (in the Derridean sense). The vaguely erotic interpellation Fernández mixes in with phrases such as "mi bien" (my sweet) and sonorous elements such as

FIGURE 2.1 Ruth Fernández as lead of Mingo and His Whoopee Kids, circa 1935. Courtesy of the Archivo General de Puerto Rico.

humming, snickering, and so forth key us to the ambivalent meaning of this not-quite-maternal figure. She inhabits a masculine space of interlocution, fronting an all-male band yet becoming permanently suspended as not quite feminine.

Fernández bridged the discourse belittling Afro–Puerto Ricans, on the one hand, and, on the other, the discourse investing music performance with a growing stature as a professional, artistic pursuit, aligned with class taste. The song uncannily mirrors the self-narrative Fernández crafted much later. The question befuddles the critic: Did Fernández tailor her narrative to echo her first hit, or does the late 1930s–early 1940s performance of "Y tu abuela onde etá" prefigure her life narrative? To this day, the original recording sounds like a riddle, a wonderful performance of ironic interlocution in a purely sonorous medium. Decidedly, the distinguishing element of the first recording is sabor, that elusive quality poorly translated into English as swing, timing, or soul.

Figure 2.1 is a very early photograph, exact date unknown, but around the same time of this early hit, which had been performed before it was recorded in 1941. The first photos of Ruth Fernández may recall Walter Benjamin's "Little History of Photography" in that they have aura, capturing a time in which subjects were simply not used to the camera, when posing required effort and subjects exhibited a high degree of self-consciousness. In other portraits of this time, Fernández donned primitivistic garb to suggest exotic blackness; in one, she held her head with her right hand in a coded erotic stance of availability. Both the respectable photo of the orchestra lead and the sexualized photo represent the singer as available, racialized "other."

The first stance, however, had much more to do with Fernández's artistic temperament. She grew up surrounded by a cosmopolitan and hybrid musical culture, in the southern city of Ponce, Puerto Rico; liked all kinds of music; and was accustomed to performing, listening to, and discussing music in her hometown. Fernández belonged to a working black middle class and was expected to pursue a respectable career. As a young artist, she was attracted to bohemia but was barred from that institution because of its associations with lewd behavior, drinking, sexual license, and loss of woman's honor.

The photo as material object relies on the visual, while recordings, obviously, stress the aural. Yet both visual and aural belong to the sensorium of racism. These archival objects are interdependent; sound and gaze, visuality and aurality work together in the perceiving subject's sensorium. Fernández's first photos, today, compel us to the gaze, but we can't obliterate the sound they were associated with, being portraits of a well-known, already iconic singer. As I have been working for some time with Fernández's archive, looking at early photos I can't help but reflect on her self-descriptions as the product of successful imperialism (the Spanish) as opposed to presumptively unsuccessful imperialism (the American); her codification of this success around erotics (describing her own lineage in terms of racial intermingling and the Spaniard's taste for black women); and how later in life she spoke of seeing her mixed European and African heritage in her own image.[20] These are all puzzling — and, at points, troubling — statements. In their looking back at us, their barely legible but present refusal, these early objects clearly reject this narrative.[21]

Despite being portraits of a raced, colonial, and clearly subordinate subject, with a compulsory artistic pose, there is inscrutability and a haunting mystery to Fernández's gaze back at the camera in this earliest period. We can divine elements of what the Martinican thinker Édouard Glissant labeled "forced poetics": "I define forced or constrained poetics as any collective yearning for expression that, when it manifests itself, is negated at the same time because of the deficiency that stifles it, not at the level of desire, which never ceases, but at the level of expression, which is never realized."[22] This "expression that is never realized" might serve as an entry point to consider Fernández's career, as a production of a "forced poetics" at the visible level and an unrecorded but present other poetics (which were closely related to circuits of blackness that did manage to survive out of the purview of the totalizing, imperial gaze).

Significantly, the flip side of the 78 recording of "Y tu abuela onde etá" (a soon-to-become iconic song), is a slow-tempo recording about self-determination, "Lamento de un boricua" (A Puerto Rican's lament). The speaker calls for Puerto Rican statehood as the just outcome of the colonial situation and secondarily for independence as the only other dignified outcome should statehood be denied:

Ay, mi patria llora
Ay, mi patria gime
Y solo pide su estadidad
O si no, pide su libertad

Borinquen mía, qué triste estás
Por qué no hablas con claridad
Es ya la hora de cantar
Nuestra canción de estadidad

My country is weeping
My country is moaning
It just wants its statehood
If not, it demands its freedom

My Puerto Rico, you are so sad
Why don't you speak with clarity
It's time to sing
Our statehood song

We cannot ascribe the song's politics to Fernández, who at this time was working for the orchestra and probably had no say in its repertoire. Nevertheless, it is striking to consider the young woman mouthing lyrics that she would not have been caught dead singing later in life, once her beloved Luis Muñoz Marín declared a new status formulation for Puerto Rico, the Estado Libre Asociado (ELA, Commonwealth of Puerto Rico). This material object, the 78 record with the two tracks, "Y tu abuela onde etá" and "Lamento de un boricua," testifies to the intersection of two underdeveloped discourses about Puerto Ricanness in 1941. First, the imperial idea that all Puerto Ricans are racially suspect or, put in more palatable, liberal terms, belong to the "tree with three roots" and as such are formally the same, if not equal.[23] The second discourse, that of self-determination, would remain a bone of contention as the third alternative of the ELA became hegemonic upon the rise of the PPD in 1952, and neither statehood nor independence were achieved. Both discourses — the new racial discourse of the 1930s and the demand for political equality — are anticolonial. Fernández emerges, paradoxically, as a symbol of both.

Fernández sang "Y tu abuela onde etá" at the Teatro Latino of New York in 1941, with other early hits: the comical "La borrachita" [The little drunk] by Rafael Hernández and the Agustín Lara bolero standard "Piénsalo bien" [Think hard about it]. She gave this 1941 performance as the origin of her enduring epithet: "The hosts, Arturo Córdova and Héctor del Villar, observed how people wept with nostalgia and they came up with 'Puerto Rico's Singing Soul'" (El alma de Puerto Rico hecha canción).[24]

Fernández accrued, as is customary for women pop singers of her stature, certain titles. These were as much honorific as they were selling slogans to aid the music industry in publicizing the singer as somehow being equal to her land of origin and therefore especially worthy. Domingo Colón's original design, of enlisting Fernández because she supplied the "class" that the orchestra presumably lacked, became refracted and displayed into an ever-widening arena composed of multiple publics. Figure 2.2 is a well-known album cover from the early 1950s neatly illustrating this changed positioning. Fernández appears in her characteristic, mature pose, quite different from that of the young woman we saw in figure 2.1. Arms outstretched as if effortlessly singing a musical note, she is dressed in a designer gown with a splendid cape and sparkling earrings (possibly similar to when, in her account, she borrowed a splendid outfit to cross color lines in a first-class hotel in the late 1930s, an anecdote I discuss below). The background features a series of snapshots of Puerto Rican life. Looking closely, we see scenes from the beach and the countryside, images of leisure time. Definitely, the cover reflects the construction of Puerto Rican singing as intimately linked to both nostalgia and tourism, presenting a revised sensorium where visuality and aurality interlock powerfully. The whole is anchored in a reinterpreted racial regime authored by the PPD to buttress the cultural arm of the three-pronged strategy Governor Luis Muñoz Marín devised for Puerto Rico during the first decade of the ELA,

FIGURE 2.2 Album cover, Ruth Fernández, *El alma de Puerto Rico hecha canción canta sus canciones favoritas*, Marvela LP-58, 1960?.

which was baptized as Operation Serenity.[25] Fernández assumed the role of primary symbol of this revised, top-down, mandated sensorium that shifted representation toward a formal new state antiracism supplanting the prior, dominant, white supremacist model.[26]

In this vinyl record, tracks originally recorded about a decade apart, from 1941 ("Tú volverás," "Cuando vuelvas") to 1952 ("Sollozo," "Luna sobre Borinquen"), as 78 rpm records are sequenced in a narrative that reflects this recalibration of racial politics. These are the artist's rerecordings, not the original tracks remastered. The album consists mostly of Latin American boleros, with the occasional ballad written specifically to induce nostalgia for Puerto Rico ("Bello amanecer" [A beautiful sunrise], "Luna sobre Borinquen" [Moon over Puerto Rico], "Tonadita borincana" [A Puerto Rican tune]). The arrangements correspond to the emerging, middle-class taste for so-called semiclassical music, featuring muted bongos, no syncopation, orchestra strings, and sweeping brass sounds vaguely suggesting the symphonic. With its highbrow yearnings, the rise of semiclassical music changed Fernández's reception; it reoriented her music toward a standardized listening ear (reminiscent of Theodor Adorno's well-known critique of the "rhythmically obedient type" in the wake of Tin Pan Alley).[27]

The epithet "El Alma de Puerto Rico Hecha Canción" stresses the spiritual; comes across as tacky (*cursi* in Spanish) to the present-day ear; and places the icon squarely in the feminine and in the purportedly colorless realm of the soul, reformulating the original icon considerably by placing her at a remove from race and closer to gender. "Canción" immediately aligns Fernández with forms of pop music considered serious or high, probably art and parlor songs, even though these were creations of middlebrow culture. The repertoire's evolution is complicated; no pop artist could survive financially singing only one genre, as they had to please heterogeneous audiences. Fernández had to sing dance music, which was coded black, if she was to make a living as a musician. Most paid work came from live singing in a variety of venues, from exclusive hotels and clubs, to the private parties of the upper classes, to the *fiestas patronales* (open air festivals) and dances in working-class clubs and, later, the New York market created by migration. Yet this new encasing of national music to approximate the "semiclassical" and perform as a collective values vessel permeated the totality of Fernández's repertoire and saturated her artistic persona. It presented an icon who was black, but also elite, a true social contradiction in mid-twentieth-century Puerto Rico. Gender, as before, operated as bridge. However much its valence changed, gender remained a gap that was useful to the extent that it was not filled but remained as a full emptiness primarily, although not exclusively, deployed through voice.

Fernández came to posit music as mostly pedagogical, didactic, as in the colonial pedagogy she learned as a child. Like other schoolchildren in the early twentieth century, she was brought up with a belief in music's edifying nature. Her first contact with music was in school, where, she claims, music was "everywhere heard" and children "learned singing."[28] It may strain credulity to believe that schools in the first decades of the American occupation of Puerto Rico could be so paradisiacal. Spanish was intermittently, but consistently, forbidden; the anthem and flag were banned; there was great violence in the country and dire economic need. Most American schoolteachers were told they would be dealing with savages. Fernández gives us a clue to what "savages" meant for these "practice teachers" (as they were called): "American schoolteachers thought all Puerto Ricans were black."[29] Clearly this statement only has meaning within the vicious American racism of the day and its white supremacist ethos. With the ascendancy of the PPD, this racial regime was substantially revised.

Fernández's value was enhanced, symbolically and practically, by her affiliation as a *ponceña*, a native of the city of Ponce, Puerto Rico, with its claims to cosmopolitanism and its mixed musical heritage. She easily slotted into the rising symbolics of racial harmony signified through wholesome popular music under the aegis of classical music. Musically speaking, 1930s Ponce offered a fascinating mix of musical culture that was more elastic than what later would be termed Puerto Rican music. In some ways, Ponce's musical scenario was heterogeneous in comparison to that of Puerto Rico's cultural center, San Juan, the capital city; in other ways, Ponce created its own stratifications and was notably Eurocentric.[30] In a cheesy but nonetheless revealing 1963 portrait of Fernández written by Abelardo Díaz Alfaro, author of several primary and secondary school textbooks of the ELA's nativist canon, indicatively titled "Ruth la negra, Ruth la blanca" (Black Ruth, white Ruth), the writer describes Fernández: "She is the typical, authentic voice of Puerto Rico, but even more so of her unforgettable Ponce, singular and provincial. The seigniorial, storied Ponce, fierce guardian of tradition, of chivalrous customs, haughty garrison of Creoleness, impregnable citadel of autochthony. Ponce, more than a city, is a passion, a feeling, a particular way of living and dreaming."[31]

Fernández described how "Ponce was a very musical town. Musicians sang in private homes, in parties. People brought serenades to other people's homes. Ponce was a very bohemian town."[32] Just as with "creoleness" (in Spanish, *criollo*, a person with Spanish parents but born in Latin America, which is odd at best when referring to a black subject whose parental lineage is traced to Africa and slavery), *bohemio* has always been a double-edged sword in Puerto Rican culture. "Bohemio" can mean someone who is unemployed or not disposed to work; it can be a designation of leisure time devoted to artistic activities; or it can indicate relaxed social mores. Its subject is most often privileged in some way. Fernández uses it here to refer to the active cultural scene and the mix of musical practices happening in the city, indicating that this mix included cross-class and cross-race contact. Managing such contact was vital to the state's new designs.

Bohemia was also gendered, associated with lewd behavior, sexual license, and drinking and partying. Women artists were vulnerable to charges of licentiousness, and black women artists were practically assumed not to have any "decency."[33] Fernández, like all young women of her background (meaning, those aspiring to the middle classes or of the middle classes) was not allowed to simply traverse the urban space at will. She had to be accompanied by a chaperone wherever she went and was required to attend university and secure credentials in a suitable, feminine profession. Fernández did so, earning a degree as a normal teacher, although she never worked as anything other than a musician until she became a politician in the 1970s. In her mature career, she refigured bohemian life as society life and turned to membership, however conditioned, in the civic ladies' society as its only black member, thus recasting the limits she had seen imposed on her as a younger woman into a privileged, though symbolically subordinate, existence.

It is a commonplace to say that the African-derived genres of Puerto Rican folkloric music were born in Ponce, but this glosses over the different forms and reception of bomba and plena, and the difference between music experienced as entertainment and music executed as labor. Fernández learned the Afro–Puerto Rican folkloric genres of bomba and plena under the sign of a conservative and Eurocentric musical vision. In the documentary *Raíces* [Roots] (2001), she stated, "The bomba and plena I grew up with resembled a minuet," emphasizing the choreographed aspects of dance and not dance's capacity to cause bodily transport in defiance of a choreography that was intended to elevate and educate, and correct the excesses of the body.[34] Silvia Álvarez Curbelo has cautioned, "To say that popular rhythm is de-popularized, is not the best approach. It would be better to speak of a hybrid created by Caribbean popular rhythms and European forms."[35] Nevertheless, it's impossible to ignore Fernández's characterization of the Ponce bomba and plena as slower-tempo music and aristocratic, in comparison to the other bomba and plena performances that Fernández implicitly refers to and to which she assigns a lesser status in culture. In dominant venues, popular music became stratified and coded as entertainment for elites. Cross-class and cross-race contact in the southern city approximated Fernández's ideal of listening and performing, limitations and all, but it's an open question whether she helped implant a truly cross-class and cross-race experience in her career and later on as a politician.

Fernández did not sing the Puerto Rican African-derived genres that she probably heard in her native Ponce during her very first years as a professional, but rather American standards and Cuban popular music.[36] This early training in non–Puerto Rican pop genres proved to be an essential preparation for the pivotal event in her career. In the late 1940s, the acclaimed Cuban composer Gonzalo Roig hired her to sing the part of Dolores Santa Cruz, a former slave, for the premiere of his operetta *Cecilia Valdés*. By this time, Fernández was a full-time musician singing dance music and boleros in competitive markets, but she had to return to Afro-Caribbean impersonations to finally obtain standing as a soloist of international acclaim.

As is well known, this operetta is considered the epic of Cuban nationality. Fernández scored a huge hit with her rendition of the tango-congo "Po Po Po," whose lyrics presume to render the vernacular Spanish of former slaves (referred to as *bozal*), after the style of Afro-Antillean poetry. No doubt her prior, acousmatic blackness — the one heard in "Y tu abuela onde etá" — is the subtext for this new performance. Dolores Santa Cruz laments the way she has been robbed of her money by "lawyers and rich white folks":

Po po po
Po po po
Po po po
Po po po

Aquí etá Dolore Santa Cru
Aquí etá

Que no tienga dinero
Po po po
Ni tienga pa comé
Po po po
Totitico lo abogao
Y caballero branco
Po po po

Le quitaron toitico cuanto tienga
Le robaron toitico su dinero
A Dolore Santa Cru

Dolores Santa Cruz is a tragicomic figure with no plot involvement in the operetta. She is presented strictly as a type. The most important element of "Po po po" stems from the declarative structure of Afro-Antillean poetry, exhibiting its "linguistricks" as well as its thematic and stylistic elements. Jacques Lacan coined "linguisterie" to suggest a fusing of hysteria and linguistics. These signifiers white writers invented to represent something they thought of as black speech strongly suggest a hysterical rendition of the black subject, identified with the colonial past remembered as a "better (cultural) time." Instead of manifesting publicly in white bodies, symptoms are transposed via writing into spectral black bodies, but they still are the white man's symptom.

Assuming the other's speech and using it as entertainment, enlisting black performers to parade the authenticity of such absurd signifiers, is also to put black performers in the psychically stressful position of being perpetual symptom bearers. Lacan's reformulation of the signified is especially useful: A signifier's relationship is to another signifier, not to any signified. Here race as the signifier, heard through its collection of phonemes, spills out of Puerto Rico and meets its Cuban counterpart, soon to travel to the rest of Latin America and to the United States. Similarly, Fernández's voice stands for the portability of speech, recasting the terms of the autoaffectivity Jacques Derrida related to the voice as the stand-in for speech: Nothing of Fernández's interiority is to be divined from her voice in these performances, or this speech, symptom of white anxiety.

For those unfamiliar with the Spanish language, it's necessary to point out the song's attempts to render black dialect: "tienga" instead of "tenga," "etá" for "está," "toitico" for "todito," and so forth. But perhaps the song's most striking sonic element lies in the repetition of a nonlinguistic refrain: "po po po," each syllable featuring a richly sonorous vowel in Spanish, the o, a favorite sound of Afro-Antillean poetry, the same literary movement that birthed the lyrics and sensibility of "Y tu abuela onde etá." It is rendered as a pure sound supposedly reminiscent of blackness, and Fernández's contralto voice becomes welded to this construction of the black subject as "entering linguistics."

(The other side of this portrayal represented the black subject as illiterate, meaning, in this view, tragically ignorant and/or inherently comical. I'm sure Fernández did not for a second intend to pose as clownish or as a buffoon, something that would have absolutely gone against her personal and musical temperament. However, the piece surely had this effect on its mostly white or light-skinned audience.)

Afro-Antillean poetry was written with performance in mind, to be executed by black *diseurs* and *diseuses* who could supposedly convey authenticity because, being black, they were taken to be more proximate to the poetry (the two most famous were the Puerto Rican Juan Boria and the Cuban Eusebia Cosme).[37] Nina Eidsheim's observations about the training of the dominant ear to perceive voices as black, and the imperative toward a vocal pedagogy to teach what blackness is (how it should be apprehended sonically), provides a supple, critical tool to understand that, in some instances, the aural cue is just as powerful (and sometimes more powerful) than the visual in the construction of blackness in music (while acknowledging the racism of both). Caribbean poetry is part of the Latin American sonic archive and its lyrics respond to phonemes imbued with meaning to condition listening beyond visuality.[38] "Po po po" was released as a 78 and stood for decades as an instantly recognizable document of "native" blackness, neatly encapsulated in a few syllables and a three-minute format.

ACOUSMATIC BLACKNESS

Documentation of the original staging of "Po po po" is not available at this time. The National Foundation for Popular Culture of Puerto Rico, fortunately, has a clip of an older Fernández, circa 1990, singing "Po po po" while dressed in character as Dolores Santa Cruz. Fernández re-creates the original character as Cirilo Villaverde's novel presents her, as deranged. She looks to the side suspiciously, smiling and giggling like a little girl. She sings in slow tempo, sometimes speaking the verses into the microphone, simulating a whisper. It's likely she was repeating closely the staging she had learned for the part, which stressed the melodramatic gesticulation, the paranoid whispering, and the insane laughter. Fernández possessed a great stage presence as well as a flair for the dramatic. However, to state the obvious, the portrayal is problematic. Fernández's other intervention in the operetta is "Tanila," in which she sings solo backed by an operatic chorus. It's staged and orchestrated to achieve the maximum folkloric effect of this representation of the stock character of the Afro-Cuban subject. Fernández's two pieces, "Po po po" and "Tanila," were released in one 78 record, which became a top seller.[39]

The Puerto Rican engineer Fernando Montilla, who financed the recording of *Cecilia Valdés*, had persuaded Gonzalo Roig to hire Fernández to sing the part. A few years later, Montilla, having become the owner and head of his own recording label, Montilla Records, hired his fellow Puerto Rican to record the LP *Ñáñigo* with Obdulio Morales and His Native Cuban Orchestra and Chorus.[40] At that point, Fernández became synonymous with the Afro-Cuban repertoire. As mentioned, *Ñáñigo* led, years later, to Rudolph Bing's invitation to sing under the auspices of the Metropolitan Opera.[41]

Light-operatic Afro-Cuban music was regarded as folkloric even though it was not, strictly speaking, culled from folkloric investigations but entailed writing songs (as Alejo Carpentier explained and others have since echoed) that sought to recreate the spirit of the original sources into learned sheet music written in Western notation.[42] The syncope, rather than rhythm, is the musical bridge between what the composers saw as the raw material of black people and sheet music they wrote as true composers. They aspired to the classical sense of writing music, of higher value than pop songwriting and therefore more worthy of expressing the authentic national essence, in this case, Cuban. The composers and producers of these records sought to embody blackness sonically or what we could better describe as dominant notions of blackness and not actual music created by black Cubans.[43]

Paradoxically, Afro-Cuban music encased the singer in the very stereotypes running counter to ideals of racial harmony and blending of the races touted by Puerto Rican and Latin American nationalism, which she came to assume (recalling her improbably celebratory vision of the blending of the races as evidenced in her own family line).[44] The operatic repertoire did satisfy one of her cherished desires: to be listened, not danced, to, as it was music for listening, through records or in the plush seats of Havana's Teatro Nacional. Operatic black music falls under art and folk discourse but is removed from the lowbrow associations popular music was subjected to. The liner notes to Ñáñigo read, "Fernández has shown the world her race's innermost temperament with hit after hit, through her interpretations of tropical popular music, of black music, with a supreme spiritual elegance . . . that is Ruth Fernández, whom her fellow Puerto Ricans call 'Puerto Rico's Singing Soul.'" As with the earlier Puerto Rican recordings in the so-called Afro style, the marketers and producers played with the idea that Fernández either identified with the content or embodied it. Ascribing "el sentir de su raza" to Fernández based on this repertoire becomes rather vexed. It asserts a homogeneous black (perhaps Caribbean) subject, resolved by the idea of a spirit that Fernández presumably embodies because she is a virtuoso. While Fernández most certainly identified as a Latin American, her descriptions of black music were always modeled on African American and Afro-Caribbean music, on soul, sabor, and feeling. The liner notes for this album appear to emphasize, however, an elite vision of blackness as racial spirit and a nonthreatening experience of feeling, instead of contemporary soul or sabor musical forms. Ana María Ochoa Gautier has spoken of a "tamed vocality" in another context, that of nineteenth-century philology.[45] Here, taming is paired with an emerging Latin Americanist variant of the semiclassical, with the caveat that Fernández's capacity for volume places her vocality nearer to a limit between tamed and unbridled sound, closer to the "extimacy" she represented than to a purely domesticated voice.

Content-wise, most of the songs in *Ñáñigo* allude to slavery as hard work that makes the subject inherently moral and portray the black subject as passively melancholic. An example of this is "Facundo," successful in the light-operatic style, musically speaking, although problematic thematically. The singing voice, marked linguistically as black, exhorts "Facundo" to work ("trabaja, negro, trabaja") so that he will not be called lazy ("pa' que no te digan vago por la calle"). Eliseo Grenet set to music a now-obscure poem by Teófilo Radillo of the *afrocubanista* movement in poetry, originally as a tango-congo. Fernández and Obdulio Morales, playing with a symphonic arrangement in all likelihood imposed by standards of taste, produced a parlor song with a tragicomic air.

The original liner notes describe this song as "humorous." It is hard to discern any humor in Fernández's interpretation, although she could not maneuver around the song's paternalism. She obviously sought to invest the performance with dignity, given its problematic portrayal of the black subject's interpellation. She employed declamatory singing featuring long end notes, the rise and fall of voice highlighting cadence, and full volume at the very end of the piece with a full orchestra accompaniment. The result to contemporary ears might be akin to a battle between her virtuosic interpretation and the song's musical portrayal of the black subject as childlike, in need of moral and parental guidance.

"Facundo" became part of the standard 1950s repertoire. Comparing Fernández's track to those of two Cuban greats, Rolando Laserie and Celia Cruz, we find different strategies to deal with the song's problematic portrayal. Laserie's is geared toward dance music; it is a slow-tempo mambo–cha cha cha; it downplays the genealogies of slavery and gestures toward a slightly more contemporary countryside. "Negro" becomes a conversational, everyday, in-group appellation, instead of the sepulchral identity of Fernández's and Morales's rendition. Cruz, in the meantime, sings in a slower tempo than Laserie, reminiscent of ritual visions of Cuban blackness (such as ones Cruz herself recorded at the start of her career and later abandoned), producing her own brand of virtuosity: switching from major to minor at various points, anticipating the beat, repeating phrases and syllables in a low-intensity soneo (improv), she succeeds in distracting the listener from the lyrics' problematic content. She turns "negro" into the familiar, affectionate, intragroup appellative "negrón."

Fernández definitely acted the song much more than her contemporaries, taking it at face value as a tale of labor and salvation. Significantly, in a column published about a decade later, she spoke of herself as a "frustrated actress" and only half-jokingly wrote, "I would have liked to work more on the stage. But, give the people what they want: My public demands that I give them my spirit in my songs."[46] This suggests a play with "spirit" that goes beyond the simple mouthing of dominant dictates about blackness; it suggests performative strategies and artistic ownership.

There is room to wonder if Fernández saw the movie *Romance musical* with the Argentinian marquee artist Libertad Lamarque in 1947, and what her reaction was. One of its musical interludes shows Lamarque performing "Facundo" in blackface. The frame is rife with crude, racist stereotypes of black people as lazy, along with the usual plantation props of bananas, fans, and palm trees. Sonically, Lamarque affects a "Cuban" "black" voice, including breaking out of the song in its chorus by literally screaming its "Ay ay ay ay" chorus as if simulating what — the savage? the buffoon? — definitely not the laborious Facundo seeking to ward off accusations of being socially unfit and inassimilable to the greater good that Fernández attempted to re-create. Lamarque's interpretation is an instructive, although unacceptable, counterpoint to Fernández's emphasis on dignity, amplified by Fernández's filiation with the classical sound of symphonic music despite all of this latter route's limitations. Lamarque, a soprano, became known as "La Novia de América" (The bride of the Americas) and was hugely influential. Clearly Fernández would never be known by such epithets, and her contralto could never have stood in for the transnational, white, European, and Christian ideal of femininity that presumably bound the emerging Latin American nations together.

With this brief sonic reconstruction, the reader may begin to listen differently to recordings such as "Facundo" and its moment, 1952. The whole of *Ñáñigo* was clearly intended to evoke the sweeping, epic misery of the black subject. To present-day ears, the record might sound brooding and somber in the cinematic sense of movie music, reminiscent of contemporary movie or Broadway scores. The effect is decidedly theatrical (although not deconstructive, as in, for example, Bola de Nieve's [Ignacio Villa] interpretations of the repertoire for cabaret, or unabashedly fervent, as with Merceditas Valdés's interpretations). Overall, Fernández switches from soft singing in major notes to full sonority, often accompanied by minor notes blasted from the brass sections of the orchestra. Fernández speaks some of the verses as if onstage. Many of the songs impel the black subject toward rest ("Drume, Lacho"). Drums are remarked upon often ("Chivo que rompe tambó" twists this appellation with a double meaning of buffoonery and religion). Orishas are called upon for help, as in "Mi Ochún." In sum, in these dominant portrayals, the black subject emerges as an emblem of universal, virtuous suffering, sometimes alleviated by the "natural" comic streak white composers often imposed on their creations. The black subject is rendered monotonously the same, always and forever, as identical to colonial times, in a decidedly archaic slant.[47]

Yet the artists' performances and the little-known story of Ñáñigo's reception belie traces of another world that hasn't been incorporated into scholarly accounts of pop music (except for salsa of the 1970s), but in which Fernández must have traveled. Obdulio Morales and His Native Cuban Orchestra and Chorus accompany her. The Native Cuban Orchestra might be a fantasy; the musicians were members of the National Symphony of Cuba, apparently repurposed for nativeness (read blackness). As Cristóbal Díaz-Ayala recounts, Morales was a believer. He consulted with the orishas before agreeing to record the album and, as instructed by the gods, he tied a red ribbon to each microphone before recording. The recording session was allegedly done in one sitting, through the night, as that was one of the religious conditions Morales had to follow.[48] Beyond the information this anecdote conveys, we can imagine the scene of the recording and how it perhaps invested the chosen songs with another interpretation not available in sheet transcription but only discernible in the traces it left on the record itself. This may contextualize Fernández's vision of her voice as anima, or spirit.

Fernández is a bit of a mystery in religious terms. Although she said in public that she was Catholic, and always spoke in Christian terms, it is well known that many Puerto Rican *santero* families revered her as a special being. It was not uncommon to see pictures of Fernández in santero homes. A freelance assistant in film and TV productions in the 1980s recounted visiting Fernández while at work and witnessing a coterie of women dressed in white — most certainly Ocha priestesses — in Fernández's home.[49] Whether or not she practiced, Fernández felt bound spiritually to the religion, which opens up the question of a divergence between her interpretation and the album's mostly bourgeois or petit-bourgeois listeners. Helio Orovio, noted Cuban music historian, cites "Facundo" as a song of praise for one of the orishas. Although he does not provide more information as to which orisha is being honored or summoned, this knowledge alters the song's layer of meanings considerably, and the album's.[50]

Fernández's interpretation of another classic with religious overtones, "Chivo que rompe tambó," is terrific, very different from the equally masterly interpretations of contemporaries such as Bola de Nieve (whose cabaret performance was also highly musically literate). Amusingly, the liner notes for *Ñáñigo* miss the most important element of the song — the sacred drum — and do not even acknowledge the myriad meaning popular sayings had in the context of religious practices that were contemporary to the 1940s, not at all relics of the past. The notes describe the song literally: "a popular saying from slavery days . . . meaning that the slave who defies customs, pays with his own flesh, a reminder of the Slavedriver's whip," either willfully or truly ignorant of the song's multilayered levels of meaning and its origins in the *patakis*, or sacred stories, of the Ocha religion.

Arguably, along with the discursive conditions for listening I have outlined, and the visual reproducibility of her performing body, the sound of Fernández's uniqueness — by then established culturally — in itself did a large amount of the work of "sounding black" for elites. This, possibly, was in a way more impactful than the re-creation of a presumptive vernacular form of Spanish or the condescending and occasionally disfiguring nature of paternalistic portrayals of the black subject (for all their assumed musical beauty). Both *Cecilia Valdés* and *Ñáñigo* represent watershed sonic interpellations and illustrate Fernández's choices as a vocalist forced into an elite-defined embodiment. Her schooling in singing is both a defense of humanity and a continuation of elite aesthetics. Neither record is out of print, and *Ñáñigo* enjoyed a later release as a four-song EP.[51]

SEMICLASSICAL

When I interviewed Fernández about her early musical experiences, certain phrases struck me as key. She referred to herself in school as "una negrita graciosa" (a cute little black girl) and "una negrita que canta en la escuela" (a little black girl who sang in school), seeming to ventriloquize others' racist depictions; she explained her success by saying, "Era negrita fea, pero tenía una gracia, en las manos, todo" (I was an ugly little black girl but I was graceful, I moved my hands well, my movements) and with the open-ended phrases, "Negra y qué, narisona y qué" (So what if I'm black? So what if I have a big nose?), echoing racist characterizations that she either heard directly or experienced as she inhabited social space.[52] In the course of her narrative, as it has unfolded in other interviews as well, she presented in infantile terms, inducing sympathy, and expressed her success in terms of psychological obstacles, inducing identification. She presented as an exemplar, as a model to follow, much like the pop ego psychology that influenced many Puerto Ricans in the 1960s, so visible in magazine spreads of the time. Yet her insistence on her racial difference as the knot through which her career should be understood is left unexplained by simply taking her account at face value, as most commentators do. It is, instead, part and parcel of her variant of the thinking voice, the result of several decades of musical labor and not necessarily an expression of any "native" Puerto Rican or Caribbean racial typology. Commercialized blackness was a marketing ploy revolving around a presumptive identification between the singer and her musical material (as was the case with nearly all black women singers of the time) and this singer's capacity to condense in one sign a dense grid of meanings that came from at least three distinct racial matrices: Puerto Rican, Cuban, and American. This capacity was made possible by virtuosity and the values it supported.

Before the 1950s, a racial matrix existed in Puerto Rico that shaped the circulation and reception of popular music, certainly, but it was only after the establishment of the ELA and the hegemony of the PPD that these formats became much more stringently tied to cultural-nationalist visions and also to the tourist market. At this point, post-*Ñáñigo*, Fernández's musical career experienced a drop in musical richness. Further, even the most perspicacious of critics fail to interrogate the elitist bent of Fernández's career and the circumstances of her successful upward mobility. I want to be clear: I am not criticizing Fernández's desire for upward mobility. As an individual, she reached her goal; she succeeded as a musician and later as a political figure. As an icon, figuration, or sign, though, she is problematic, and unpacking the conflicts inherent in her mature persona is crucial, particularly regarding how populist understanding of popular music and their concomitant uses of racial discourse at once claim exceptionalism while only partially disclosing or symbolizing the racial rejection upon which their claim for racial progress rests (the "policy of the ostrich" I alluded to earlier).

Fernández clearly sought to present blackness and black people as moral, responsible, educated, and hardworking, and not lewd, lascivious, party going, and irresponsible, as the racist discourse would claim. Whether she espoused this moral discourse as publicly during her first decade and a half as an artist is unclear. It would saturate her persona after the 1950s, once she became completely aligned with the middle- and upper-class modalities of taste via her recordings of the Afro-Cuban, light-operatic repertoire. After her most estimable recording and performing period (the late 1930s and the 1940s), Fernández turned to an intense symbolization of "local color" during the 1950s and 1960s. In this endeavor she received the full backing of the government and the media.

The discourses and the actual push toward progress and Americanization clashed with older musical formats and former class-based tastes, changing music culture vertiginously in 1950s Puerto Rico. Fernández's enlistment by the PPD had to do directly with the successful implantation of a public perception of the artist as a vessel of values and protector of the national patrimony against foreign (read American) values and cultural artifacts.[53] At the time, her internationalist projection and musical sophistication fit into the push to reassure tourists and investors that Puerto Rico was safe, that they could find entertainment and culture during their financial ventures or vacations.

Fernández adjusted her music to fit a middle-class aesthetic and started to address the working classes in the populist mode embodied most perfectly in Luis Muñoz Marín, who, according to Álvarez Curbelo, had long been her idol ("Ruth came from a tradition where Muñoz Marín and Roosevelt ruled Olympus").[54] While her musical education was shaped by the vivid 1930s in Ponce, a city that provided deep musical knowledge through practices inherited from the nineteenth century, and also new information coming in through the airwaves since radio's inception in 1922 (via radio stations like WKAQ and WNEL), Fernández set aside these musical pursuits and passions and conformed to being a singularly fixed sign heavily dependent on the elite's sensorium and their expectation of acousmatic blackness.[55]

At home, she became the unofficial, cultural spokesperson of the PPD and local elites. Abroad, she functioned as their cultural ambassador. Her repertoire advertised a vision of Latin America that was calibrated to the Good Neighbor Policy and the Alliance for Progress. The manipulation of local culture, and the insertion of the local in a universalist paradigm, was key in this venture. (Other stars in this vein include the Mexican Jorge Negrete who, like Fernández, pursued Pan-Americanism in the semiclassical, operatic style around this same time. Having failed to secure work in his first option, the opera, this tenor enjoyed a hugely successful career decked as a *charro* who sang *rancheras* with a full symphonic orchestra, and also became a symbol for changing U.S.–Latin American relations. Libertad Lamarque,

MARTES — 7:30 P. M.

CANAL 6 WIPR-TV

presenta

CANTEMOS CON RUTH FERNANDEZ

Ofrecemos al pueblo puertorriqueño esta nueva serie de progra- mas, en que una vez más nuestra máxima exponente de la can- ción popular hará ga- la de su gran tempera- mento artístico.

Con la dirección musical de:

TITO ENRIQUEZ

Al piano: JOSE LUIS SIERRA

TODOS LOS MARTES A LAS 7:30 P. M.

FIGURE 2.3 Advertisement, *El Imparcial*, April 4, 1961, for the TV show *Cantemos con Ruth Fernández*, on the state channel, WIPR. The channel was named for the phrase, "Wonderful Island of Puerto Rico." "We offer the Puerto Rican public this new series of programs, in which, once more, our most esteemed popular music singer will showcase her artistic temperament."

mentioned earlier, toured the region incessantly. She made stops in U.S. cities too, singing not only her core Argentinian repertoire but also boleros and folk music of various countries.) Supported by the newly founded ELA, Fernández was a regular in New York. She filled the Teatro Puerto Rico in the Bronx in her performances, as well as multiple Latino spaces in the city. Her capacity to embody the ELA's promise of symbolic inclusion as a joyful and assured destiny is marvelously encapsulated in a newspaper ad for one of her television shows, *Let's Sing with Ruth Fernández* (figure 2.3). One cannot help but think of "the grace with my hands" of the little girl when seeing this image today.

One of the highlights of Fernández's career happened when the Metropolitan Opera House held "An Evening of Latin American Music" on July 17, 1966, during the Met's open-air summer season concerts at the Lewisohn Stadium of the City College of New York. The Lewisohn, now demolished, stood on 138th Street between Amsterdam and Convent Avenues. A spectacular setting, adorned by an elaborate Doric colonnade, it had hosted landmark concerts, including several Gershwin concerts (he played the solo piano part of his *Rhapsody* in 1927 and premiered his *Cuban Overture* in 1932); Marian Anderson in her first concert performance on August 26, 1925; and Ella Fitzgerald in concert with the Metropolitan Opera Orchestra in 1965. It was indeed an honor to be chosen to perform at this concert, and it aligned Fernández with one of the great debates of the century, regarding the boundaries between classical and popular music.

The Lewisohn programs were conceived, as a whole, as educational ventures, bridges between the classical world and popular music. Gershwin's music straddled the boundaries between classical idioms and the American songbook; his oeuvre included both classical pieces and Broadway music. As we saw, Fernández had sung roles modeled after Gershwin in the Afro-Cuban operatic repertoire, in which she had sought to invest popular music with the values thought to inhere in classical forms. The Lewisohn concert opportunity presented as an occasion to showcase her beloved popular music but also to envelop it with the aura of classical music, as she had learned to do.

During the interview I conducted with Fernández, I was struck by her testimony about her music lessons and how they ran counter to her passion. I asked if she was trained, to which she responded that she had taken music lessons and had been taught some piano but, "When you start singing popular music, you immediately go out of your training. I wanted to sing popular music, not what I was being taught in formal lessons. I liked sabor [soulfulness, funk], and also sentimental music. . . . I don't know how to tell you — it's so hard to talk about oneself like this . . . but the truth is, I liked all music, music as a whole." As a musical subject, she existed between the official interpellation hailing classical and virtuosic modes as the most refined execution of music and the everyday practices of popular music surrounding her and those she heard on the radio, which were diasporic.

I was intrigued by her description of the phonetic method she had used to learn English and how this connected her to hundreds of Puerto Rican schoolchildren who were forced to learn English as the subjects of empire, during the beginning decades of the twentieth century. The phonetic method coexisted with the "linguistricks" of Afro-Antillean poetry, linking Fernández's to minoritized discourses of "nativeness" as well as the grand ones of progress. Yet it was evident that the use of phonemes to learn English helped her orient her desires toward other musics she felt just as deeply connected to, breaking the mold of nativism as Ponce, despite its classism, previously had.

Part of this Lewisohn episode concerns how deeply Fernández admired the legacy of African American singing. She emphasized her special affinity with American black music and how she loved singing in English:

I used to sing in English a lot. I recorded "Stormy Weather," "St. Louis Blues." I used to learn songs written in English; I had a knack for them. They had an impact and still do; I loved them. We had a teacher who taught us English with the Morrin Phonetic method. I will never forget her, Teresa Carrera. I loved the English language. "A tisket, a tasket, I love my yellow basket." . . . I sang it since I was a child, from about seventh grade on. I loved the blues. Black music. I loved it. I loved its strength.[56]

I heard her sing several bars of "A-Tisket, A-Tasket" and "Summertime," priding herself on her ability to sing in English and claiming a musical lineage that included the first ladies of jazz. She voiced reverence for Anderson, a singer who must have been a model and who was frequently referenced in magazine articles portraying Fernández's magnificence and social value. Perusing the complete list of Met-sponsored concerts at the Lewisohn, one finds that African American sopranos sang opera roles (Gloria Davy sang *Aida* in 1958 and Leontyne Price had a recital under solo billing in 1966), and that Marian Anderson returned to this stage the same year that Fernández sang (on July 3, 1965, Anderson performed part of Aaron Copland's *A Lincoln Portrait* and spirituals with the Met Orchestra, a fact that must have impinged heavily on Fernández's desire to be invited and her consequent acceptance of the invitation). Although, in her by-then typical public persona, Fernández feigned surprise and waxed humble at being picked to sing at the Lewisohn, I'm certain she was well aware of what this platform meant.[57] I'm also certain that she was moved, not just by her imperative to represent Puerto Rico (particularly the still-young ELA), but also by the musical desire to share the space of the African American women singers she so admired.

Why was it important for Fernández to label herself the first singer of Latin popular music at the Met? What cultural work did the epithet "semiclassical" perform in the context of Puerto Rican/Latin music? In one of dozens of articles on her in the early 1960s, we read, "She insists on her will to internationalize Puerto Rican music. 'There's a lot of work ahead for our folklore. All countries are known through their music. A musical ambassador is sometimes worth ten diplomats. A song can achieve a lot more and more quickly than several speeches. We have to fight to take our music everywhere. Plena says a lot. It's popular, but not vulgar. I always include danzas, plenas, boleros, even bombas in my repertoire. I aspire to one day be able to say: "I have done something for Puerto Rico." ' "[58] The notion of folklore had a long shelf life in the twentieth century, and it's clear that popular music is a demarcation of a boundary separating what should be included as the expression of a nation and what should be left out because it is vulgar. "Vulgar" appears in shades of black. Fernández claims that the plena is never vulgar, while she qualifies the bomba. Tomás Blanco, recall, categorized plena as a miscegenating genre, specifically stating it was not vulgar, claiming a moralizing potential to its mixing and clarifying its status as Hispanic music. He went so far as to claim that plena, while having an "elemento negroide" (Negroid [sic] element), "in every other respect [it] is — plainly — white."[59] Bomba was never whitened in intellectual discourse. Fernández here stresses her willingness to represent the popular, "even the bomba" (read: even black music), in service to Puerto Rico. If we go back to her 1940s repertoire, neither bomba nor plena were prominent or possibly even present prior to the ELA's rise in the 1950s.

On the island, semiclassical appealed to middle-class taste. In New York City, semiclassical performed nostalgia for the homeland as defined by middlebrow culture, as it was geared specifically to Latino immigrants in New York. It proffered a version of the "civilizing mission," a message to immigrants in the city living through the turbulent 1960s. A political will dictated the employ of Fernández's musical voice in her role as cultural ambassador, as she characterizes her life endeavor repeatedly during this time. In the 1970s, she would define her entry into politics as derivative of music: "The language of music will serve as the pious background to my work as senator. . . . Art is a universal language, capable of bending wills and unifying hearts."[60] This "language of music" masks the cold rationality of many political maneuvers in the ELA's heyday, starting with the massive migration of Puerto Ricans to New York. They were left to survive as best they could, with no real government aid and facing several decades of being derided in their own homeland.

Figure 2.4 is the program for "An Evening of Latin American Music," for which Fernández was paid 850 dollars. She chose the repertoire for the evening. Fernández assumed a didactic, even paternalistic role through music, that would be increasingly calibrated toward the explicitly political. Here musical respect for popular music (albeit with qualifiers) mixed with calculus, dovetailing with Fernández's own belief in music's pedagogical mission and her championing of the music industry's development in Puerto Rico and Latin America as evidence of progress. Excerpts of her statements to the press clearly indicate her belief: "Now that I am older . . . I realize that I did not just come into this world to entertain. I have a responsibility as an artist and as

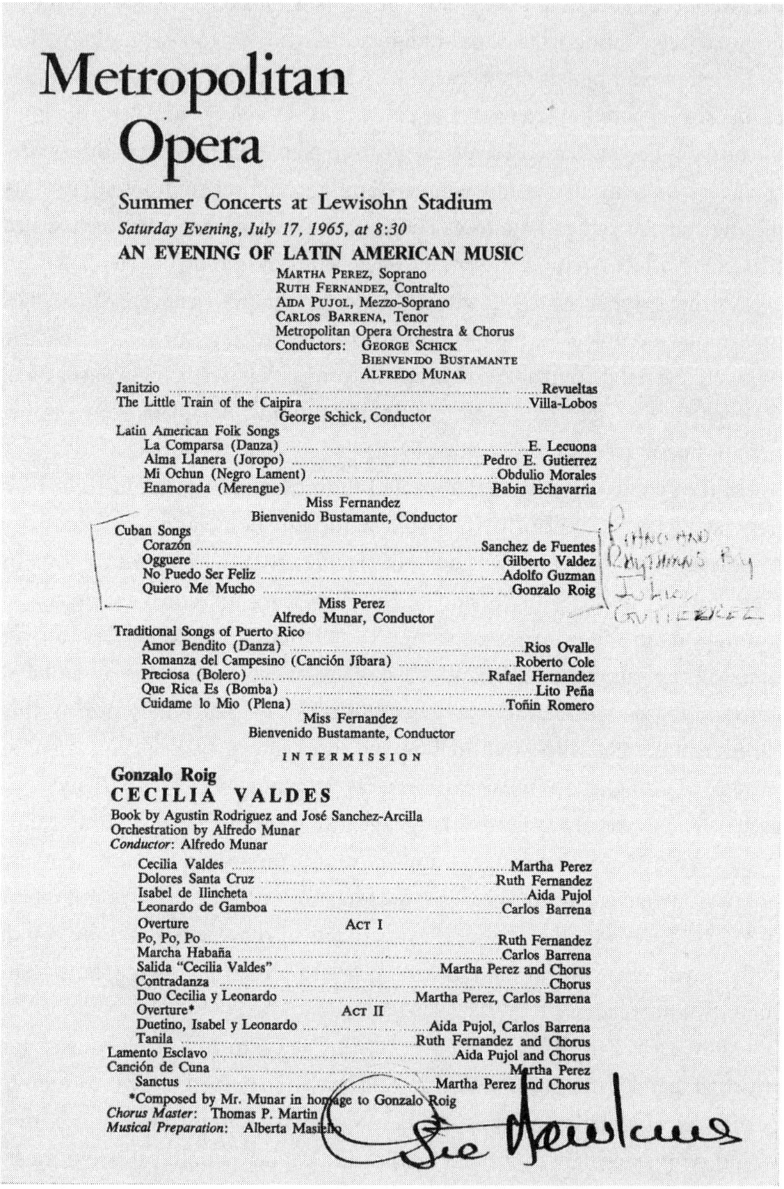

Metropolitan Opera

Summer Concerts at Lewisohn Stadium
Saturday Evening, July 17, 1965, at 8:30

AN EVENING OF LATIN AMERICAN MUSIC

MARTHA PEREZ, Soprano
RUTH FERNANDEZ, Contralto
AIDA PUJOL, Mezzo-Soprano
CARLOS BARRENA, Tenor
Metropolitan Opera Orchestra & Chorus
Conductors: GEORGE SCHICK
BIENVENIDO BUSTAMANTE
ALFREDO MUNAR

Janitzio .... Revueltas
The Little Train of the Caipira .... Villa-Lobos
George Schick, Conductor

Latin American Folk Songs
La Comparsa (Danza) .... E. Lecuona
Alma Llanera (Joropo) .... Pedro E. Gutierrez
Mi Ochun (Negro Lament) .... Obdulio Morales
Enamorada (Merengue) .... Babin Echavarria
Miss Fernandez
Bienvenido Bustamante, Conductor

Cuban Songs
Corazón .... Sanchez de Fuentes
Ogguere .... Gilberto Valdez
No Puedo Ser Feliz .... Adolfo Guzman
Quiero Me Mucho .... Gonzalo Roig
Miss Perez
Alfredo Munar, Conductor

Traditional Songs of Puerto Rico
Amor Bendito (Danza) .... Rios Ovalle
Romanza del Campesino (Canción Jíbara) .... Roberto Cole
Preciosa (Bolero) .... Rafael Hernandez
Que Rica Es (Bomba) .... Lito Peña
Cuidame lo Mio (Plena) .... Toñin Romero
Miss Fernandez
Bienvenido Bustamante, Conductor

INTERMISSION

Gonzalo Roig
CECILIA VALDES

Book by Agustin Rodriguez and José Sanchez-Arcilla
Orchestration by Alfredo Munar
Conductor: Alfredo Munar

Cecilia Valdes .... Martha Perez
Dolores Santa Cruz .... Ruth Fernandez
Isabel de Ilincheta .... Aida Pujol
Leonardo de Gamboa .... Carlos Barrena

Overture   ACT I
Po, Po, Po .... Ruth Fernandez
Marcha Habaña .... Carlos Barrena
Salida "Cecilia Valdes" .... Martha Perez and Chorus
Contradanza .... Chorus
Duo Cecilia y Leonardo .... Martha Perez, Carlos Barrena
Overture*   ACT II
Duetino, Isabel y Leonardo .... Aida Pujol, Carlos Barrena
Tanila .... Ruth Fernandez and Chorus
Lamento Esclavo .... Aida Pujol and Chorus
Canción de Cuna .... Martha Perez
Sanctus .... Martha Perez and Chorus
*Composed by Mr. Munar in homage to Gonzalo Roig
Chorus Master: Thomas P. Martin
Musical Preparation: Alberta Masiello

FIGURE 2.4 The program for An Evening of Latin American Music, Summer
Concerts at Lewisohn, Metropolitan Opera House, July 17, 1965.

a citizen to speak out for my ideas."[61] And, queried by a reporter for the top entertainment journal *Bohemia* in 1967:

— What do you think of today's art?

— That it should not develop only along the lines of entertainment. . . . Art has to respond to deeper goals and objectives. . . . It should spark patriotism . . . advocate for the fraternity of nations . . . and of races.[62]

The evening's repertoire buttressed an agenda not only to reaffirm *puertor-riqueñidad* (Puerto Ricanness) but *latinoamericanismo* (Latin Americanism), the prevailing discourse governing notions of cultural ambassadorship and mediating relations with the United States as the economic power throughout the hemisphere.

Fernández, attentive to populist detail, married folklore and populism to the prestige associated with high forms of music, as represented by the symphonic orchestra. The *New York Times* reported Fernández had distributed "five or six *favas* [*sic*] . . . so she could feel more at home"; in the Puerto Rican press, the *pavas* multiplied to ninety so that, in the Puerto Rican imagination, the entire orchestra had donned pavas during Fernández's performance. The pava or straw hat worn by farmhands to shield themselves from the sun had become the foremost symbol of the PPD. Purportedly, it symbolized the Puerto Rican peasant, the jíbaro, he whom the PPD had saved and also modernized (or saved because it had modernized). We will turn to this figure in chapter 3; suffice it to say that this symbol of whiteness, aside from erasing the racial identity of many jíbaros, directly occluded Afro–Puerto Ricans in the mandated imaginary and its requisite sensorium as the century progressed. Fernández's distribution of pavas entails the joining of two dissonant cultural and social signs.

The penchant for hyperbole in the colonial press ran deep, because the same article reported that Fernández's voice "could be heard throughout the island of Manhattan" because of "a specially outfitted machine capable of disseminating her canticles to all the limits of this great city."[63] I cannot verify what this machine was. However, we can note the importance of technological reproduction and how it alters the perception of Fernández's vocal success, augmenting the potential of her vocal virtuosity for political marketing internationally. We can also verify the mystical prestige of operatic singing in this national context (pop songs referred to as "canticles"), already instilled as the preferred pedagogical model of the Commonwealth of Puerto Rico.

Fernández was, undoubtedly, the thread of the entire program of "An Evening of Latin American Music." After an opening instrumental set (consisting of "Janitzio" by the Mexican composer Silvestre Revueltas and "The Little Train of the Caipira" by the Brazilian Heitor Villa-Lobos), Fernández took the stage in her Latin Americanist persona, in a set titled "Latin American Folk Songs." She sang two songs from Ñáñigo, a Venezuelan joropo, and a Dominican merengue. The soprano Martha Pérez was slated to follow with four songs labeled simply "Cuban" (this singer was not marked as folkloric, like Fernández) but had to skip the set because of a "slight indisposition." The selections for the climactic section of Act I, "Traditional Songs of Puerto Rico," clearly conformed to the dominant, official folkloric appreciation of Puerto Rican music at the height of the 1960s: a danza, a canción jíbara, a bolero, a didactic bomba by Lito Peña, and a festive plena. (No Nuyorican bugalú, jala jala, or working-class plenas and bombas, even in the wildly successful, crossover Rafael Cortijo style, were included; the concert did not feature any jíbaro musicians, although they were hugely popular in 1960s New York.) After the intermission, Fernández reprised her role as Dolores Santa Cruz, the former slave, in the Cuban operetta Cecilia Valdés, which she sang with Martha Pérez, the Cuban soprano, and Aída Pujol, a Puerto Rican mezzo-soprano. The Dominican Bienvenido Bustamante and the Cuban Alfredo Munar shared conducting duties.[64] Clearly, the repertoire and the musicians represented a proto-Pan-Latino ensemble responding to shifting paradigms of identity in the city, while emphasizing the overwhelmingly Puerto Rican numbers among the concertgoers. The Puerto Rican press described the Lewisohn concert as an opportunity to "vestir a nuestro folklore de etiqueta" (dress up our folklore in a tuxedo), and this reporter states, "It is up to Ruth Fernández and Bienvenido Bustamante to impose our music on the world."[65] Although a grand stage, one internationally known, with three operatic singers, the selection of three women singers and the framing of their work as folklore suggest the work of the feminine as implanting and sustaining a state mandate to domesticate unruliness.

The New York Times review described the concert as "an evening of fun." According to the reviewer, the introductory set "gave no hint . . . of the infectious high spirits about to burst forth in the person of Miss Fernández. . . . The contralto revealed a dark, creamy voice and an utterly irresistible musical personality." The reviewer also praised Fernández's performance in Cecilia Valdés ("she was just as impressive in the operetta as in her songs"), although he described the operetta in decidedly minor language, calling it "this colorful little work."[66] I need not point out the evident racism of the review, couched in benevolent language treating Fernández as quasi-infantile. And yet the reviewer did note how Fernández worked the huge crowd and commandeered the music. This must have required great musical chops and vocal dexterity, given a professional orchestra of symphonic size. By contrast, the *New York Herald Tribune* reported, with no apparent irony: "Inter-hemispheric relations, music-division, were appreciably strengthened Saturday at Lewisohn Stadium when the Metropolitan Opera, in a Latin-American evening, played host to a variety of artists and compositions not generally heard in concert halls." The reporter described Fernández as a "sultry-voiced Puerto Rican contralto," who "swept onstage to sing folk songs from pre-Castro Cuba, Venezuela and Santa [*sic*] Domingo, as well as a traditional group from Puerto Rico, including the haunting 'Preciosa' of Rafael Hernández." He remarked on Fernández's educational and humorous running commentary, describing the repertoire and performance as "a series of warmly sung, expressively interpreted selections, occasionally with what she slyly referred to as 'the Metropolitan touch.' Giulietta or Judy she may not be, but Miss Fernández proved herself a unique addition to any OAS (Organization of American Singers)."[67]

In this review, Fernández is obviously belittled, yet differently from the *New York Times* review. "Sultry" seems to sexualize her somewhat; saying she "swept" onstage would have been uncharacteristic, given the displays of coolness and reserve Fernández usually exhibited, proceeding from her stated mantra of "I always make people want me" through a performance of studied indifference. It may be that she was overwhelmed emotionally by the occasion; I don't doubt it. (Expediency cannot narrate the entire story of her investments.) However, in the absence of properly musical descriptions of her contralto in performance, there is room for doubt of the *Herald Tribune*'s description.

More important is the crass comparison to Giulietta and Judy. Giulietta might be the mezzo Giulietta Simionato. Judy is of course Judy Garland. The statement is not vague about Fernández's inferiority to the two, but is vague about where exactly this inferiority should be located. Is it within the coordinates of classical singing or virtuosic popular singing? Is there a quarrel with her contralto being out of place in both realms? Naturally the reference to the "Organization of American Singers" lays bare the direct intervention of Cold War uses of culture, something Fernández surely knew all too well and, more likely than not, embraced.

Fernández's affiliation with both popular and classical registers, which can be condensed as the semiclassical, was woven into her discographical work of the 1960s, responding directly to the Puerto Rican state project. The liner notes to *Yo soy la que soy* (I am the one), released the same year as the Lewisohn concert, 1966, read, "For quite some time now, when speaking of the Puerto Rican entertainment industry it is imperative to mention the name of Ruth Fernández, the woman from Ponce who has gained the love and respect of all of Latin America not just thanks to her magnificent interpretations of Puerto Rican folklore but because she has known how to elevate the name of her Enchanted Island to faraway stages, and gain fame among the popular element and also the fans of semiclassical music."[68] "Música semiclásica" refers to the operatic Afro-Cuban music LPs. Fernández never recorded this music again, but it remained at the center of her figuration as an icon of normative blackness. Semiclassical is presented in counterpoint to an ambiguous "popular element." The boundary between the two might have been a source of anxiety: Where did popular music and semiclassical meet? The unstated question was: How to elevate popular music away from its unruly inclinations? Along with her LPs and television shows, Fernández had a tight concert schedule, which included presentations in the United States (such as the concert described above and others at Carnegie Hall, where *Cecilia Valdés* had been staged in October 1962). Increasingly, Fernández's message in all of these performances closely aligned with the ELA's message to its nationals abroad and the potential tourist: Puerto Rico was a paradise with very minor racial problems. Afro-Cuban light-operatic music was performed as a relic of a distant, colonial past, while Afro–Puerto Rican forms were invariably enlisted to provide sonic examples of the present's increasing state of harmony. Although not made explicit in the records, it is obvious that the point of comparison was the United States, particularly the segregated South, which Fernández mentioned in her interviews.[69] On occasion, Fernández performed American songs, as was the norm in the repertoire tailored to tourists in San Juan; most of her late repertoire, however, circulated a nativist signifier of race, either via songs thematizing ethnic harmony or via her splendidly costumed body and her multiply layered, virtuosic contralto voice.

Fernández exhibits, as a figure, colonialism's temporal and ideological obfuscations. The recipient of virulent racism, her public persona nevertheless harkens back to the pre-1898 colonial order extolled by Hispanophiles to uphold the modernizing, pro-American impulse of Luis Muñoz Marín. In the 1960s, specifically, at the heyday of developmentalism, Fernández emphasized the watered-down, easy listening folklore that catered to a homogenized and sanitized vision of Afro–Puerto Rican music in the face of the forms reigning in New York, seen as wild and lascivious. These ethnically and musically mixed, hybrid forms would presage the diasporic masterwork of salsa. Silvia Álvarez Curbelo observes, "The cultures of taste experienced a very important mutation. I believe this also holds true for Puerto Rican musical cultures. The middle classes adopt the taste for semi-classical music, with its American bent, but they also recover the Spanish zarzuela. All of this to counter what they saw as the 'plebeianization' of Puerto Rico."[70] Commenting on the selection of tracks for the contemporary record *Yo soy la que soy*, Eleuterio Santiago-Díaz points out the album's conformity to the PPD ideology and their cultural program aimed at the hotel industry and tourism: "On the island, racial and identity discourses have usually privileged conciliation. . . . The more radical gesture would be to shed light on the racial conflictivity that is contained in that zone of continuity."[71] Fernández would come to "shed light on racial conflictivity" in her later, political career as "the singing senator," although not in any directly confrontational way. Simply her embodiment and how it was received cast these zones into relief very plainly. And, as mentioned, it is hard to adjudicate her racial analysis, unpalatable as it is at times, due to an entire infrapolitical experience we still don't know about but that, undeniably, existed.[72]

THE ARTISTIC CLASS

It was around this time that Fernández began championing the "artistic class." This artistic class, Fernández claimed, would safeguard the nation's most cherished values and its highest ideals in the face of accelerated modernization and seemingly successful progress. Fernández took it upon herself to embody Puerto Rico's Operation Serenity (a name straight out of Cold War culture), Governor Muñoz Marín's symbolic and cultural operation that was parallel to the better-known Operation Bootstrap, the economic program of the ELA. "Artistic class" sounds a lot like "political class." The first term came to mean an entity that was parallel, sometimes a shadow, to the second, gaining an ambiguous but powerful political role. Fernández called on the government's duty to nourish and protect this class because it performed work that was intrinsic to the establishment of Puerto Rico's modernity and the creation of a space for the new citizen, who did not regard himself or herself colonially anymore but as the new subject of the ELA, heading toward progress.

Serenity was never passed formally into law; nevertheless, it created the country's chief institutions of music culture, enduring and indeed venerable institutions that survive to this day. A focus on Serenity shows how the state project relied on music as a stand-in for culture, as evidence of progress, and as a placeholder of the aspirational mode of class interpellating most Puerto Ricans in the ELA. Ernesto Ramos Antonini, a prominent lawyer who had a long career in the House of Representatives (1940–1963), eventually becoming its speaker and president, an Afro–Puerto Rican not yet given his due in official historiography, a *ponceño* like Fernández, was instrumental in the shaping of the Instituto de Cultura Puertorriqueña (Institute of Puerto Rican Culture), the Escuelas Libres de Música (State-Funded Music Schools), the Orquesta Sinfónica de Puerto Rico (Puerto Rico Symphony Orchestra), the Conservatory of Music, and the public radio and TV stations (WIPR), all government-run venues in which Ruth Fernández starred or was linked to, all linchpins of Operation Serenity.[73] The economist Teodoro Moscoso, chief architect of Operation Bootstrap, went on to head the powerful agency Compañía de Fomento Industrial. Fomento was assigned oversight of a festival to promote tourism in Puerto Rico and assuage tourists and investors about its civilized nature and its stability for investment, the Festival Casals de Puerto Rico (Casals Festival of Puerto Rico).[74] Fernández became good friends with the festival's namesake and chief draw, Pau (Pablo) Casals, who, as mentioned, had compared her voice to the sound of his cello.[75]

Woefully little has been written about Ramos Antonini's thought process regarding the establishment of a national network of musical education and uplift through a curriculum in music appreciation. One can surmise, along lines relevant to Ruth Fernández as well, as lone black star body in the ELA, that Ramos Antonini was very influenced by the postwar discourse of the rights of man and by liberation and decolonization movements in African and Caribbean societies, including their recourse to aesthetics. Keeping in mind watershed theorists of negritude and decolonization, such as Léopold Sédar Senghor and Aimé Césaire, who both became involved in statecraft directly, we can add depth to the incursions of Ernesto Ramos Antonini and Ruth Fernández into the political sphere. In addition, it should be noted that Fernández fully assumed a role exercised primarily by black men internationally, of linking cultural endeavor to the political solution of colonialism.

By the close of the decade, Fernández argued that artists in Puerto Rico had no work because the country's "folklore" was not showcased.[76] She compared Puerto Rico to Mexico where, she opined, the government took better advantage of the potential of native forms of cultural expression to spearhead business and especially tourism.[77] Of course, Puerto Rico is a tiny market compared

to Mexico. But, at the dawn of the 1960s, it existed in a complex colonial relationship to the United States, functioning symbolically as a showcase for
progress and a beacon of liberty during the Cold War. In truth, progress and
liberty were myths, not realities; what is certain is Puerto Rico's function, materially, as a military strategic point for the U.S. Army and tax haven for U.S.
companies. The rest of Latin America looked to its capacity to be an economic
and political bridge between the United States and the southern countries,
despite the routine cultural scorn it dispensed to the island-nation. Puerto
Rico played an enormous role in Cold War politics and U.S. expansionism,
as is well known, due as much to its Latin American character (sold by Luis
Muñoz Marín in various speeches for its value in the cultural Cold War) as
to its status as American military outpost. (Recall that both Myrta Silva and
Ruth Fernández were sent to entertain Puerto Rican troops during successive
wars and in various army bases, underscoring entertainment's relevance to
cementing gendered, militaristic, colonial patriotism.)

The defense of the artistic class is inseparable from the molding of Fernández's life narrative of social mobility and her ascent into the social elite. It
is very illuminating to consider Fernández's increasing repetition of this tale
of racial trauma as generative. I mostly reference Marvette Pérez's Smithsonian oral history, with the clarification that it has appeared verbatim in other
sources. This latter discourse is different from the one that led to her status as
Puerto Rican symbol of harmony and her Senate seat. Up to 1973, Fernández
had claimed never to have experienced racial discrimination: "I know it has
existed, but it has always been in muted form."[78] The factual accuracy of this
claim is suspect, but what interests me here is the artist's discursivity, her shift
in presentation to a racial warrior.

Fernández begins with a racial analysis of her childhood and family (which
she refers to as a "rainbow") and then proceeds to describe the skin color and
hair texture of all her sisters, as well as the origin of her mother, father, and
grandparents (meaning she identifies the white grandparents, the black ones,
and the mulatos).[79] She remembers her childhood as a paradise where color
was irrelevant: "I did not know what racial prejudice was. I was not conscious
of it, children played together."[80] According to the artist, she was inaugurated
into the realities of racism through an incident that happened in the child's
first true social space, the school, where she belonged to the choir and was
"la única negra en el coro" (the only black girl in the choir): "The first time
I became conscious that I was black (I didn't realize it until then) was a very
painful experience. Nevertheless, it shaped me for life."[81] In this incident, she

is passed over for a choir trip and is not given a satisfactory explanation. Then: "When I was walking home, my friend calls me and says, what teacher said was a lie. . . . I saw her when she was telling the other teacher, well Ruth is the best, but we have a problem, she's too black, and the girls in the choir are all white. . . . So what if I'm a little black girl? What does that have to do with it? I saw how in my house I had white sisters with kinky hair, a black grandmother, and a white grandfather. I was so confused. I cried and cried." She seeks solace (and an explanation) in her grandmother, who delivers a long speech about racial equality, culminating with the following message: "That has nothing to do with anything. Your teacher is wrong. She is wrong because there is no difference between blacks and white people. Black people are prepared. The black person must study, must improve, he has to be educated [fino], have manners, he has to have everything or more than the white man because then, when there is a discussion on this topic, all you have to say is, so what if I'm black?"[82] The discourse exhibits some of the classic elements of racist discourse under colonialism: the importance of values, forgiveness for the American schoolteacher, tropes of common humanity, and the harmonizing potential of *mestizaje* (miscegenation). Yet it also enacts the classic diva quandary: Faced with an enormous obstacle, the diva or, more accurately, the diva to be, already a solitary and misunderstood figure, proclaims, I will sing![83] In this case, Fernández explicitly racializes the diva cry: It becomes "negra, ¿y qué?" (So what if I'm black?). Not yet an adult, she receives the intimation of her destiny in puberty, another classic trope of the diva narrative.

Fernández insistently places music performance in a social context and speaks at length about segregation in Puerto Rico. She spectacularly narrates how she broke racial barriers by refusing to enter the exclusive Hotel Condado Vanderbilt through the back door, as was customary for all black musicians playing in white establishments. Commenting on this episode, she states she was about sixteen or seventeen years old: "Todavía quedaban los blancos resabiosos que todavia creían en los prejuicios" (There were still some holdouts, some resentful white folks who still believed in racial prejudice).[84] Fernández states that her greatest satisfaction of the evening came from making the dance couples stop dancing and listen to her voice — a scene of diva vindication that has to do with both racial pride and the creation of a space where race would momentarily evaporate. Clearly, Ruth Fernández stages the Hotel Condado story as her scene of vindication.[85] Her objective, she narrates, was to stop the dancing and fixate everybody's eyes upward, to her mouth, the source of her voice. Everyone had to listen and fixate on the singer, the opposite goal of dance music: "Once I started to sing, everyone stopped dancing. When I was done, a thunderous applause broke out. It was so loud that I turned to Mingo and asked him, feel better? I always make people want me."[86]

The idea of racial paradise is undercut by her description of having been excluded from musical pursuits when she was a small child. Fernández displaces racism into an American schoolteacher, thus indirectly bolstering the myth that Puerto Rican society was not inherently racist. Instead, a foreign, temperamentally alien element came in and "brought the racism," tainting a paradisiacal environment. Fernández opts for a cultural forgetting of racial trauma, symbolized in her childhood experience, and sutures the issue of Puerto Rican racism by creating a tale of vindication where she resolved both traumas — individual and social — by putting into practice her grandmother's recommendations.

Despite her polished discourse, I have no doubt that Fernández resented her role as representative and, despite her multiple references to her own ugliness, there is room to wonder if she truly felt shame or if past a certain point she mobilized elements of abjection as part of another operation (one that may be labeled political) and which she channeled through the artistic class.

I AM THE ONE

Fernández's grandmother emphasized the importance of strategies to defend against societal conventions of beauty. The more personal question remains unanswered: Did the grandmother consider her granddaughter beautiful or simply capable of overcoming the obstacle that she thought her granddaughter's body was? The self-narrative does not proffer details about the intimate aspect of this quandary. It is possible, however, to verify how Fernández's abject portrayal as ugly clashed with the magnificence of her photographic image, which represents the theatrical femininity of the diva in publicity stills and album covers. Her iconography as revealed from the 1950s onward in album covers, publicity stills, and film appearances presents a woman identified visually with high fashion, elite circles, and successful African American models. The visual record establishes that Fernández did not shy away from being photographed and considered attractive. She was photographed (and presented herself) as normative, but certainly not as ugly or undesirable.

In her battle to "educate" the colonial subject, Fernández often discusses the importance of dress. She was a fashion plate.[87] As is evident from the album covers with place name markers from local to hemispheric, *Ruth Fernández*

FIGURE 2.5 Album cover, *Ruth Fernández con la Orquesta Panamericana*, Rumba Records LP 55572, 1960s, shows Fernández in a Motown pose.

con la Orquesta Panamericana (Ruth Fernández with Pan-American Orchestra, figure 2.5) and *Ruth Fernández, Es de Borinquen, con Machito y su Orquesta* (She comes from Puerto Rico: Ruth Fernández with Machito and His Orchestra, figure 2.6), she dressed to suggest refinement and a certain degree of aloofness. "I am obsessed by clothes. I like very feminine attire, with plenty of ruffles and lace."[88] She told Marvette Pérez how her experience in the Hotel Condado Vanderbilt involved some decisions about dress and how it contributed to fighting racism: "My grandmother always told me, Ruth, you have to be well dressed. The first impression is the most important moment for an artist. . . . If you arrive well dressed, you can be ugly, black, have a big nose, all that, but if you have a magnificent gown, that's all they look at. . . . If you can't dress up, then don't go."[89]

An alternate cover of *Ñáñigo*, retitled *Ruth Fernández Sings*, shows Fernández in costume, possibly as the ex-slave Dolores Santa Cruz from *Cecilia Valdés*, likely an earlier picture from the 1940s. It presents Fernández's image as a guarantee of the singer's connection to the music and its raced sound (figure 2.7). It shows Fernández dressed to represent black identity as corre-

FIGURE 2.6 Album cover, Ruth Fernández, *Es de Borinquen* with Machito and His Orchestra, Tico LP 1101, 1963?.

sponding to plantation life. Apparently the 1960s required a repeated return to colonial myths, since for *Fiend of Dope Island* (one of the island movies so popular in the 1960s, which used the colony as a cheap movie set and portrayed its people as either savage or country bumpkins), an older Fernández is dressed similarly to her costume for *Ruth Fernández Sings* (figure 2.8). In contrast to this vaguely colonial costume, contemporary publicity stills show her fully inhabiting her more usual diva persona. Her extremely self-confident poses suggest the cool, reserved sensuality of American jazz divas. *Ruth Fernández con la Orquesta Panamericana* (figure 2.5) used as a cover one such still, colorized, showing Fernández with a *rumbera*-style dress but no musical instruments (typically rumberas were photographed with percussive accouterments, such as maracas). With its sideways pose, looking down, arms spread, and the artist dressed in a refined, long gown, it intimates a cool sensuality that alludes to both respectability and femininity, very similar to the Motown photos of Diana Ross. The Motown influence is also evident in the cover of *Es de Borinquen* (figure 2.6), with hands tossed up and a slightly twisted body.

FIGURE 2.7 Album cover, *Ruth Fernández Sings*, with
Obdulio Morales and His Native Cuban Orchestra and
Chorus, Montilla FM 54, 1955. The album was released
in Cuba, the United States, Spain, and France. The
cover shows Fernández in vaguely colonial dress, very
different from her usual high-fashion persona.

Fernández was photographed dozens of times; there are many extant publicity stills across various decades, such as the one shown in figure 2.9, which
appears to be from the early 1960s. Gazing at this image, it would seem that
the feminine had no trouble being established in the scopic register, almost
promising a jump forward beyond racism. Its representation was more vexing
when it came to sound, where it was inextricably linked to notions of "sonic
blackness."[90] In the LP *Yo soy la que soy* (I am the one), Fernández recorded
two songs that appeal directly to her figure as an icon of Puerto Rican and
Caribbean blackness, and specifically as a black Caribbean woman.[91] These
can be considered signature songs, but, in contradistinction to Myrta Silva's
performance of "Nada" (chapter 1), these songs did not function as a letter
supporting meaning while simultaneously displacing it. Their relationship to
the signifier of "Ruth Fernández" is not as successful. Ruth Fernández operated, to use a Lacanian approach, as an imaginary, not a symbolic construct.

FIGURE 2.8 Ruth Fernández as "Tula," in a nonspeaking film role as a bartender. From the cult movie *Fiend of Dope Island*, 1961.

The first is the album's title track, "Yo soy la que soy." It differs from the second song I discuss, "Yo soy mulata," in significant ways. The bandleader, Lito Peña, who worked closely with Fernández throughout her ELA musical career, wrote the first song for Fernández. He incorporated a second title she had accrued during this time, "La Negra de Ponce" (The black woman from Ponce) and referred to bomba and plena in the lyrics. "Yo soy la que soy," however, was not recorded with any bomba or plena instruments. The lyrics celebrate the ideal of racial harmony, as signified discursively by both bomba and plena, but stripped of their musical signs and hence disfigured in their black identity. They re-create the view of racial harmony and the certainty of unqualified love on the part of her listeners (something we know to have been false, from the constant jokes about Fernández's physiognomy, shockingly alive to this day). In this sense, the song mirrors exactly Fernández's self-narrative as having resolved the ravages of racism through her personal itinerary, where the final destination is national music:

Yo soy la que soy, la que soy
Cuidado que aquí llegó la Negra de Ponce

FIGURE 2.9 Publicity still of Ruth Fernández, photographer unknown, 1960s. Courtesy of the Archivo General de Puerto Rico.

La que baila la bomba
La que canta la plena
La que dice con gran orgullo soy pura . . . puertorriqueña

Pa' mí no hay problema racial
Yo soy muy feliz con to' lo que Dios me ha dado
Yo no puedo quejarme
Todo el mundo me quiere
Y nací en esta bella islita en que todos somos hermanos

I am the one; I am the one
Be careful, the black woman of Ponce has arrived
She who dances the bomba
She who sings the plena
She who says, with great pride, I am a pure . . . Puerto Rican woman!

For me, there's no racial problem
I'm very happy with what God gave me
I can't complain
Everyone loves me
And I was born on this beautiful island, where we are all brothers and
    sisters

Fernández can be heard attempting to inject some irony and edge to the song, for example in the ellipsis creating a distance between "pure" and "Puerto Rican": "yo soy pura . . . puertorriqueña." It appears that Fernández was playing with saying "yo soy pura negra" (I am a purely black woman) especially because she sings, in a mockingly warning tone, "Be careful, the black woman from Ponce has arrived." The possibility of a challenge to the dominant racial order is quickly quashed in the next stanza.

The song "Yo soy mulata" (I am a mulata) is a dated racial portrayal, a resurrection of the 1930s and 1940s ideal of the mulata as a more acceptable version of the black woman, yet not fully integrated into the normative ideal, either. Despite its datedness and the lack of transparent references to "Puerto Ricanness," Fernández's performance strikes a deeper chord, functioning as a negative to the more straightforward signature of "Yo soy la que soy." Rafael "Bullumba" Landestoy, a Dominican composer active since the 1930s, wrote "Yo soy mulata." Landestoy wrote the song for Milagros Lanty, an Afro-Dominican singer. Upon visiting the Dominican Republic while on tour, the Mexican great Toña la Negra (Toña the black woman) took the song with her to record in Mexico. Thus, we have three Afro–Latin American singers, at least, who performed the song; in theory, there could be more, as the figure they represented was repeatable across various nations and collectives.

In a nutshell, the song attempts to respond to racial shaming by presenting a celebratory account of mestizaje. On the surface, the song responds to the same dominant vision of music's capacity to resolve racial tensions. Yet while in "Yo soy la que soy," the singer adopts a contrived joy, when listening to "Yo soy mulata," the listener can divine at the very least her ambivalence via a superior vocal performance.

> Yo soy mulata
> Y a orgullo tengo
> Llevar la sangre de negro en las venas
> Yo soy mulata
> Y no me importa
> Que me critiquen
> Si yo tengo bemba
>
> Yo no sé por qué la gente
> Se preocupa porque tengo [jajaja]
> Y que pasa dura [ja ja]
> Yo no sé
>
> Y si visto de colores
> Me critican y me dicen
> Bueno negra pero qué mal gusto [jummm]
> Y que tengo yo
>
> Y no me importa
> Si tengo ñata
> A orgullo tengo
> Tener piel tostá
> Y no me importa
> Yo soy mulata
> Yo soy mulata
> Mulata en verdad
>
> Soy mulata
> De verdad

I am a mulata
And I feel proud
Of the black blood in my veins
I am a mulata
And I don't care
If people criticize
My thick lips

Beats me why folks
worry that I have
so-called kinky hair

Who knows why?
If I wear lots of color
People criticize me and say
Well, girl, what bad taste (hmmm)
I supposedly have

I really don't care
About my flat nose
I'm very proud
Of my brown skin
I don't care
I am a mulata
I am a mulata
A true mulata
I am mulata
A true mulata

The performance is punctuated at every turn with displays of vocal virtuosity, particularly soaring into high notes, descending into very low notes, and employing operatic phrasing throughout. Fernández also speaks some of the verses, and incorporates laughter, as she did on "Y tu abuela onde etá." She sings this song triumphantly, but the ambivalence is palpable. The identities, negra and mulata, are not collapsible into one another and create virtually impossible quandaries for the singer to settle in her preferred mode of triumphalism. Fernández never performed a song in which her name could come to signify a social "working through," referring to herself instead by racial epithets, such as "la Negra de Ponce," "negra," or "mulata." In "Yo soy mulata," singing "I am a mulata" is as much an affirmation of pride as it is a re-creation of the racial taxonomies and practices restraining and shaping her musical career. Whether the song is ironic in its repetition of the markers of supposedly benign racist discourse, including its ideal of sexualized feminine beauty, the mulata, is up for grabs. The performance doesn't resolve one of the central problems of this repertoire and of Latin Americanist racial discourse — whitening as social policy — even if on the surface the lyrics celebrate the mulata ideal. The performance of the fabulous that Fernández achieved, visually and vocally, is not enough to render the problem sutured, much less confronted. On the contrary, her diva incarnation seems to have worked even better to suit the political needs of the PPD, which were to decree that racism in Puerto Rico was a minimal affair.

One of the puzzles of Fernández's conditional admission into elite circles was just how she managed to enter this white supremacist world. Her excellence in music and star quality were likely insufficient. The colonial feminine was the gateway, as it evolved in early century Ponce.[92] It's possible that, at some point, Fernández became friends with the legendary local society lady "Doña Fela," Felisa Rincón de Gautier, who before her segue into a long political career as San Juan's mayor (1946–1968) owned the Felisa Style Shop in Old San Juan. She might have become acquainted with Fernández because of their common passion for high fashion, the most interesting element in Fernández's tale of star inception. Rincón may have sold Fernández dresses in the 1940s. We still lack information as to how exactly Fernández assumed a didactic role for the PPD, but do know she became particularly notable for performing a Rafael Hernández song, "Lamento borincano," at multiple PPD rallies, celebrations, and, just as importantly, events sponsored by ladies' society circles, often spearheaded by the first lady, Inés Mendoza de Muñoz. Dress was a common denominator among these women, signifying their inclusion in a social class. Fernández also entered because of her vocal capacity, harbinger of her strangeness in this supremacist environment. This white or light-skinned world surely regarded her paternalistically, or might one say, maternalistically, finding it difficult to cope with their feeling of discomfort while also experiencing a simultaneous fascination for their "pet." Personally, I doubt the description of Fernández as a mulata would have had any purchase in this group, although elites generally would never disclose their feelings of contempt for and superiority over Fernández by calling her "negra" to her face, with all the word meant in that circle. Her songs of self-interpellation remain a puzzle. "Yo," whether in "Yo soy la que soy" or "Yo soy mulata," is a gap.

"Lamento borincano" is a melancholy song about a peasant who tries to sell his agricultural products in the city and comes back empty-handed, condemned to a life of poverty. It was a celebrated anticolonial song until it became Luis Muñoz Marín's unofficial anthem. This gesture changed the song's valence considerably, turning it into a cultural-nationalist defense of the spiritual independence of the nation and the stock values upon which it rested, irrespectively of self-determination (the professed theme of the song cited in the beginning of the chapter, "Lamento de un boricua"). The transmission of the song rested, to an extent, on Fernández's raced and gendered body, similar to Farah Jasmine Griffin's description of "the recognizably black woman — singing rather than speaking . . . a familiar sight for American audiences. While each instance, each woman, each voice is unique — these women do not 'sound' alike — the physicality is familiar. The woman stands before a crowd in front of a microphone, mouth open, positioned to sing."[93] Like the singers Griffin names, Fernández is a social sign: the black woman with her mouth open and, eventually, the singing senator. [94] On top of that, as with the pavas she had distributed at the Lewisohn among the orchestra, "Lamento borincano" refers the listener immediately to the whitened social figure of the jíbaro. Here is an example of the sign of the "black woman singing," prior to her properly political career, when the first lady called on Fernández to sing "Lamento borincano" at the height of her musical career:

> The meeting ended after Ruth Fernández, the Puerto Rican songstress, performed "Lamento borincano." Mrs. Muñoz Marín introduced her as "a great Puerto Rican woman."
> Most of those who attended the meeting were women, and they joined Ruth Fernández in the song that has served and still serves as the musical backdrop of the political meetings of the Popular Democratic Party.
> According to the organizers, a thousand people attended the gathering, which proceeded with the utmost order and enthusiasm.[95]

Fernández later borrowed a page from Mendoza, starting to underscore her own variation of republican motherhood in the press and stressing her value as someone who could appeal to women voters specifically across class stratification: "Women should participate in the politics of today, to give politics a touch of love, femininity, and warmth, to balance things out and calm violent dispositions. . . . I think Puerto Rico's future is in women's hands, and if we can have better girls, through preventive homes, we will have better women tomorrow."[96]

By the time the 1970s rolled around, Rafael Hernández Colón, the PPD's rising star, tapped Fernández to be senator at large on the party ticket that he headed as candidate for governor. Undoubtedly their common roots in and identification with seigniorial Ponce played a key role. Just as clearly, her symbolics of femininity, coded along the musical, and simultaneously exhibiting and downplaying race, did too. She avoided giving details about how she got tapped for the Senate: "By the time I realized it, I was already in politics. It had been laid at my feet."[97] She spoke of friends who had approached her with the idea, and gave the impression she never sought out the nomination.[98] Her campaign for Senate was baptized "La Negra Va" (the black woman's in it to win).[99]

Figure 2.10 is a detail of the 1972 election ballot on which Fernández was a candidate, along with other candidates for senator at large for the PPD, all men. Fernández appears represented by a musical instrument, a guitar. For her second ballot, in 1976, it was mandatory for all candidates to print their picture. Fernández appears once more against the backdrop of a guitar, the only candidate from the senator at large bracket to supplement her image with a symbol. As in music, in politics she was the lone black figure. Figure 2.11 is a scene from her 1972 campaign, possibly singing, in the Aibonito PPD headquarters. Fernández won election to the Senate both times, garnering a large number of votes. The idea of the musical figured prominently in Fernández's political persona; she drew heavily on understandings of popular music as the spirit of the nation, or, as Álvarez Curbelo puts it, most succinctly, as a grid of identity in 1970s Puerto Rico, alongside sports.[100] (She did not run in the 1980 elections; another artist and woman, the actress Velda González, replaced her on the ballot. Fernández served instead as the special assistant for cultural affairs during two consecutive terms of Rafael Hernández Colón, 1985–1993.)

Fernández was eventually and unevenly admitted to Puerto Rico's elite circles, arguably because, in the racist interpretation of her voice, she was thought of as nonfemale, a characterization that Fernández countered by foregrounding femininity in her public persona. Yet she also sought to represent respectability out of conviction and was promoted by the colonial government as the cultural ambassador of Puerto Rico abroad and later as a cultural icon in her career as senator. She decided to embody the ideals of racial harmony so dear to Puerto Rican cultural nationalism and, in retrospect, redefined the terms upon which to understand this decision through a carefully constructed diva narrative of triumph and restitution. She went beyond her personal recollec-

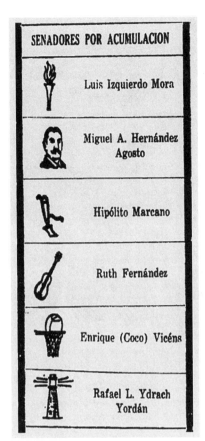

SENADORES POR ACUMULACION

Luis Izquierdo Mora

Miguel A. Hernández Agosto

Hipólito Marcano

Ruth Fernández

Enrique (Coco) Vicéns

Rafael L. Ydrach Yordán

FIGURE 2.10 Detail, election ballot of 1972. Ruth Fernández is listed as a candidate for PPD senator at large. Her symbol is a guitar.

tion to define the national act of recollection, upholding a Latin Americanist raced paradigm. "We are a single America, of indigenous, black, and Spanish origins. That's why Puerto Rico is at the vanguard among the Latin American countries."[101]

During her Senate years, Fernández established the Compañía de Variedades Artísticas (Company for artistic shows) and the Comisión de Arte y Cultura (Arts and culture commission). She cut a formidable figure. As the singing senator, Fernández became the avuncular figure instructing all colonial citizens to obey the new colonial state, the ELA, for their own good, like children. She justified the PPD hegemony in politics by calling Puerto Rico "la Isla del Progreso" (Progress Island), a take on the patriotic phrase "la Isla del Encanto" (Island of Enchantment).[102] Talking to an interviewer in the 1990s,

FIGURE 2.11 Ruth Fernández in her 1972 campaign for the Senate, speaking at PPD headquarters in Aibonito, Puerto Rico. The walls are plastered with the PPD symbol, a profile of a jíbaro with a pava (straw hat) and the logo "Pan, Tierra, Libertad" (Bread, land, liberty). Images of Luis Muñoz Marín and the 1972 PPD candidate for governor, Rafael Hernández Colón, are visible. Fernández's candidate poster is partially visible in the center, and reads, "Ruth Fernández, El alma de Puerto Rico, Para el Senado" (Ruth Fernández, Puerto Rico's soul, for the Senate). Courtesy of the Archivo General de Puerto Rico.

she clarified that her role in politics had been "public relations": "When the governor needed me, I was sent to the projects, barrios, and towns. I was sent to sing."[103] Through the tool of respectable femininity, in its incarnation as feminine song, Fernández instilled a devotional tie to the artistic class and its version of popular music, fully utilizing music's political potential.

In the twenty-first century, *Raíces* (Roots), a 2001 Banco Popular special honoring the legacy of Afro–Puerto Ricans in national music, re-created the scene of Fernández singing lead as a young woman in Ponce. It staged the scene to present a celebratory, nostalgic look back at a supposed golden age, with the express intent of targeting a neoliberal consumer. In the video, Fernández repeats her life narrative once more and sings "Y tu abuela onde etá" as an example of the roots music the video purports to honor. Her performance of the Fortunato Vizcarrondo poem in *Raíces* departs significantly from the one she performed as a twenty-year-old live and on the recording preserved on a 78 rpm record.

When Fernández performed the song at the Escambrón Beach Club in the late 1930s, she was a very young woman, improbably leading an important orchestra, launching her career. By the time Fernández rerecorded it for *Raíces*, she had sung it on TV specials in Puerto Rico a fair number of times, often as part of greatest-hits medleys recalling the past. In almost all of these presentations, Lito Peña arranged the song. Peña is the bandleader who wrote "Yo soy la que soy" (I am the one) for her and whose orchestra frequently served as Fernández's accompaniment in 1970s and 1980s Puerto Rico. Peña's later arrangement for "Y tu abuela" echoes the sonic clichés of "Yo soy la que soy": blandly orchestrated Afro–Puerto Rican music catering to the middle classes. None of the original bite of Fernández's first recording of this song with Mingo and His Whoopee Kids is recalled. Extant videos show Fernández cavorting in an expensive designer dress while performing, sometimes punctuating the ending with, "Mira, y que decirme negra a mí" (Can you believe he said I was black). We simply cannot know if she was avowing or disavowing her black identity. Given my certainty that another conversation existed between Afro–Puerto Rican musicians exclusively, there is ample room to believe it was an ironic address.

The original recording of "Y tu abuela" is auratic because it's imbued with an unrecoverable pastness. A disturbing normalization of this song's history unfolded when Fernández became senator; it was only slightly revised in *Raíces* along the neoliberal format of nostalgia. Later performances could have revived the importance of "Y tu abuela," elucidating its witness to a problematic past of segregation, while updating its arrangement.[104] Perhaps in bomba? Or in salsa? Or jazz, a genre Fernández clearly enjoyed singing in? *Raíces* is not quite triumphalist, but it does suture the clear wounds Fernández incurred.

I have attempted to touch this past or *arkhé* in this chapter, get close to this black diva of Puerto Rico. A diva is not supposed to have any markers next to her name; she must simply be, transcendent and unique. Fernández thought of herself this way. Her protestation, "¿Negra, y qué?" (So what if I'm black?), traces her life according to this calling, from her grandmother's words, famously presaging not only her artistic triumph but also her political career, through a series of obstacles overturned, principally, by her presumptively strange voice.[105] The remark has overtones of the mournful, however. As a looking back at her inclusion on the problematic terms of a society stratified by race and class, it has been read as heroic. I've tried to pry open the phrase to reveal the wound. I've also sought to listen more carefully: voice's potential to become a thinking voice, to intimate the voice that's been suppressed, lives spectrally on as a battle cry: ¿Negra, y qué?

THREE

TECHNE AND THE LADY

The career of Ernestina Reyes, "La Calandria" (San Lorenzo, 1925–Bronx, 1994) illustrates mid-twentieth-century historical processes in a gripping way through the career arc of her voice. She became a star in Puerto Rico in the 1950s, just when the Estado Libre Asociado (ELA, Commonwealth of Puerto Rico) was born. Calandria was the first woman *música campesina* (country music) singer to appear on both radio and television. Over the course of two decades, she recorded an uncommonly large number of tracks for a woman, a feat made all the more remarkable because she routinely received sole or main billing, collaborated with the very best vocalists of the country music genre, and was as a matter of course backed by master country music *cuatro* players, certifying her revered standing. She became the epitome of country music's so-called female voice, towering over her female colleagues in terms of a recording career, live presentations, and iconic impact.[1] Like other "greatest women artists," her colleagues and the wider public insisted on understanding her voice through a gender separation that rendered her secondary to men, notwithstanding the equality of her prowess.

Calandria participated in country music radio programs just when the Popular Democratic Party (PPD) was asserting its hegemony over Puerto Rican politics, around 1948. Circa 1951 she was featured in a popular radio program, *La hora del volante* (The driver's hour), with Florencio Morales Ramos, known as Ramito, regarded as "the greatest jíbaro singer" (male singers did not suffer from being marked by their gender). Over the course of this pivotal decade, Calandria, Ramito, and a host of notable country musicians participated in heavily promoted goodwill tours to the United States (especially New York) to aid in the ELA's quest to present itself as the migrants' *amigo* (friend), a positioning illustrated in two state-produced educational videos of 1952 and 1956, *Un amigo en Nueva York* and *Un amigo en Chicago*.[2]

Ernestina Reyes was the fifth of nine siblings. Calandria was not formally trained in music, but she did receive some music lessons when she was young and was able to play some guitar. She began singing professionally with her sister, Carmen, as part of the duet Las Hermanas Reyes (The Reyes Sisters). The young girls listened assiduously to the radio. They were fans of the *radionovelas* of the 1940s (radio soap operas), especially *El derecho de nacer* (The right to be born), with Lucy Boscana and Mona Marti, two well-known Puerto Rican radio stars who went on to become two of the most recognizable character actresses on television soap operas. These radionovelas, as is to be expected, veered toward the melodramatic. They targeted women — particularly working-class women — as their audience.

Las Hermanas Reyes debuted on a musical segment of the radio news program *La correspondencia* (Correspondence), hosted by Rafael Quiñones Vidal (Puerto Rico's founding radio personality and impresario).

> I recall the microphone hung from the ceiling . . . I was 12; Ernestina was 10. We were going to sing 'Sin bandera' [Without a flag] but it was banned because it was considered a Nationalist song. . . . 'Sin bandera' was all the rage; people sang it on the streets. [Sings] *We Puerto Ricans, we do not have a single corner to call our own.* . . . My father was a Nationalist and close friends with Pedro Albizu Campos. He was the godfather of one of my brothers, along with his wife Laura Meneses. . . . Probably my father chose the song, I don't remember. Since we couldn't sing 'Sin bandera' we sang 'Campanitas de cristal' [Glass bells]. Rafael Seijó and Pedro Dávila played guitar. Ernestina sang melody and I sang harmony.[3]

Calandria sang with her sister until approximately 1948, when Carmen got married. Carmen recounts they first sang boleros and *danzas*, and that she never liked jíbaro music. According to Carmen, Ernestina started singing jíbaro music at around eighteen.

Ernestina gave birth to the first of two daughters when she was sixteen.[4] She quit school to take care of the baby while Carmen attended university. Carmen was not eager to take a job, preferring to stay at home, even though her husband did not forbid her from singing. Ernestina, by contrast, was passionately involved with music and could not wait to launch herself as a professional. "Germán Nigaglioni was recruiting talent for a show he had brought with him from Cuba, the *Colgate Show with Calandria and Clavelito*. They paid seventy-five dollars a week. . . . My father made eighty dollars a month as a sanitation employee. . . . Ernestina was making more than a schoolteacher!"[5] It was as hired talent for this program that Calandria started singing the traditional *décimas* of the countryside, over the radio, in the capital city of San Juan.[6]

There were a couple of topics per show, which were fodder for *controversias*, sung competitions between two singers who followed the rule of the *pie forzado*: a refrain ending each stanza, dictating both topic and rhyme scheme. The singers were expected to act out the jíbaro persona — a clowning, straight-talking entity mostly performed by the male voice, with the female voice usually reproving of his ways. The popular appeal of controversias could not have been lost on the advertisers who sponsored the programs (Colgate, in this case). The stage name Calandria (Songbird) referred initially to this character which she played on the *Colgate Show*, which they took from the stage name of the Cuban singer Nena Cruz, who had been part of the identical radio show singing Cuban country music (*puntos guajiros*) with Clavelito (Miguel Alfonso). (It's worth noting the multiple singers were baptized as Calandrias at some point or another during their careers, for example, Rita Vidaurri in the ranchera tradition, Inés Arce in tango, and others we still don't know about.) Jesús Sánchez Erazo, "Chuíto el de Bayamón," who was by then an experienced hand in radio programming, was hired to play Clavelito. After this contract, Calandria kept the name artistically as she went on to a professional recording and performance career. She starred in other radio shows at the dawn of the 1950s, such as *Alegrías campesinas* (Country delights) and later in *La hora del volante* (The driver's hour) with Ramito.[7]

In "La Calandria: An unforgettable sufferer," an article published December 26, 2004, in Puerto Rico's major newspaper, *El Nuevo Día*, Jaime Torres Torres wrote, "When Ernestina Reyes 'La Calandria' sang a *seis* or an *aguinaldo*, the *patria* [motherland] wept along with her, lamenting the fatigue, pain and frustration of colonialism."[8] His article, while well meaning (he describes Calandria as "one of those minds that appears only once every four or five generations"), still draws from a problematic, gendered narrative: "Ever since her youth, misery and trouble hounded her. In spite of many divorces and failed loves, her successful performances and records earned her the rank of diva, heroine, queen and empress of country folklore, titles that she still holds." However unintentionally, Torres Torres exhibits a regressive approach to Calandria's musical career; he sketches the singer's biography as a sustained failure. The hyperbole inherent in the succession of titles does not by itself tell us anything about the singer's career or musicianship. Despite echoing earlier times, in which such hyperbole cemented illustrious personas and countered the social belittling of jíbaros and their music, the repetition of hyperbole falls flat on our ears without careful unpacking and insertion into their listening context. Further, it reinforces the gender separation: the ideology of the great woman singer.

Torres Torres concluded that "the sociological phenomenon known as La Calandria has not yet been studied in Puerto Rico as it deserves." Although classifying her as a "sociological phenomenon" is overstated (substituting an individual for an entire society), he was correct in calling for her study. His final word on this "diva" is: "In between drinks, and armed with a guitar, Ernestina personified melancholy. Melancholy smiles at life during the day and consumes itself at night, while sobbing its pain away." This characterization has two troubling aspects. First, it ascribes a melancholy mood to the singer (who, according to her closest associates, was anything but a melancholic). Second, it recurs to familiar tropes of artistic women as consumed by an un-specified bohemian lifestyle. A construction of women as downfallen, the need to keep girls under tight and constant surveillance, mirror the strictures of Ernestina's own life as a young woman in San Lorenzo.

The linking of migration and melancholy disguises the stark decisions of the newly established ELA. The economic planners of the new status knew that they could not create enough jobs for the total number of workers on the island. Thus they sponsored an unprecedented migration to the United States, especially to New York City. A large segment of the audience for coun-try music was literally evacuated from the national territory. Simultaneously, the state constructed a binary anchored in two interpellations — those who "stayed" and those who "left" — which stands as very unfair to the thousands of people who emigrated thanks to policies that squeezed them out of the economy. To allay the severity of its program, and aid in creating consensus, the state installed the symbolic Puerto Rican peasant and the Puerto Rican countryside as dyad in its mythology of belonging, creating a "melancholy cage" to facilitate the state plan.[9]

In its personalization of a brutal, cold economic decision — its deployment of the illusion of caring for its suddenly inconvenient national subjects — the state enlisted music in the campaign to induce compliance from those it had expelled under pretense of a bright economic future in the U.S. city. The event of mass migration altered the course of country music more par-ticularly. The state manipulated jíbaro music to correlate with its creation of new myths. It inserted country music in a hierarchical relationship to the other musics it was promoting in Puerto Rico: on the one hand, classical music via Operation Serenity's venerable institutions (chapter 2), on the other, pop music for tourists and the middle classes, including a type of nativist peasant music regularly featured on TV and in stylized revues in the capital city's posh hotels.

When Operation Bootstrap emphasized consumerism and modernity, requiring new musical formats to correspond to new cultures of taste on the island, the Puerto Rican folk genres of plena, bomba, and jíbaro music became explicitly aligned with national-popular visions that rewrote music history as a racialized narrative of predominantly Hispanophile origins. The ELA exalted the peasant figure and relegated Afro–Puerto Ricans to a heritage role. Country music was routed into folkloric understandings of string-based music, while Afro–Puerto Rican music was classified as rhythmic. Both occupied the lower rungs on the scale of musical worthiness, as defined by the state. Schools and the university taught this musical pedagogy uninterruptedly through developmentalism's first phase (1950s and 1960s) and well beyond, into its decline (1970s and 1980s). In this pedagogy, both genres were esteemed as folklore, not as pop.

While dominant visions coded both black and jíbaro as *zoe* and regarded their "bare life" as revealed in music, state designs on jíbaro music differed from official appropriations of black music (chapter 2).[10] Compared to the Afro–Puerto Rican subject, the symbolic country dweller lived on, however spectrally, while the descendant of slaves faded away as a relic of the past. What both raced imaginaries had in common was that both were expected to play a role in citizen identification with a dominant state project. In addition to the burden of representation that constrained musicians, both genres suffered the fate of not being documented in all their breadth, since the focus of dominant interpretation became narrowly confined to substantiating the state mandate regarding national music.

Classified as melancholic and lost, the thousands belonging to the working class and peasantry became removed from island listening circuits. They forged new spaces for music making and vastly complicated the entire insular definition of values listening that the ELA implanted. Jíbaro musicians were key in these articulations. Despite being participants in the state mythology, and despite their considerable travails and the very real losses faced by individuals as they were uprooted and separated from Puerto Rico, jíbaro musicians and the migration at large creatively navigated this minoritarian space. Among the most aware of an alignment with the moment was Calandria, who first migrated to New York City in 1960.

Even under the auspices of the state, musical labor had been underpaid and hard to come by. Like Calandria, many jíbaro musicians migrated to New York City in the early 1960s and became icons for the migrant community. Some shuttled back and forth between New York and Puerto Rico over the course of the decade. Calandria was one of these musical itinerants, with varying periods of residence between Puerto Rico and New York until she settled permanently in the Bronx around 1970.[11] In the words of jíbaro singer Joaquín Mouliert, "El Pitirre de Fajardo" (The kingbird from Fajardo), "Se dieron cuenta que había más todo para nuestra música" (They realized there was "more everything" for our music).[12] Following on Mouliert's insight, this chapter seeks to address this "todo" (all) that musicians like Calandria accurately perceived. I go beyond the paradigm of mere economic need, which does not suffice to explain the magnitude of their artistic decision. Certainly the state showed a knack for manipulating culture to "educate consent," but that's far from the whole story, and maybe it isn't the main story.[13] Calandria's musician's desire — her devotion to jíbaro music, to her profession — impelled her to migrate along with her audience. She was adventurous and unafraid to venture out of all strictures, including that of the great woman singer.

CALLING ALL CRITICS

The jíbaro (a difficult word to translate: peasant, farmhand, peon) has been, for decades, the foremost Puerto Rican national symbol. The ELA implanted a fantasy of national meaning: life in the countryside, recast as peaceful and idyllic. On television and radio, in school textbooks, in booklets the Division of Education for the Community (DIVEDCO) issued, all were hailed as descended from this mythical jíbaro and his way of life. The audio recordings and live performances of jíbaro music, in which Calandria participated, played a crucial role in identifying with this abstraction.

Puerto Rico's "lettered city" worked discursively toward décima's incorporation and of its presumptive practitioner, the jíbaro or farmhand of the countryside, as emblems of Puerto Rican difference. They waged their anticolonial struggle primarily in the university and other, lettered venues.[14] Poets such as Luis Lloréns Torres and Juan Antonio Corretjer sought to incorporate the jíbaro décima into cultured Puerto Rican poetry. Intellectuals from Miguel Meléndez Muñoz to Antonio S. Pedreira wrote treatises about the jíbaro temperament (as nineteenth-century intellectuals had done before them, most notably Salvador Brau).[15] Julia de Burgos, Puerto Rico's esteemed poet, contributed her "Coplas jíbaras para ser cantadas" (Jíbaro verses to be sung) to the radio program *La Escuela del Aire* (The school of the air), a program similar to those found throughout Latin America.[16] In Puerto Rico, it was sponsored by the Department of Education (Departamento de Instrucción Pública) in the early decades of the U.S. colonial occupation of Puerto Rico. As a crucial element of its national-popular pedagogy, this entire corpus sought to translate the sound of jíbaro vernacular into print and elucidate the jíbaro temperament via language, through a catalog of speech patterns, popular sayings, and other such markers of jíbaro orality.

Abelardo Díaz Alfaro, a staple of the public school curriculum, created a running series called *Estampas de la vida de Teyo Gracia* (Scenes from the life of Teyo Gracia), which became the standard text introducing the ever more modernized schoolchildren as well as elite nationals to the jíbaro. It was derived from a radio program sponsored by the Department of Education and aired on its radio station, WIPR, beginning in 1951.[17] Music was often used as a backdrop, and Chuíto el de Bayamón (who had starred with Calandria in *The Colgate Show*) performed décimas, reportedly at the request of Governor Muñoz Marín. Occasionally programs presented peasant musical practices (cleaned up, to be sure). Chuíto invited his jíbaro musician colleagues to perform with him on air, including La Calandria. Sadly, very few original recordings survive. Here is a typical excerpt, in its print version, from *Alma Latina* (Latinate soul) of November 15, 1962. It likely sticks close to the actual scripts of the program: "From such sadness, his sobbing, mournful singing arises; it's like an audible heartbeat of the native bird. The jíbaro is afraid of what his singing portends. He heard this intimation the day he found his wife motionless on the cot, the day he had to take his son on his hammock to the town hospital, the day he took the elderly woman's corpse in a box to the town cemetery, which is like a field of crosses. . . . The jíbaro asks God for his mercy every time he hears the native bird singing."[18]

Díaz Alfaro and other commentators offer a biopolitical assessment of jíbaro music by affirming that the humanity of the jíbaro's existence rests on his capacity to create music and by characterizing musical talent as innate to the peasant body. They place this singing jíbaro at exactly the line separating those who will be "allowed to die" and those who will be "let live," to employ the axiomatic Foucauldian formulation. This biopolitics extends to the stock instrument, the cuatro, as imitating the abject nature of jíbaro singing, as incapable of producing any other sound than those of the sorrow and resignation that comes from being at death's door. With the example of Díaz

Alfaro's *Teyo Gracia* series, we see how the state manipulated music and singing to create a consensus that the jíbaro was better off with modernization,
despite the loss of the natural beauty in which he lived. This became a tenet
of the ELA's official pedagogy. In this fantasy (here I'm using "fantasy" in its
psychoanalytic sense, as unconscious symbolic structure), the only remnant
worth preserving as a kind of memorial to the countryside is music. Music
becomes the jíbaro's only creation and the sum total of his creativity. Other
than music, he is definitely zoe, bare life.[19]

The PPD leader Luis Muñoz Marín (the most powerful political voice in
Puerto Rican history), almost single-handedly created this myth of the jíbaro.
He spoke of politics in the 1950s as a "jalda arriba," an uphill trek, using a
vernacular expression directly targeting the voters' ears. (Most, at the time,
were impoverished and functionally illiterate. In fact, the PPD anthem is titled
"Jalda arriba.")[20] Notwithstanding the accelerated industrialization of developmentalism, Muñoz Marín called for the preservation of the "buen saber
del jíbaro" (the jíbaro's noble wisdom) and the spirit of the *campo* (countryside).[21] This "buen saber" should be installed in the citizen psyche, and
music did a significant share of this work. During the first half of the twentieth century, musicians participated in various radio shows across the island,
showcasing "música de la montaña" (mountain music), as jíbaro music was
known in those early decades. For the ELA at midcentury, music became a
form of therapy, coinciding with the increasing professionalization of jíbaro
musicians. On more than one occasion, Muñoz Marín, surely influenced by
the pop psychology of the time, spoke of the populace's need for solutions
to the neuroses caused by vertiginous social change; he referred to this set
of loose precepts as Operation Serenity (chapter 2).[22] With ventures like the
Teyo Gracia series on WIPR and other such state-sponsored media efforts, the
ELA arrived at the image of jíbaro music as somber and sorrowful, a memorial to life in the underdeveloped countryside that the ELA purportedly saved
peasants from.

Despite the official, abstract admiration, societally speaking, jíbaros were
close to being loathed. Their music was never truly exalted and it was not
institutionalized like the literate musical forms that became the backbone of
musical education in Operation Serenity (chapter 2). The ELA did not invite
the musicians to join the Escuelas Libres de Música (founded 1946) or the
Conservatory (founded 1960) to teach their music. It was unthinkable to create a running festival of jíbaro music to attract tourists and investors, like the
Festival Casals. Jíbaro music remained confined to the unofficial pedagogy

regarding the popular, loosely presented in handbooks that cataloged seises and recorded décima examples to suit the official mythology only. Its full repertoire has not survived in the official record. Plainly put, the government did not take care of jíbaro music's preservation as a musically valuable expression in its own, musical right. And since it did not overtly reject or censor it (unlike the reception of race records in the United States; I think of the various myths surrounding figures like Robert Johnson, or the deviant discourses attached to notable women blues singers), researchers lack a negative record to draw on to at least read against the grain.

It's crucial to unsettle the primacy of native, elite visions of jíbaro music as the last word on its interpretation, starting with rejecting a static, millenarian rurality as its axis. David Monod asserts about another presumptive rural genre, the American blues: "Can the fundamentals of blues scholarship really be overturned . . . and are we ready for a thorough re-assessment of the origins of the blues music?"[23] While not discounting traditional elements in the blues, Monod contests the idea that blues is a millenarian music and as such a vessel of timeless values, or that it is, in its strictest sense, only African American.[24] In a similar vein, music critics should contest the PPD's narrative of origins along with the idyllic vision of the countryside as an untainted space of rightful dwelling lost to modernization but that modernization should preserve in its "values."[25]

Commercial jíbaro music began with the very first radio programs of the twentieth century and continued through various radio programs and eventually, television segments. The music was able to survive the changes of Operation Bootstrap and thrive thanks to the vibrant soundscape in New York City and other cities where Puerto Rican migrants settled (such as Chicago) and in places far from the migratory epicenter of New York (such as Hawai'i).[26] The stylized costumes and learned mannerisms of many jíbaro musicians on television and in concert catered to the colonial imaginary, but were in all likelihood received in multifarious forms by their audiences. We don't know nearly enough about this reception. I'm certain that kitsch was sometimes received as precisely that—kitsch—and not always as a solemn, brooding, suffering statement on loss. The clowning attributed to jíbaro musicians, their celebrated wit, could also extend to their audiences.

Although migrant loss is quite palpable in the adoration jíbaro musicians experienced while performing abroad, loss could coexist with savvy about cultural objects and their figurative function. The thousands of migrants were the audience for shows such as the ones memorialized in the marquee of

FIGURE 3.1 Marquee of the Teatro Puerto Rico in the Bronx, New York, where scores of Latin American artists performed through the 1950s and 1960s. This evening advertises El tribunal de la montaña, un sainete jíbaro (The court of justice of the mountainside, a jíbaro musical farce), circa mid-1950s. La Calandria was a regular at these shows. Courtesy of Grego Marcano.

Teatro Puerto Rico announcing a *sainete jíbaro* (jíbaro musical farce) and a program flyer for *El Gran Show de Navidad* in 1954, which include Calandria as a marquee artist (figures 3.1 and 3.2). Near the New York epicenter, the musicians played their music live in Las Villas, the collective name for concerts sponsored by multiple businesses in the Catskills region of New York State, seventy-five miles or so north of New York City, and at La Montaña del Oso (Bear Mountain), about forty-five miles away. Buses carried migrants by the thousands to attend these outdoor events. Calandria and her colleagues worked a steady stream of open-air festivals between Puerto Rico and the mainland. They recorded 78 rpm records and eventually LPs in Puerto Rico and the United States. Their 45s were constantly played in *velloneras* (juke-boxes) for collective listening and dancing. Their singles sold in the thousands. At a dizzying pace, jíbaro music fast became an urban music, as much part of the city soundscape as the Greenwich Village scene happening at the

FIGURE 3.2 Promotional flyer for Gran Show de Navidad (Grand Christmas Party) at the Teatro Puerto Rico, Bronx, New York, circa mid-1950s. Calandria is featured with other jíbaro greats. Courtesy of Grego Marcano.

same time. Writing for *New York, the Sunday Herald Tribune Magazine* on July 4, 1965, Tom Wolfe described the "kind of invisible jíbaro universe that New Yorkers, even those in the music business, barely knew existed." He continues, "Invisible! This is the great new age of troubadours, and the great new folk singers, Joan Baez, Peter, Paul, and Mary, Dave Van Ronk . . . they're not ever anywhere because they are all hunkered down being *authentic*."[27] Jíbaro musicians carried the aura of the big city all the way back to Puerto Rico, as potently as the symbolic umbilical cord of the Puerto Rican countryside traveled to New York via their sounds. New York City sounds have been explored in myriad ways, including the 1960s downtown, Village scene; bebop; avant-garde experiments; and bugalú. Jíbaro music, however, is summarily excluded from any account of folk music in the 1950s and 1960s city. If there are only outdated handbooks and a couple of studies of jíbaro music in Puerto Rico, it's fair to say that jíbaro music in New York is completely absent from the historical and musicological record, even though it enjoyed great currency in the diasporas of the 1950s and 1960s.

Monod makes the point that the line between creation and commercialization in folk genres is quite blurry, and that commercialization does not equal falsity or adulteration but is part of pop music's evolution and creative adaptation to formats of circulation and reception. What we think of today as jíbaro music is a modern and, indeed, a pop music. This is not to affirm that it was not played in the countryside of Puerto Rico or that the rural way of life was extinguished in one fell swoop, or that some of the 1950s exponents were not members of rural communities. Yet while a good number of jíbaro musicians were raised in rural Puerto Rico, others belonged to a working class that was already urban, as planned and executed by Operation Bootstrap. Moreover, jíbaro musician entrepreneurship was clearly a quality the audience recognized and rewarded. The musicians used the available codes and adjusted to the market, selling authenticity at times and, at others, surely, dancing around its strictures.

WOMAN, THE ALWAYS ALREADY

Women musicians navigated an extra layering of encoding and faced a much more restrictive arena when it came to authenticity and its affordances (however limited). Within dominant discourse, symbolic womanhood appeared in multiple guises. In poetry and literature and in political discourse, the patria (motherland) often was cast as a suffering damsel in need of a bard to save her (as is well known, Luis Muñoz Marín cultivated this persona of poet or bard in his political career). In nationalist writings, motherhood was the primary articulation of womanhood. The modern schoolteacher preoccupied intellectuals like Antonio S. Pedreira. The new housekeeper was targeted in radio, print ads, and television as the ideal consumer and blank slate on which to create progress. The jíbara was ignored. She was a symbol of a terrifying nothing, portrayed much like her precursor, the peasant woman (in admittedly scant writings), as derelict or doomed.

If the fantasy scenario never truly existed, gendered moral discourse pro-vided its psychic grounding, a measure for its impossible certainty. Benigno Trigo, a literary critic, has written about "the representation of the 'white' peasant woman's body as invaded by a curable disease," a "figure to govern the colony" in early twentieth-century Puerto Rico.[28] Eileen Findlay, a historian, discusses how morality, as discourse, shifts and repositions itself continually according to vectors of race and class among women in turn-of-the-century Ponce.[29] Ivette Rodríguez-Santana, a sociologist, illustrates how the jíbara carries a burden of representation in addition to that shouldered by the jíbaro, defined by the polarities of degeneration/regeneration, promiscuity/purity, rootlessness/fixity, infirmity/strength, antisocial/malleable, dangerous/future laden. Rodríguez-Santana demonstrates that gender is seamlessly integrated into the signifier that is the jíbaro (although gender is most certainly occluded symbolically).[30] The esteemed historian Fernando Picó wrote memorably of the precariousness of country life and how women (presumably jíbaras) were continually in danger in Utuado, Puerto Rico; his book *Los gallos peleados* (Cocks locked in battle) defies any collective remembering of the countryside as a haven, even less so for women.[31]

Thus, jíbara musicians had few templates on which to base their staging of requisite authenticity, which created a peculiar space that was, to use the Lacanian formulation, extimate, included and excluded. Jíbara musicians were on the edge of both jíbaro music's privileging of masculinity and class-based discourses about proper femininity, and on the edge of the racial con-structions of jíbaros as white. Calandria is an example of a female body that proved difficult to classify racially. She was always described as a *trigueña* or *trigueñona* to me (brown skinned).[32] Although in interviews I learned only a few details about Calandria's music making, I heard several times over that she was *oscura* (dark), clearly indicating she was not white and separating her from notions of the pure racial makeup of jíbaros.[33] Silvia Álvarez Curbelo re-counts that the music Calandria performed was seen pejoratively as "música de sirvientas" (maids' music), approximating Calandria to the unacceptable class *bios* more than her male counterparts, who were more protected from blatant characterizations of amorality, even though they shared a class stand-ing.[34] Calandria astutely navigated this extimacy and understood the con-tradictory affordances of the nothing. She played with the empty set of the female singer to disassociate her performance from the standards expected of women singers. This process took some time and was not linear. Nor did it arrive at a final, serene state of triumph. What I propose is not an exaltation of the nonplace but an investigation into its productive density, accounting for the material and discursive difficulties Calandria faced for creativity and success.

Visually, jíbara musicians were less beholden to a fixed persona, as compared to their male counterparts. There was simply no visual language for this figurative body or template for their persona. They could not carry machetes onstage, or comfortably wear the wide-brimmed straw hat, the *pava* that shielded the farmhand from the bruising sun. (The pava had become a symbol of the PPD, so much so that the party itself came to be known as La Pava.) Admitting the existence of women's labor as peons ran counter to their idealization in the new racial regime as faithful wives and selfless mothers.[35]

Figure 3.3 is Calandria performing the jíbara in the Teatro Puerto Rico, Bronx, New York, in the 1950s. This performance is in all likelihood very similar to the series of live performances in which the musicians participated in New York City as part of the state's program to provide a cultural palliative for the trauma of migration. Calandria wears the pava, symbol of the jíbaro. She displays a wonderfully confident demeanor and obvious delight at the adoring feedback of her fans in New York City. We see a *bohío* (hut with a straw roof) in the left corner.[36] A sunny sky with cumulus clouds and a conspicuous palm tree to the right transmit the tropics, while a young boy is in charge of roasting a pig, apparently with no company. The Puerto Rican flag is in dead center, sealing the paradisiacal, but oddly spare construction of the lost island. Jíbaro music always featured cuatro, guitar, and *güiro*, visible in the photo. As it became recorded music, trumpets, bongos, and other instruments were added to evoke the commercialized, Pan-Latino, ethnic sound that promoters and the recording industry desired. In this picture, we see a *timbalero* to the right and accordion and piano players to the left, signaling this commercial period.[37]

The principal symbols — backdrop, pava, and cuatro instrument — evoke images of the preindustrial countryside, fast disappearing by the mid-1950s, supposedly built on traditional ways in which men and women play out their natural roles. The migration itself flew in the face of this fantasy, but demanded the fantasy nonetheless, revealing the importance of a psychic structure that bound them to the lost homeland. Like her counterparts, through the act of singing Calandria portrayed this desired jíbaro of identification: a peasant figure, whose singing springs from labor in a close connection to the land. That this is a persona is obvious in Calandria's case; she was from a small-town working-to-middle class and her supreme desire was to pursue a

FIGURE 3.3 Calandria performing at the Teatro Puerto Rico, Bronx, New York, mid-1950s. The backdrop stages an idyllic countryside back home. Calandria wears the large straw hat known as a pava, which became a symbol of the jíbaro with the hegemony of the Popular Democratic Party. Justo Martí Papers, Archives of the Puerto Rican Diaspora, Centro de Estudios Puertorriqueños, Hunter College, CUNY.

music career. All jíbaro musicians assumed this identity as their persona, even if they happened to be from the rural areas. This doesn't mean that they were false in their presentation of patriotic feelings or yearnings for a lost homeland or countryside but points to a more intricate understanding of their self-presentation and theatricality.

Calandria learned to convey the "rustic" via well-traveled techniques of rasp and nasality; she also recurred to shrill tone, which sounded uneducated to the middle classes, a fact she must have been well aware of. What I'm indicating is that Calandria, like all good singers, deployed a technique that jíbaro musicians developed in their progressively professional incursions into music. Jíbaro artists underwent an accelerated education in poise and pose at the dawn of the 1940s and the early 1950s, in sync with the accelerated industrialization program happening at the time in Puerto Rico. Just as all Puerto Ricans were expected to become familiar with progress and its technology in various arenas (nutrition, literacy, baby formula, washing machines, and so forth), musicians had to come up to speed. In short order, jíbaro musicians became familiar with sound and visual technology. As they were recorded, photographed, and filmed, they adjusted their up-to-then unrehearsed and sonorous personas (they were only heard live on the radio and in live, community events until then) to assume fully modern musical personas, scripted in many instances, with a visual image and the ability to present a body that up to that point was graspable only through sound.

In 1951 Calandria, along with Jesús Sánchez Erazo (Chuíto) and Florencio Morales Ramos (Ramito), who were, together with Calandria, already touted as the three greats of jíbaro music, participated in a brief, didactic movie made for television by DIVEDCO. A seminal government agency that produced films, graphic art, and booklets targeted to the educational needs of the barely literate peasantry, DIVEDCO incited their participation in state campaigns of literacy and hygiene and tackled various social issues, including, eventually, migration (as seen in booklet no. 8 of *Books for the People*, "Emigración").[38] For *Trulla* (Impromptu Christmas party), the government enlisted the best jíbaro musicians in addition to the best jíbaro singers: Maso Rivera and Francisco Ortiz Piñero on cuatro, Felipe Rosario Goyco "Don Felo" on guitar, and Patricio Rijos "Toribio" on güiro.

Most of these films had companion books released in conjunction with the new literacy campaigns of the ELA, and various Christmastime booklets bore the same name, "Trulla." One stated, "Vemos que el espíritu de noble alegría existente en el siglo pasado para la época navideña, sigue aún vivo entre nosotros. . . . Ni el tiempo ni el progreso han podido matar las costumbres buenas de nuestro pueblo" (We see that the spirit of noble happiness that existed a century ago during Christmastime is alive and well in us. . . . Neither time nor progress have been able to kill the good customs of our people).[39]

The film's setting re-creates the porch of a traditional "casita en la montaña" (mountain dwelling). *Trulla* refers to Christmas music, played for the delight of neighbors and friends, in a surprise visit happening at any hour of the night. The short does not attempt to re-create the liveness of a trulla, but it does seek to present it as a stock form of Puerto Ricannness, oscillating between the comical and the tragic. Its opening credits capture the moment when the musicians are tuning their instruments; they appear as professionals. The

FIGURE 3.4 Scene from the DIVEDCO (Division of Education for the Community, Commonwealth of Puerto Rico) short film, *Trulla*, 1951, directed by Jack Delano. Calandria is seated between Jesús Sánchez Erazo, "Chuíto el de Bayamón," and Flor Morales Ramos, "Ramito." She sings a décima in a controversia with Chuíto.

artists look uneasy in front of the camera. They alternate between formality and slight amusement. Clearly they were instructed to act solemnly. One of the movie's ironies is that very little of jíbaro music's trademark witticism or continual banter comes through and nothing of its often rambunctious side. Chuíto goes first, probably because he is the oldest. He sings a humorous décima, corresponding to his role as the trio's clown. Calandria, who is seated between the two standing singers, assuming a feminine role, does not sing on her own (figure 3.4). Instead, she goes second, as Chuíto's sidekick in a controversia about the differing natures of women and men. She is the picture of concentration. In their décima, Chuíto sings of women as evil. Calandria sings about how it is men who are evil for forcing women into certain behaviors. Ramito, cast as the serious singer of the three, ends the movie with the third song, "Mi toro barcino" (My spotted bull), about the end of the *estancias* (plantations) in Puerto Rico. The last bars in the movie consist of this lament of both singer and *mapeyé* (the slow-tempo, brooding melodic line of the cuatro, instantly recognizable to jíbaro music listeners):

Ya se acabó la abundancia, bendito hombre
Y este dolor me acrisola
Ya se secó la amapola
Ya murió el buey que pitaba
Murió el que lo pastoreaba
Y quedó la estancia sola

Abundance has ended, my friend
And sorrow burns in me
The flower dried up
The ox that used to whistle died
The man who took him out to graze died
And the farm was abandoned

These verses end the movie with gloom. The speaker includes himself in the stanza and names, in turn, elements of the dilapidated landscape he surveys: flower, ox, and man, all aligned with literal death. Allegorically, they stand in for a larger sense of cultural dissolution. The stanza joins the scopic sweep to the sonic recapitulation of loss, signified by the mapeyé. The camera underscores this juncture offered by the décima, as it pans away from the singers and the scene fades to black just as the singer ends the song. In these early TV productions, the state began to disseminate the widespread construction of jíbaro music as a mostly melancholy genre, as about the always already past.

Jíbaro music changed from a traditional to an urban folk music because of the populist impulse of the PPD, and the musicians adapted creatively and intelligently to the reign of media. However, the complex metaphorical and metonymical operations through which the jíbaro comes to stand in for authenticity became condensed in most accounts to an almost arrested insistence on the elegiac narrative. This is problematic in the case of all jíbaro singers but especially onerous for women, since their forced positioning in an earlier temporality (prior to "progress") entailed a double or triple fixity. In a sense, *Trulla* partakes of the "epistemological work of purification" that has so influenced the genre's interpretation.[40] Yet the eruption of the musicians on TV — their learning of the ways of the market and technology — is also a moment of new creativity. *Trulla* is a precious document because so few of the performances of jíbaro musicians are preserved for the historical record. It enjoys a new life as a YouTube clip with about 200,000 views as of this writing.

Jíbaro song posed an inherent challenge to the industry's manufacturing of fixity and the state's injunction to remain immemorial, particularly charged to the symbolic woman that the jíbara singer should represent. First, it became, for all its touting as roots music, a music of displacement and migration. Second, while it was tethered, in official accounts, to orality (which, as Jonathan Sterne has argued, regarding Havelock Ellis's influential theory, implements a "denial of coevalness" and mandates that the jíbaro live in a time preceding modernity),[41] as a performance, jíbaro music is characterized by its "verbal art."[42] As such, it leads us squarely to voice's presence in the music's grain, what Roland Barthes famously theorized as the moment in which the bodily aspect of vocal performance is crystallized in the encounter between a language and the voice.[43] This art began in "the times of Spain" but is always already an art of the present, an art of change.

When I spoke to the *trovador* Joaquín Mouliert, he was quite serious in avowing allegiance to the ancient form of the décima, credited to Vicente Espinel (Spain, 1550–1624). However, his was not a simple imitation of the prestige of lettered forms but a kind of expression that had its own logic, not dictated by dominant culture. The sung décima is based on techne, skill. The challenge is to produce a perfect and if possible dazzling and delightful sync between speech and the seis, showcasing the meeting between the singer's voice and the words that (in theory) he or she must produce on the spot. To appear spontaneous requires an apprenticeship in music, despite the rhetoric of innocence and good times and the use of place names and simple verbs, such as "to be" (*ser* and *estar*), as transparent allocutions of identity. Innate talent will never be enough to create décimas; study and practice are required. Jíbaro music, at its best, provokes admiration for this virtuosic skill set. It is a verbal art but never identical to declamation of poetry. It is a dialogue with the seis line, in musical call and response to another master musician, the *cuatrista*. Popular décimas are meant to be sung and require voice and persona. Calandria towers along with Ramito and Chuíto because she had the innate talent, put in the study and practice, understood the stage, and could hold her vocal own with the seis.

Despite well-meaning appreciations, she has never been granted this equality. Mouliert described Calandria as the most important exponent "en el sexo femenino" (among the feminine sex) of jíbaro music's techne, separating his evaluation of her prowess from those of male singers, who are always assumed to be superior to the entire group of female singers:

Ernestina was the Golden Voice . . . a singer with such sweetness in her voice. She played a little guitar. She was not an improviser or songwriter. Priscilla [Flores] was more professional than Ernestina; she had more class. What Priscilla didn't have was Ernestina's bohemian disposition. Once Pagán [Herminio Pagán, Ernestina's husband] and Ernestina arrived on a Thursday and left on Monday. It was the most beautiful weekend of my life. She loved the *décima jocosa*, the double entendre décima. Of all the women, she definitely was the one who recorded the most. Among the women, she definitely was the one who brought the décima to greatest heights.[44]

Flores (whose career, incidentally, Calandria helped launch) was an excellent singer in her own right. Compared to her, Calandria's voice sounds less feminine according to dominant dictates, which may be what Mouliert meant by saying Flores "had more class." Yet he may have also been describing Flores as appealing to bourgeois taste, whereas Calandria clearly espoused a working-class aesthetic in her persona. "Sweetness" is not really explained as such, but it is not an adjective that would first come to mind when listening to a classic Calandria recording. An important gender distinguisher appears to be the belief that Calandria was not an improviser, the highest standing among jíbaro singers, given the degree of difficulty and creativity required of improvisation.

Some of her contemporaries have told me that she did improvise when the occasion called for it and even composed a handful of songs. By now it has been established among connoisseurs that few of the renowned trovadores actually improvised, including Ramito and Chuíto.[45] Regardless of whether Calandria improvised, and sidestepping the debate on the absolute merit of improv in this genre, Calandria's "greater heights" seem to be lower than the least of the great achievements of the male group of singers, improvisation or no. The philologist and folklorist Marcelo Canino, long the recognized authority on folk singing in Puerto Rico, mentions Calandria as the foremost female exponent of jíbaro music. He also relates, "Aside from singing décimas in singing duels, our female singers also interpret the traditional lyrical repertoire, known by all in our island. They likewise participate in public contests and competitions, and are members of native ensembles that play in dance gatherings. Above all, they are mostly heard during Christmas and Easter celebrations, since, on the whole, they are true specialists in the divine topics of Nativity and Christ's passion. *However, even though they do not lack for feminine grace, our female troubadours have not achieved the absolute mastery of our male troubadours in the aforementioned traditional forms."*[46]

Jíbaro music's gender discourse is difficult to navigate. Woman could be the measure of progress or the measure of the downfall caused by progress; she could be the bearer of purity, including linguistic purity, or the seed of all degeneration; she could be the loyal, faithful wife to a husband (no matter how philandering) or the vixen breeding way too many children and therefore burdening the family. An example of the imbrication between women and cultural degeneration and the need to prop up the jíbara as the stalwart upon which culture must depend (an example perhaps lesser known outside of jíbaro music fan circles) is "Muriendo nuestra cultura" (Our culture is dying), penned and sung by José Ángel Ortiz, "El Jíbaro de Yauco." It is one of the oldest of extant jíbaro recordings. Ortiz first praises Puerto Rico's path to progress, then illustrates the dangers of this progress by recounting the sad tale of a father who, intending to help his daughter as progress recommended, paid for her studies at the university. All he got for his trouble was the daughter having a child out of wedlock. The father proceeds to give the daughter a beating and sends her off to New York City, since she has disgraced the family. Although the city offers many good things, the singer says, the daughter cannot handle the city's licentiousness and comes back to Puerto Rico with "a dozen children."[47] Woman is the measure of Puerto Rico's state of cultural degeneration in the face of progress. Ortiz takes a swipe at university education and aspirations to enter the middle class, thus aligning the figuration of the jíbara with another figuration I alluded to earlier as a source of fear: the university-trained woman, often a schoolteacher.

Calandria's incursion into music entailed entering the middle classes, as they were defined in 1940s and 1950s Puerto Rico. Recall how Carmen, her sister, said that Calandria earned "more than a schoolteacher." However, such ascension through popular music was bound to be limited, as pop music represented a hotbed of immorality for women. Calandria was associated with the bohemian aspect of jíbaro music in a particularly intense way. All women occupied this space almost automatically, as the negative of dominant visions of the jíbaro. As much as the male ideal was zoe (bare life), woman, bereft of a true symbolic encasing, emerged as a little too close to *bios*, a little too fond of sociality outside of any mandate. Jíbaro music was partly acceptable to the dominant gaze because it strictly defended the policing of women. Although jíbaro music is melodic, pleasant to listen to, often hopeful, and abundantly witty, we cannot forget that looming over this as well as other musics is the contemporary reality of male-female relationships and the particularly vulnerable status of women — symbolically, and also materially, and in the most urgent sense of personal safety and prospects of survival. The spaces of invention for women singers mirror the prescriptions of this corpus, while male musicians enjoyed greater musical freedom without, it goes without saying, the weight of stigma.

Compare "Muriendo nuestra cultura" to "Nací llorando" (I was born weeping), by the same songwriter, in an outstanding Calandria recording. Here Calandria occupies the masculine voice of the jíbaro singer, momentarily crossing gender boundaries to assume the construction of the male as solitary, antisocial, distrusting, and surviving on innate guile.

Nací en el mundo llorando
Desnuda, yo se lo juro
De madera en piso duro
Como un reptil arrastrando

I was born weeping
Naked, I swear to you
On a hard slab of wood
Just like a slithering reptile

This song, a soulful *mapeyé* like "Mi toro barcino" (My spotted bull), portrays the jíbaro singer and the act of singing jíbaro music more generally as a traversing of the trials and tribulations of life lived under dire circumstances from birth. In tune with Ivette Rodríguez-Santana's Foucauldian analysis of the campo as a laboratory — not to defend from, but to create disease and decay, a frontier ruled by death — jíbaro singing is coupled with death and miserable conditions.[48] Aside from the fact that it is men who sing in most recorded jíbaro music, the mapeyé's place of enunciation might also be seen as a space of the band of brothers of the defeated, a locus defined by the melancholy male.[49] The jíbaro voice in "Nací llorando" alludes to friendship but also to a fighting attitude in an existence dictated by turmoil and extermination. The human figure is zoe, bare life, naked. The song echoes Díaz Alfaro's characterization of the jíbaro as zoe, of his singing as animal, as a reptile, correlating with Díaz Alfaro's bird, resonating in turn with Calandria's stage name of "songbird."[50]

The repeated description of Calandria's voice as "sweet" responds to these gendered coordinates, to the distribution of the sensible in jíbaro music.[51]

Perhaps unconsciously, the insistence on sweetness sutures her gender difference and serves the purpose of separating her from that hallowed space of the trovador who improvises (a figure more than a fact among professional musicians, as is widely acknowledged today). In fact, her voice was husky, rough around the edges, at times shrill, at others raspy, reflecting her musical decisions to inflect a given song with the appropriate tone and mood. Calandria's timbre was immediately distinctive, marking her voice as singular and unpredictable. As Luis Miranda, "El Pico de Oro" (The golden beak), told me, "What was distinctive about her was her timbre."[52]

Related to her impure class and racial status, she lent her voice and skill to discussions of purity in other realms, all of which correlated with the official mandate of purity that jíbaro music was charged with representing. One was language purity, a recurring topic of discussion. Following a trope of Puerto Rican literature (the corruption of language in colonialism), Calandria recorded "Un jíbaro en Nueva York" (A jíbaro comes to New York) for RCA Victor in 1947. The track features a young Calandria playing sidekick to Chuíto el de Bayamón, performing with El Conjunto Típico Ladí (one of the most respected bands of Puerto Rican popular music at the time). It is, to my knowledge, her earliest recording. She asks him, in Spanish, how things are named and expressed in New York City, in the English language. She challenges him on the grounds that he cannot improvise in the new language. Chuíto then sings brilliantly hilarious lines, playing his persona to perfection (of the witty jíbaro with innate, but not learned, knowledge). Although funny and dexterous, the track still leaves the young Calandria out of the space of jíbaro creation. She does sound muted and sweet (as in docile) in this recording, when compared to later ones. She has not yet developed her mature style, typified by a number of musical recourses to convey tone, rasp, and break.

In "Ayer y hoy" (Yesterday and today), of approximately 1952, Calandria sings a controversia with Félix Castrillón and El Conjunto Típico Ladí. The singers debate the merits of progress from a gendered perspective, similar in content to the male speaker in "Muriendo nuestra cultura" but with distinct female and male parts reflecting contrasting, gendered voices. The male singer begins his intervention in the competition by defending the modern woman, singing, "Ella vive con soltura / ella misma se gobierna" (She lives relaxed / she takes care of her own business), insisting that she "trabaja y viste a la moda" (works and dresses fashionably) and even finds her own boyfriend and plans her own wedding. The young Calandria assumes the conservative position, defending the traditional vision of womanhood as upholding sexual purity: "Porque en época pasada / la señorita o señora / no vestía como ahora / una moda exagerada" (In olden times, the woman, married or yet a virgin, did not dress like women today, too stylishly).

Another controversia with Castrillón and Ladí finds Calandria defending the dark-skinned woman, "la trigueña," whose merits vastly outshine those of her competitor, "la rubia" (the blonde). Several singers recorded variations of the competition between rubias and trigueñas. "Trigueña" and "rubia" were not fixed feminine and masculine preferences. The singers occupy different positions in each rendition. The recording I was able to consult is an earlier, Cuban version with Calandria and Clavelito, but we can safely assume the lyrics are similar if not identical. The two types, rubia and trigueña, represent women's obfuscations. It is simply the point of view that gives them a negative or positive valence. The song is not a defense of any one type, or an affirmation of racial pride. Upon close examination, what is being debated is, once again, gender purity. It is women's temperament and their capacity to mold to consumer society. Calandria here sidesteps the question of dominant morality into an affirmation of pride, but the terms of the entire debate seem spurious: whose body is the most attractive, who grooms herself better, who uses consumer products (beauty products in particular) in the wisest fashion, and so forth. Calandria's sister, Carmen Ortiz, recounts that after this song was performed, radio listeners were asked to vote for their favorite that day, the blonde woman, or the brown-skinned woman.[53] (Since controversias are essentially situational battles of wits, it could well be that Calandria performed as la rubia in some competitions, although her sister assured me she always sang the part of la trigueña.) I do not know the results of these competitions, but more likely than not, they varied. What was really being upheld was women's positioning within consumer culture. In Clavelito's verses, he ends up not even alluding to women, just store mannequins.

The anticommercial pose of stalwart against mass production and forms of standardization regarded as inauthentic is presented against the backdrop of women as corruptors of men and society. Men pose as singers against financial gain, interested only in expression of feeling. Multiple publics, across communities and in this case, cities and territories, responded to the persona of the male folk singer as being personally sincere, *un campesino de verdad*, a true peasant. Simultaneously, they held women and by extension trovadoras under constant examination.

A TALE OF TWO PERSONAS

Jíbaro music was not a music Calandria grew up with in her native San Lorenzo. She most likely sang boleros and rancheras when, as a child, she entered competitions on radio programs. She became acquainted with folk music on the radio and possibly danced to it in town gatherings, like many across Puerto Rico. After her debut in the *Colgate Show with Calandria and Clavelito*, she developed affection for and identification with jíbaro music as a musician's music, which became a genre thanks to professional musicians who created a rich and rewarding musical world along with their faithful, vibrant audience. These musicians, Calandria among them, were in sync with the moment and the market, capitalizing on the selling of nostalgia and authenticity during the 1950s.

In these 1950s records, jíbaro music circulated among city dwellers and was shared through records and other mass-mediated technology. Most were released by Ansonia Records, a company that, thanks to its huge catalog, repackaged 78s into later LPs with covers suggesting the tracks were new, and which later rereleased the vinyl albums as CDs when the CD format emerged. We know precious little of record buyers and radio play in Puerto Rico; we know recordings were done in New York and Puerto Rico, and that small labels existed. Ansonia was by far the biggest. If we take only the Ansonia catalogue as paradigm, recorded jíbaro music might be interpreted as strongly retaining the associations with traditional folk music. Ansonia's covers reflected images akin to the Bronx performance briefly examined through a surviving photograph: Men with machetes and pavas abounded, dressed in bright folkloric wear, with scarves tied around necks and sashes at the waist. Sometimes cocks, wheelbarrows, roast pigs, straw huts, and green mountains appeared as elements in this construction of the authentic jíbaro.

Ansonia released *Brisas navideñas* (Christmas airs) as an LP around 1960, the year of Calandria's migration to New York City. The LP's temporal mix was enabled by new technologies that made possible the transfer and remixing of 78 tracks into the "stereo-like sound" of 33-1/3 rpm.[54] The voice we hear is temporally separated from the voice we perceive in the album cover art by a few years (figure 3.5). Calandria is decked out in a vaguely folkloric dress: a low-cut, shoulderless shirt with a skirt. She smiles slightly and looks to the side, the picture of confidence. This portrait is meant to suggest everything women in folk music should stand for: a distance from glamour, a celebration of stock values, and closeness to the land (even if it appears figured here by

FIGURE 3.5 Album cover, La Calandria, *Brisas navideñas*, Ansonia SALP 1275, 1960?. The studio backdrop suggests a mountainside setting.

a tacky studio background). Calandria, as a jíbara, is tasked with projecting simplicity and lack of interest in worldly wiles or personal gain. She should be attractive, but somewhat comely, and never overtly sexual. The singer injects grace and a sense of cool into the portrait, striking a common pose of live, jíbaro performance, as if mentally composing or rehearsing her next intervention. She sports a slightly deprecating, faint smile — a smile of challenge.

In the original liner notes, Herman Glass, Ansonia's founder and owner, wrote:

ERNESTINA REYES, better known as "LA CALANDRIA" is probably the greatest of the female "Jíbaro" (mountain music) singers. Her fame has spread from Puerto Rico to New York and each year because of her popularity, she is invited to appear at different theatres and clubs of this great metropolis. With each yearly appearance, the ovations given to her by the public become more and more sensational. . . .

It is easily understandable how LA CALANDRIA has become one of our most loved "Jíbaro" singers. Her powerful voice engulfs us with sweet and nostalgic tones. Sometimes, a huskiness in her voice causes a listener who might well be impervious to sentimentalism to concentrate on the artistry of this polished professional, to rejoice while she sings happy tunes, to be remorseful when she is crooning her laments.

Glass acknowledges Calandria performing in New York as a fully professional musician; his description of Calandria's voice is, though brief, more complex than is usual in contemporary accounts. Although he has recourse to that neutralizing adjective "sweet" at first, he speaks of sweet tones, acknowledging the selection that all singers make when singing. Glass does not limit her voice and vocal performance to the stricture that women's voices must match societal conventions of femininity. He correctly describes her voice as "powerful" and introduces the "huskiness" that made it resonate with the masculine sound of most jíbaro music. Her artistic difference from the lot of female singers kept it from being merely sentimental; she was focused on musical execution, the true residence of musical affect. Hence the adoration of migrants who, as I have suggested, were in the know about performance and persona and ran the gamut of jíbaro's affective register.

The Spanish version of the liner notes tames or elides Glass's perceptions. Perla Pérez, their author, describes Calandria's voice as "melodiosa y dulce" (melodious and sweet) where Glass had written that her voice was "powerful" and had a "huskiness." Glass described Calandria's tones (which she chose in execution) as "sweet and nostalgic," foregrounding her vocal performance. Pérez describes the tones as deep, speaking of "tonos más graves según la música que interpreta" (deeper tones called forth by the music she is interpreting). She hesitates to describe the singer's voice as deep, favoring the explanation that music itself "authors" the performance heard on the record and sidestepping Calandria's potentially unfeminine sound.[55] The entire English-language section about sentimentalism and its limitations is ignored, as is Glass's ending reference to the pleasure audiophiles will obtain (he calls them "discriminating critics of folkloric music"). Pérez's ending address is more generic, to an audience of "lovers of the folkloric music of the beautiful island of Puerto Rico," suggesting an interesting language politics in which English-speaking consumers collect records as an exercise in musical knowledge based on their distinction,[56] while Spanish-speaking followers listen to the record based on its capacity to convey the timeless connection to a native land.

The album proceeds along a domesticated narrative, tailored as much to insular Puerto Rico as to metropolitan Greater New York. Three tracks from the 1950s that were repackaged for a different type of circulation — inserted in a narrative of expulsion from Eden into the hard life of the city and ending in an affirmation of agency — might serve to illustrate the willful manipulation of the jíbaro repertoire in the market of nostalgia and begin to illustrate the way in which migration changed the music's meaning and uses in the Puerto Rican context. The first is a lovely guaracha jíbara titled "Somos boricuas" (We are Puerto Rican), which reached the Puerto Rican Hit Parade. This song corresponds to the principal narrative of jíbaro music, that is, the idyllic nature of the Puerto Rican countryside and the tranquil existence of the jíbaro before this way of life was uprooted. The first image is of the sunrise and the jíbaro heading to work. Images of work as conferring decency and providing happiness are reinforced by the presumed harmony between man and landscape. Puerto Rico is "mi" Puerto Rico, marked as a place of belonging by the fact of physical birth in the territory. The jíbara in this portrayal is in her proper place, the home, and she sets out to do housework for the family. While the man is paired with nature in complete harmony, in the second stanza woman is paired with temporality, with the fixed nature of national identity. The years may pass, but tradition will always rule, and the woman will always be present, washing clothes by the river. (The scenario was highly unlikely in the contemporary economic situation, more typified by families broken apart by dire economic need and lack of social support networks. The state was literally phasing the working class out of the economy at an accelerated pace, which is the reason, as is well documented in history books, that the 1950s migration of Puerto Ricans to the United States took place under government auspices.)

The speaking subject in "La jíbara se va" (The jíbara is leaving), a hit when it was first released as a 78, employs a completely different tone, expressing anger at being in the city and stating "she" will go back to Puerto Rico. The cuatro has picked up tempo and the tone differs from the placid contentment of "Somos boricuas." This song revolves around actual anecdotes of life in the city, not an idealized rural landscape. It is unclear for how long or when exactly the singer is planning to leave New York (the present tense in Spanish is often used to indicate futurity). This plan might or might not happen. It could simply remain a wish, or perhaps a gritty urban lament, to share with equally disgruntled jíbaros in the city. The refrain, in a call and response with the other musicians, gives us a clue that leaving will be, at best, temporary (the refrain states that she is leaving to escape the snow). The song proceeds through four interventions by the singer. The first, above, is about cold weather and the discomfort of winter clothes; in the second, the speaker is horrified at the loss of identity signified by a jíbaro addressing another jíbaro in the street in English ("How yu feel what yu say"); the third relates the presumed isolation of city life in the absence of kinship relations and the reciprocal hospitality of neighbors; and the final stanza enlists food as a marker of national cohesion, when the speaker complains that her friend Paquito did not offer her Puerto Rican finger food when she visited his home ("cuchifritos," recalling Myrta Silva's performance of the Rafael Hernández standard discussed in chapter 1). As we can readily see, the song revolves around anecdotes and not images. People interact; some even have names (José, Paquito), while in "Somos boricuas" there were no actual people, just the twin, stylized images of an jíbaro and jíbara quite solitarily, even prophylactically encased in a picture-perfect countryside. As far as we could tell, they had no neighbors or *compadres* to speak Spanish to, share home-cooked dishes or taste cuchifritos with. Perhaps the sole advantage of the "Somos boricuas" jíbaro dyad was that they did not have to wear coats or endure cold weather.

Ansonia did not include any controversias on this record. There is one song that presumes a male addressee and thus can be read in light of the themes of controversias and the structuring meaning that man-woman relationships have in the definition of the national character, along with women's displacement and purity. It engages migration directly and is unabashedly self-referential: Calandria names herself as the subject who will migrate. The song is titled "El que se va no hace falta" (He who leaves will not be missed). The first two stanzas feature Calandria addressing a partner. She resolves to accept his behavior as a wanderer and home abandoner, the opposite of the idealized pair in "Somos boricuas." The singer states that she will remake her life, despite any "accusations from her father-in-law" (presumably that his son left her because she was an unfit wife and mother). She also sings that she enjoys the support of her community, which comforts her by stating, in the refrain, that "he who leaves will not be missed."

Up to then, a generic woman had expressed the strength and resolve of the stock jíbara. The third stanza, however, jumps to a surprising, new referent in a song that had only addressed a failed love relationship:

Sabrás que soy Ernestina
Mejor dicho La Calandria

Pequeña cual salamandria
Pero artista culta y fina
Si a la ciudad neoyorquina
Vuelo cual rápida carga
Allí hallaré quien comparta
Con esta humilde cantante
Y aquí te diré al instante
Que el que se va no hace falta

Let me tell you, I am Ernestina
Or better put, La Calandria
Small as a salamander
But a cultured and refined artist
If I go to New York City
In the blink of an eye
I will find people there to be
With this humble singer
And this very instant I tell you
He who leaves will not be missed

In the third stanza, the singer herself becomes the one who will leave and not be missed, as she speaks of her decision to migrate to New York and predicts that she will find a new life in the city as well as people to share it with. (At the moment of the recording, which happened earlier than the release of this LP, none of this was actually happening to the singer; it is a pose.) What interests me the most about this song is its meta quality as statement. Calandria sings, "I am Ernestina, or better put, La Calandria." Naming herself, and describing herself as "artista culta y fina"(cultured and refined artist), her name is not that of an acquaintance (like José and Paquito in the previous song) but a figure, mixing in the trope of jíbaro humility with the assertion of musical mastery (the latter is also an important trope of this music).

Musically, in the tracks gathered on *Brisas* and the other few dozen 78s Calandria cut in the 1950s, the change in her musical style from the very first recordings is everywhere in evidence. No longer "sweet," she sings with full volume, employs the shrill tone and vocal rasp that would become her hallmark, and effectively embodies the lack of sentimentality or corniness, a fact that Glass remarks upon in his liner notes to *Brisas navideñas*. She delivers a viscous sound, thick, unruly, disobedient to convention, willful, full of body, hoarse, with more timing and sense of swing in counterpoint to the lines of the cuatro than the very first recordings discussed. With this vocal execution, Calandria inhabited the meaning making of jíbaro song, whereas in her beginnings she had been more of an echo chamber for the male word, for its logos or authority.

In an interview with Cristóbal Díaz Ayala, Mercedes Pérez Glass states that most of the Ansonia catalog is *música jíbara*. Pérez Glass recounts that thousands of 78s and hundreds of LPs were recorded, and that the 45 was mostly for jukeboxes.[57] There was money to be made from jukebox sales. *Billboard* published a series in 1966 called "Money Programming"; in "All-Alike Music in Latin Locations Is Loco," Ray Brack recommends matching music to the particular Latino group that a given business caters to, using "imaginative jukebox advertising." "This article suggests ways to win a loyal phonograph following in your Latin locations" (77). "Should your locations get good Puerto Rican patronage, you can offer folk music by Ramito (Ansonia Records), La-Calandria (Ansonia) or the Cuarteto Mayarí" (86)."[58] The sheer numbers Glass cites indicate Ansonia's dominance of this ethnic market in the 1950s. In the 1960s, the musicians were able to record with Canomar (the musician Piquito Marcano's label) for about six years. We witness a new diversity of topics and playing styles that Ansonia, despite its status as the single most important venue for jíbaro recordings, might not have favored, since it catered so directly to the nostalgia market from the beginning.

Figure 3.7 is an LP of approximately 1965, *La Calandria canta . . .* (Calandria sings . . .). The location of this photo is unknown, but it appears to be from the same photo shoot that produced the album covers of two records with Ramito, *Los dos gigantes* (The two giants) and *Vuelven los dos grandes: Calandria con Ramito, vol. 2* (The two greats are back: Calandria and Ramito, vol. 2; figure 3.8), albums dating from when both artists resided in New York and, importantly, which were recorded as complete albums (not concocted out of remastered 78 tracks). Calandria's persona is markedly different from that of *Brisas navideñas*.

In *La Calandria canta . . .* she strikes a completely bohemian note. The setting is bucolic. Dressed in modern garb, her pose suggests dreamlike absorption. In *Vuelven los dos grandes*, Calandria brandishes the guitar she holds in *La Calandria canta . . .* , as if ready to strike her colleague Ramito with it, while he, decked out in nativized jíbaro attire (contrasting with Calandria's modern clothing) appears just as ready to teach her a lesson with his machete, feigning a stern macho look while touching her elbow. For this second cover, Calandria has donned a small pava to provide a feminine balance to Ramito's

FIGURE 3.6 Group picture documenting a musician's gathering in the home of Pedro "Piquito" Marcano, Caimito, Puerto Rico, circa 1959. Calandria is standing third from left; Herman Glass of Ansonia Records stands eighth from left, near the center; and Piquito Marcano of Canomar Records is standing at far right. Courtesy of Grego Marcano.

masculine pose. In *Los dos gigantes*, Calandria and Ramito rest peacefully on the grass. Ramito is grinning and looking straight at the camera, while Calandria has assumed her aloof, bohemian pose once again, as if she had just released the guitar into his reassuring grasp. The pava now rests on the grass in front of them. The machete is laid casually over his body, comically suggesting phallic and also musical dominance (Ramito has also taken control of the guitar). Calandria, sans guitar, pava, or tree trunk props, simply is the absorbed figure in her dreamlike, feminine stance, a version of woman as enigma not matching Ramito's jíbaro persona at all.

Taken together, the three covers indicate fun and play. Nothing is taken seriously, and the gendered poses are clearly assumed as roles to be acted out in the music, not as any true recommendation for everyday life. Still, the difference between the two artists' poses is telling. Calandria seems to be situated visually between two irreconcilable poles. These covers show Calandria occupying the space of the bohemian singer and the jíbara simultaneously.

FIGURE 3.7 Album cover, *La Calandria canta* . . .
Canomar CLP 511, 1960s. Shows Calandria out of the
jíbaro persona.

Her vocal performance embodied these two opposing positions as well, at
one and the same time. Notably, she is given equal billing with Ramito as a
gigante and a grande.

It wasn't always the case that she appeared on the covers as a player equal
to her two illustrious counterparts. The cover for *Ramito en controversia con
La Calandria* gives Ramito principal billing, and her name appears in the
lower right-hand corner only. Ramito is now playing the guitar, wearing, as
usual, his jíbaro accoutrements. The most delightful detail of this cover is its
Fillmore lettering and psychedelic design, with the *pascua* boughs typical of
Puerto Rican Christmas standing in for the more American details of the Fillmore publicity. Although Ramito is the voice of tradition in the controversias
he recorded with La Calandria, here his nostalgic re-creation of the jíbaro
persona is clearly offset by the decorative aspects of the cover, so U.S. pop.

By contrast, on another record where La Calandria receives secondary bill-
ing and also doesn't appear in the cover art, except through her name, *Puerto
Rico canta* (Puerto Rico sings), with her other famed counterpart, Chuíto el de
Bayamón, she appears suggested by an unidentified woman in the background,

FIGURE 3.8　Album cover, Calandria and Ramito,
Vuelven los dos grandes, Canomar CLP 513, 1960s.
Taken during the same photo shoot as *La Calandria
canta* . . . , Calandria now wears a small pava to mark
her standing as jíbara.

standing by the doorway of a presumably jíbaro hut, calling out to her mate
while he very conspicuously tills land manually in the foreground of the
photo. Here the appeal is to tradition and the images that this music is taken
to evoke, of simpler times in the countryside. Is the unexamined, possibly
unintentional implication that Calandria cannot be the jíbara who calls out
from the hut to him in the picture (at once a soothing and demanding figure,
typical of women's presumptive double-agent nature, but certainly very feminine in dominant terms)? On these records, Calandria may appear on one or
two tracks only, as was the norm with LPs of the time that mixed and matched
various artists, even including people who were not billed on the cover.

Perhaps because her timbre stood up so well to the voices of her male counterparts, because she infiltrated the masculine register dominant in jíbaro music
thanks to her wondrous ability to create a tough, uncompromising sound,
Calandria was a favorite in male-female controversias. Although she recorded
important controversias with Chuíto el de Bayamón and Claudio Ferrer, for
her most memorable controversias she partnered with Ramito. Calandria and

Ramito recorded controversias about male-female relationships, trading many a barb concerning their avowed sexual potency and options. (In one, "La finquita de La Calandria" [Calandria's little farm] Ramito tells Calandria that her "finca" [farm] is no longer in working condition, while she accuses him of not being able to "soplar" [blow].) Undoubtedly they raised the roof in live performances, which were much more obscene than any double entendre preserved in recorded music. Would that these live versions had survived in any form.

As anybody who has attended live competitions knows, the audience typically responds to a set number of repertoire choices. The themes that stand out are the motherland, return, the flag, religious belief, the cantador or trovador mastery of the genre, and the contentious nature of man-woman relationships, explored in controversias that can become as insulting as any game of the dozens, cut short when one singer accepts that the other has surpassed him in wit and style. I wish to call attention to three Canomar controversias from the early 1960s, when both Calandria and Ramito resided in New York City. I posit them as examples of the music's evolution and capacity for change. The singers debate the pressing issues affecting insular and mainland Puerto Rico: first, cultural assimilation, as in preferring cultural goods that are foreign to Puerto Rico ("Seis contra twist" [Seis versus twist]); second, language purity and the philological definition of nationality as being Spanish speaking and Hispanophile ("Dos idiomas en porfía" [Two languages do battle]); and third, the presumably American, individualist desire to make and spend money ("Ambición al dinero" [A passion for money]). These controversias depart from the genre's established repertoire and offer us a vision of music's incorporation of a new environment and the genre's capacity to renew itself, especially when it comes to creating new lyrics, the backbone of jíbaro music as a verbal art.

In "Seis contra twist," Calandria chides Ramito for preferring native music to the twist; she presents as being "de la muchachada" (into youth culture) and claims, "No quiero lo de mi país" (I reject everything that comes from my country). Of jíbaro music ("épocas pasadas" [bygone days]), she sings, "sólo queda un aleteo" (only a flutter remains) (not to be taken at face value, since the controversia they perform is, obviously, much more than a flutter and completely in their performance present). Calandria's stanzas accuse Ramito of being old-fashioned and resistant to change. With that, a challenge is launched toward the entire establishment of jíbaro music, particularly in its populist versions. Should the genre remain in a state of timeless purity? Could it survive? Shouldn't it incorporate the experience of Puerto Ricans from something other than abjection, the evanescence or emptiness they were called on to symbolize? Ramito's stanzas accuse Calandria, in turn, of forgetting the Eden that they came from and abandoning their "música de cuerdas" (acoustic string music) in favor of electric guitars and mainstream pop music. Amusingly, the cuatro — the instrument of authenticity in this music, the veritable musical stand-in for Puerto Rico — embodies the controversia sonically by switching between seis and swing lines. This is possibly the first time a cuatro was recorded playing something other than Puerto Rican country music.[59]

In "Dos idiomas en porfía," Calandria incorporates Spanglish expressions into her décima ("Whastsu matter con Ramito / You have problem qué te pasa," and "Listen esquius me Ramito / Yu crazy nada te escucho") to exemplify the reverse of what she had embodied in the first record she appeared in, RCA Victor's "Un jíbaro en Nueva York." Part of the intention is comical, positing the migrant who supposedly loses his language as buffoon. There is a self-deprecating quality in this and the other such socially oriented controversias that indicates that neither singer truly inhabits the polarized role they vocalize. Instead, they examine the reality that new, and sometimes pleasurable, elements have come into their (musical) lives. Calandria plays the role of accusing Ramito, once again, of being behind the times and also of hypocrisy. She sings that Ramito appears quite comfortable in English when they are having a "plain old conversation," the opposite of the disregard for English that he expresses when he is singing a décima. Ramito responds that he only speaks English for practical reasons, that it is not a language of creativity or love. He equates Spanish with native instruments, such as the güiro, and claims he is "latino de verdad" (a true Latin male/national). The challenge is whether Calandria has ceased to be a true décima singer. Their exchange is playful and serves to acknowledge the new traditions of a new, migrant community, who will obviously use both languages, possibly for practical, everyday reasons at first but eventually in creative and personal ways.

In "Ambición al dinero," Calandria personifies materialist greed. Her desire to find a fellow male singer to together cultivate the décima is replaced by the desire to find a man who will fulfill women's avowed addiction to consumption and expenditure. The female voice states, "Si en rica yo me convierto / Yo te aseguro coplero / Este cantar chacharero / Jamás lo volveré a hacer" (If I do become rich / I assure you, verse maker, / that I will never again engage in / this pointless singing); the female speaker will renounce her cherished vocation as a jíbara singer in favor of riches (and, implicitly, a completely different way of life, having nothing to do with Puerto Rican official values). I don't think any listener took this statement as a true expression of Calandria's wishes; they knew it was unthinkable for either Ramito or Calandria to walk away from making jíbaro music.

In these controversias, Ramito and Calandria exemplify how jíbaro music did not remain frozen in time. Ramito wrote the controversias, probably in collaboration with Calandria, with some improvisation thrown in at the time of the recording. The verses imagine two highly gendered voices, as the male voice assumes the role of bastion of tradition and defender of native cultural values, while the female voice embodies the unexamined, pleasure-ridden, live-for-the-moment quality of the too-quickly assimilated. It would be simplistic, however, to hold the singers to these notions. It would be inadvisable to take the conventions of this music as transparent discourse. Such a position would also not take into account the performative dimension evident in the recordings as much as the visual poses struck in their cover art, which, we can imagine, were even more salient in live performance, accompanied by the singer's gestures, bursts of laughter, audience reaction, and, let's not forget, food and drink.

Back in Puerto Rico, jíbaro music experienced a kind of last hurrah in the 1960s, arguably the best decade for many jíbaro musicians who could be best described as active in two places simultaneously. The city of Caguas, just south of San Juan, was especially welcoming to the jíbaro group. It boasted a strong jíbaro circuit, including one of Puerto Rico's most interesting grassroots cultural institutions of the 1960s. The Caguas bohemia, a group of local intellectuals, artists, poets, and surely a few dilettantes, gathered around the figure of Caguas native Ramón "Moncho" Osorio in his home in Caguas, Puerto Rico, just south of San Juan.[60] According to the testimony of people who frequented the circuit in their youth, Calandria was its only woman member. Gilberto Almenas dates this group at 1965–1968; according to him, "it was a golden age for them," during which they sang on *La Montaña Canta* (The mountains sing) radio show broadcast from Caguas (inaugurated in 1961), and performed regularly at the Rancho de Trovadores (Trovador ranch) in Guavate Reserve, where folks danced to their tunes. Almenas describes the group as "bien elegante" (well dressed, polished) and Calandria as "viva, alegre, habladora" (sharp, lively, talkative). During this time, jíbaro musicians enjoyed Operation Bootstrap's heyday, its short-lived plenitude. In the 1970s, they would experience Bootstrap's downfall directly as a chronic lack of work for jíbaro musicians, who surfaced from oblivion only at Christmastime.

CIRCUITS OF DEBT

Traditionally, jíbaro singers include multiple moments of self-reference and self-expression in which they take as a topic their own importance and mastery as singers. The hyperbolic titles used as marketing devices — *los maestros de los cantores* (master singers), *los decanos de los cantores* (the deans of singing), *los gigantes* (giants), *los grandes* (greats), *invencibles* (invincibles), and so forth — stress virtuosity, in stark contrast to the music's minoritarian status. The singer must always prove superiority, expressed by his or her capacity to deliver sheer personality and force through voice, poise, and successful manipulation of the genre's staple themes. Two songs, probably from the later 1960s, expand and transform these distinguishing tropes. In the first, "La Peluya," Calandria sings about the art of singing and her own place within the tradition of *decimar* (creating décimas). In the second, "La infortunada" (The unfortunate one), Calandria looks back on her life as years of torment.[61]

"La Peluya" sounds like a place name, but it is actually an off-color pun on a woman's sexual organs. In my ignorance, I asked Calandria's sister, Doña Carmen, what it meant, thinking it was a place name of the kind that one encounters often in jíbaro music. Laughing gently, she explained that this was an obscene word, part of a game, used as in the dozens to insult another person's mother, all in good cheer.[62] I shook my head at how off I had truly been in my listening, simply because I completely missed the obscene pun.

Calandria's fast-tempo, passionate performance is a dare to a number of interlocutors: other singers, the Catholic Church, broadcast media, other women singers. It is a defense of La Calandria against unnamed detractors or perhaps against the national morality so prevalent in her youth (and through the decades, if we take articles such as Torres Torres's "Calandria: An Unforgettable Sufferer" as paradigmatic).[63] I include the complete décima she delivers at full volume and with full vocal technique of rasp and break, and the deliberately slightly out of tune singing of jíbaro music:

> Yo canto por La Peluya
> Canto por el peluyón
> Y canto por el sermón
> Que dijo el cura en Jayuya
>
> Cuando yo empiezo a cantar
> Música de tierra adentro

Soy más feliz y me encuentro
Un tipo a quien vacilar

En eso de improvisar
No me gusta buscar bulla
Pero si alguno me puya
O en versos me desafía
Si él me canta astronomía
Yo canto por La Peluya

En este campo señora
Aunque malo se me tilde
Quiero ser la más humilde
De todas las trovadoras

Son muchas las cantaoras
De poca preparación
Que van a televisión
O a la radio a cantar prosa
Y yo por cambiar la cosa
Canto por el peluyón

Yo en décimas por ejemplo
Si nadie me obstaculiza
Le canto hasta por la misa
Del Viernes Santo en el templo

Junto al trovador contemplo
La Divina Concepción
Y si por cierta razón
Al coro se me ha invitado
Después que el cura haya hablado
Yo canto por el sermón

Me gusta que el trovador
Sea un sujeto apostólico
Para entrar en lo católico
Sin cometer un error

Si es de la Biblia un lector
Y si quiere que lo instruya

Yo canto por La Peluya
Canto por el peluyón
Y canto por el sermón
Que dijo el cura en Jayuya

I sing for the Peluya
I sing for the peluyón
And I sing for the sermon
The priest gave in Jayuya

When I start to sing
Music from the heartland
I feel happier and find
A guy to poke fun at

When it comes to improvising
I don't like to pick a fight
But if someone dares me
Or challenges me in verse
By singing about astronomy
I will sing for the Peluya

In this field of ours, ma'am
Although they might say I am bad
I wish to be the most humble
Of all the trovadoras

There are a lot of cantaoras
That lack preparation
But go on television
Or on the radio to sing their poor prose
But I, to change things here,
Sing for the peluyón

In my décimas, for example
If no one gets in my way
I'll even sing in the temple
For the mass on Good Friday

With the trovador I ponder
the Immaculate Conception

And if for some reason
I've been invited only to sing in the choir
After the priest has finished speaking
I will sing the sermon

I like it when the trovador
Is an apostolic type
So we can get into Catholicism
Without making a mistake

If he reads the Bible faithfully
And wants me to give him lessons
I sing for the Peluya
I sing for the peluyón
And I sing for the sermon
That the priest gave in Jayuya

In the first stanza, the words "sermón" and "Jayuya" seem to appear strictly due to the needs of the rhyme scheme. They are loaded with meaning in this context, however. The sermon is clearly the most important discourse traditional jíbaros heard in any formal manner. Long before the government of Puerto Rico became organized as such, jíbaros listened to sermons and paid heed to what the priest told them to do, more than to any official word from legal venues. The name of the Father, without a doubt, was the priest's. Calandria here states that she sings "to pay homage to the sermon the priest delivered in Jayuya." So far, the sense of the song is not altogether clear, although we know she is going to talk about her singing and why it happens.

In the second stanza, she introduces the elements of fun ("vacilar") and sex ("un tipo con quien vacilar"). This activity is directly in opposition to the gravity of the sermon. She also qualifies her singing as "música de tierra adentro," music from the heartland. Now the place name Jayuya makes more sense, because Jayuya is the town in Puerto Rico that is located in the very center of the mountainous area of the island. As such, Calandria is locating her singing metaphorically in the heart of the tradition, and staking her place as a full member.

In the next three stanzas, Calandria sings of accusations against her singing (and her value as a person; recall that in this folk genre the two are taken to be the same). She says she doesn't want to pick a fight (this is a convention of this tradition, as we have seen in the controversias), that she wants to be "the most humble among all the trovadoras" (female improvisers), another trope. Then she states indirectly that she is not like the majority of these female singers, whom she in turn accuses of singing only for personal glory and gain (to appear on the radio and television, and sing prose, not true oral poetry), yet another trope of this music. Calandria portrays herself as a continuation of the tradition that others defile by twisting its true nature. "Yo canto por cambiar la cosa, canto por el peluyón" (I sing to change things; I sing for the peluyón) might mean a number of things: She will not corrupt the genre, so she will go her own way; she will introduce innovations to the genre; she will not cave in to the expectations for women singers, and will sing in the male manner ("peluyón" is obviously both an obscene superlative and a masculinization of "peluya").

In the concluding stanzas, the references to religion multiply. She sings that if no one gets in her way, she would sing the Good Friday Mass. Obviously, the Good Friday Mass is the most important Mass of the year. Those familiar with the history of the Catholic religion also know that women were strictly policed in the church. Calandria doesn't stop with the sermon, though; she says she will discuss the miracle of the Immaculate Conception, bringing the Blessed Virgin Mary into the mix and toying with an oblique allusion to sex. If someone has invited her to merely be a member of the choir (because she is a woman, and possibly also a national away from home), she will wait until the priest has given his sermon and then redo the sermon as a décima, the ultimate test of skill. The sermon is Logos, supreme patriarchal meaning (as is the Bible or, more accurately, the exegesis of the Bible she sings about). Despite any obstacles, the singer will demand her place in the creation of that meaning, which, in this genre, means the right to be considered a master of the décima, on equal footing with any male singer ("junto con el trovador"), with no holds barred in topic or style.

In "La infortunada" (The unfortunate one), Calandria's tone is vastly different. Jíbaro music possesses a true panoply of seises to correspond to subject matter, mood, and requirements of execution.[64] This is a seis de San Lorenzo, named for the town Calandria was born in, which employs a moderate tempo. Jesús Sánchez Erazo, "Chuíto el de Bayamón," is the registered songwriter, but probably Calandria at the very least had a say in some of its lyrics, and in "La Peluya" too. Jaime Torres Torres cited this song as a source or document to substantiate his claims about Calandria's misguided nature from birth and accelerated demise. In his opinion, the song was proof that Calandria lived out her years unhappily, mired in melancholy. As a kind of signature song, it does have self-referential aspects, but perhaps not in the literal sense Torres Torres deployed. I cite the complete décima, whose melodious sound is different from the preceding, employing Calandria's more melodious tones:

A ver si ya infortunada
Soy desde que vine al mundo
Y en el tormento iracundo
Vivo triste y apenada

Vine un día destinada
Al mundo para cantar
Pero al verme declinar
En este valle de hastío
Le dije a los ojos míos
Ojos míos, no llorad [sic]

Logré triunfar en amores
Como toda una mujer
Y en mis años de placer
Viví mis ratos mejores
Luego caí en los peores
Días de mi desenlace
Nada, nada me complace
Desde que mi amor se fue
Porque pierde hasta la fe
El que desgraciado nace

Los campos de San Lorenzo
Me vieron nacer un día
Y desde allí pretendía
Surcar el espacio inmenso
Más tarde me hallé en descenso
En un mundo de insolvencia
Y en mi infame decadencia
Invadida por el llanto
Yo dije en mi desencanto
Lágrimas, tened paciencia

Aún sigo siendo Ernestina
Jíbara sanlorenzana

Y de mi garganta emana
La música campesina
Y aunque mi marido opina
Que no he quedado indefensa
No logro que me convenza
Ni me arranque esta fachada
Pues la mujer desgraciada
Desde la cuna comienza

Let's see if I have been unfortunate
Since I came to this world
And lived sadly and full of regrets
In this angry torment

I arrived in this world one day
Destined to sing
But after seeing myself decline
In this valley of tedium
I told my eyes
Eyes of mine, do not cry

I was triumphant in love
Like a real woman
And during my years of pleasure
I lived the best of times
But then I fell into my worst days
When my life unraveled
Nothing, nothing gives me pleasure
Since my love departed
Because one who is born unlucky
Loses everything, even faith

The San Lorenzo countryside
Witnessed my birth one day
From there I believed I could
Plough through immense space
Later, I found myself declining
In a world of debt
And in my infamous decadence
Invaded by my tears

I said, disenchanted
Tears, be patient

For I am still Ernestina
A San Lorenzo jíbara
And jíbaro music
Still flows from my throat
Even though my husband chides me
Reminding me it hasn't been all that bad
He hasn't been able to convince me
Or to tear away this pose
For the ill-fated woman
Is so from birth

Here the female speaker espouses normative gender discourse and employs traditional jíbaro musical tropes, apparently with no discernible irony, all the while singing peacefully, melodiously, although with a wonderful, expansive use of rasp. The lyrics literally state that women should remain in their place of origin and follow the trajectory that has been outlined for them; any deviation will entail moral lapses and therefore suffering. Such is the standard reading.

In my reading, Calandria refers to the melancholy state of jíbaro singing, not to her own life. When she says she came into this world to fulfill her destiny, to sing, and then concedes that she declined, it is more likely she refers to her struggles to keep this music alive in the face of so much work (in other words, she refers to the precarious nature of singing jíbaro music, as musical labor). She steers away from the moral consideration (that she was responsible for her personal downfall) to the larger question of the uses of the music itself and her responsibility in keeping the national birthright alive (the verse "ojos míos, no llorad" [eyes of mine, do not cry] does not indicate quite clearly the object of mourning, but it occurs in a stanza about singing the music of the countryside).

As she sings in the décima, she was successful in love, had her moments of pleasure, and is now reflecting on something larger, which is the singing she was destined to fulfill ("vine un día destinada / al mundo para cantar" [I arrived in the world one day / destined to sing]). In a gentle jibe at the narrative of woman's triumph as being about securing a man, she even mentions her husband chiding her for her complaints. She concedes that in the face of economic hardship ("mundo de insolvencia" [world of debt]) she was almost broken ("invadida por el llanto" [invaded by tears]), but then implores her tears "to be patient," indicating that perhaps the end of the tale is not completely revealed during the singing.

"Aún sigo siendo Ernestina / jíbara sanlorenzana" (I am still Ernestina /a jíbara from San Lorenzo) returns the singer to her roots before she left the island; "y de mi garganta emana / la música campesina" (and jíbaro music / flows from my throat) is a reminder, as much to herself as to the audience, that the music, the genre is not dead, despite the oblivion and selective commercialization it has suffered. "No logro que me arranque esta fachada," referring to her self-description as "unfortunate" as a "pose," is a description of her pose of melancholy. It is not exactly insincere or a put-on; it is a reality that the conventions of this music making, and the fate of the genre itself, have cornered her into. "La mujer desgraciada / desde la cuna comienza" (for the ill-fated woman / is so from birth) could be read as a fatalistic bow to the misogynistic portrayals of woman as Eve, burdened with sin since birth, but for me this is a misreading. "Desgracia" is a trope of fatalism seen often in décimas, not a personal statement of Calandria's own disgrace. It can be read with ironic distance into an open-ended conclusion, because the ending notes of the décima are not sorrowful or abject. Rather, they range from reflective to tongue-in-cheek. In fact, one can hear an ever so slight but distinct chuckle at the end of some of the verses about misfortune.

Calandria sounds contemplative, yet playful. She is illustrating how she had to negotiate various gender and genre expectations that were heavily shaped by the historical changes the Puerto Rican communities, island and mainland, had been subject to. This could well be what "infortunada" means in this song. "Woman" goes from being the placeholder of tradition to tradition's most vile betrayer, since she is also modernity's cipher. She is materialism and greed, and the polar opposite, infinite sacrifice and love. The song "La infortunada" illustrates the arc of this constant double positioning.

I'm particularly interested in "insolvencia" (debt) as the key to "La infortunada." Joaquín Mouliert opined that jíbaro musicians never did well living off their music, and suggested that only their supreme devotion to their art kept the music going.[65] Ana María Ochoa Gautier has critiqued models of music performance that explain everything away with the culture-as-resource paradigm. She sets out to theorize the vast majority of Latin American musical labor within a matrix of debt as well as networks of reciprocity and solidarity that make possible certain musical productions while not resolving single artists' actual debt.[66] Ochoa suggests that there is a need to better account for and theorize the "allure of art as beyond its reduction to a logic of expediency."[67] "La infortunada" speaks directly to the tension between the "allure of art" and the reality of debt, a point Torres Torres completely missed in his 2004 profile, when he employed this song as a biographical narrative about the artist that would confirm her misery, melancholy, and addictions.

Most country musicians relocated to Puerto Rico definitively at the close of the 1960s, living out the rest of their days as symbols of the jíbaro, eking out a living as best they could in the later, economically depressed times of the failed ELA. Unlike most of her counterparts, Calandria lived in New York during the 1970s and 1980s until her death in 1994. She settled in the Bronx with her husband, the Judge Pagán she names in songs. She continued her performing career when and where she could. She made the occasional trip to perform in Puerto Rico, particularly at Christmastime, when country music was in most demand as Puerto Rico's values music. She appeared on television shows during the holiday season catering to the nostalgia jíbaro music came to represent (such as the long-running Tommy Muñiz show, *Borinquen canta* [Puerto Rico sings]). Irma Morales, "La Jíbara de Salinas" and Ramito's widow, told me, "Ernestina se murió y nadie hizo mención de la muerte de ella. Todo el tiempo estuvo cantando su patria, su pueblo. Tenía una voz brillantísima" (When Ernestina died, no one mentioned her. She sang her motherland, her people, at all times. She had a brilliant voice).[68]

Despite having attained unofficial status as the "folk diva" of Puerto Rico, she did not record very many new tracks. Long-playing records compiled from her large output were released regularly. A cartoon image of Calandria with a Puerto Rican pava, presumptive jíbara wear, and the cuchifrito (memorably exalted in Myrta Silva's brilliant recording; chapter 1) underwrite twelve tracks of uninterrupted *Alegres navidades borincanas* (Joyous Puerto Rican Christ-mastime; figure 3.9). In another record, *La Calandria Vol. 3*, Ansonia reprised Calandria's image in the earlier *Brisas navideñas* (Christmas airs), with the studio countryside replaced by a snazzy beach. This creates an odd juxtaposi-tion between nativist and tourist-attraction images, in her own body and the studio background, respectively. We can see that the cover of *Brisas navideñas* is the model for Calandria's cartoon wear as the authentic jíbara, albeit with the added pava and cuchifrito props. *Ernestina Reyes con Mariachi* is not a full mariachi record, as the title promises. Only one of the tracks is recorded with a Mexican folk instrumentation, "Respeta mi pollo" (Stay away from my cutie). The other tracks are selected from those she had recorded in the 1950s that were not jíbaro décimas but Latin American standards by renowned and

FIGURE 3.9 Album cover, *La Calandria en alegres Navidades borincanas*, Regio R 71, 1970s. The cartoon portrays Calandria in the commercialized attire of jíbaro musicians. Older recordings were rereleased during Christmas time to celebrate autochthony.

hugely popular songwriters, including Rafael Hernández and Agustín Lara. The liner notes to *Mariachi* pair Calandria with the *pueblo* (people) and their assumed simplicity, equating her singing with an unmarked realism of every-day life (targeting women consumers one would imagine, given the sentimental address). Two other records without any images of the singer (one showing the Three Wise Men, one a picture of a man playing a guitar with a tropical-looking woman beckoning a welcome over a pig roasting in a pit, an image used on records by other artists) associate Calandria with Christmastime (*Christmas Party with La Calandria* and *La Calandria Wishes You a Merry Christmas*). It is unknown if she was paid for any of these reissues of her recorded music. Other such compilations exist; these are but a few examples.[69]

One record, the 1977 *La Calandria "En salsa,"* contained new recordings (figure 3.10). This was a Christmas release that took advantage of the new sounds of salsa to revitalize the jíbaro genre, with remakes of old hits. The esteemed trumpeter Mario Ortiz recorded two such albums, one with Ramito

FIGURE 3.10 *La Calandria, "En salsa," con Mario Ortiz y su Orquesta*, Borinquen ADG 1322, 1970s.

and one with Calandria: "These albums were due to the success of Bailables Navideños. Darío González, the owner of Borinquen Records, hired Dad [Ortiz] to produce these albums of well-known Puerto Rican folk singers. Dad was very good at arranging typical Puerto Rican Christmas songs. Dad had a passion for Christmas music."[70] Obviously, the two folk greats were enlisted to boost sales at Christmastime. Jíbaro music began its sad reduction to being heard only at Christmas. One song refers to Christmastime in New York City: "En la Navidad, señores / que pasamos en Nueva York / no es igual que en Puerto Rico / pero hacemos lo mejor" (Christmas in New York / isn't the same as Puerto Rico / but we do our best). Other tracks revive the ancestral, peasant past: "Ya la Misa de Gallo va a empezar / levántate Juana / que las campanas repiquetean vístete ya / ve colando un poco de café / y avísale a Pancha / que la gente del campo va para la ciudad" (Midnight Mass is about to begin / get up Juana / make the coffee / let Pancha know / that folks from the countryside are starting to go to the city). The first example addresses the larger community; the second is particularized, addressing a woman, a comadre, Juana. In the first, the location is New York, the metropolis; the home country, Puerto Rico, is named as the absence that gives sense to the endeavor of celebrating Christmastime. In the second, it is the countryside, standing in spectrally for the island of Puerto Rico at Christmastime. The most sacred of holidays, Christmas Eve, is the symbol of autochthony. One need only remember the dire situation of Puerto Ricans in 1970s New York City to understand nostalgia as a disavowal of the profound abandonment of the Puerto Rican migrant community by the very homeland it had revered for decades — a reverence fostered and sustained mostly through pop music.

Jíbaro musicians' relative success in the 1950s under the contradictory patronage of the ELA and the recording industry shows that, like all successful professional musicians, jíbaro singers were entrepreneurs who knew when and how to adapt to market niches. The decade produced a splendid body of recordings; the main resource at this point for the country music of Puerto Rico consists of this rich trove. I approached this invaluable archive with the caveat that it does not contain the entirety of the performed repertoire and that it tends to reflect dominant politics that created the jíbaro corpus as a perpetual elegy and statement of loss, aided by an ethnic niche market that profited handsomely from selling a somewhat facile, although deeply felt, nostalgia for the homeland. This dominant reception doesn't factor in the spaces in which most recordings circulated, which were more communal than individual, more joyful than sorrowful. The last five songs discussed, "Ambición al dinero" (A passion for money), "Dos idiomas en porfía" (Two languages do battle), "Seis contra twist" (Seis versus twist), "La Peluya," and "La infortunada" (The unfortunate one), recorded in the 1960s, are all examples of reworking classic tropes of the jíbaro corpus without falling into the mandated abjection of state-spurred melancholia.

This chapter specifically considers gender as a place to reconceptualize jíbaro music. Throughout the decades, measured against female singers only (by her living colleagues and also by ethnomusicologists and aficionados of this music), the not-so-subtle implication is that Calandria is always already inferior to any male singer in the genre. Instead, she should be considered and clearly was received by the listening public as one of the very best: una grande, in the genre's parlance. Calandria's thinking voice points the way into the nothing of the historical record, on jíbaro musicians generally and women musicians especially. At times one has to do with nothing, one has to deal with nothing, one has to wade into nothing to divine those nothings that are not empty. I have treated this nothing that jíbaro music generally, and Calandria specifically, have been consigned to as a clearing to reconstruct the event of voice in multiple displacements: of migration, temporality, and gender. Calandria dealt head on with the nothing to which she was assigned and her remarkable achievement is preserved in the "resonant tombs" — to use Jonathan Sterne's beautiful phrase — that make up the jíbaro corpus.[71]

Sterne makes the following observation: "The phonograph as a way of preserving the dead: its contemporaries thought themselves brilliant and the invention wonderful for contriving such a possibility. Yet this peculiar construct of sound recording did not simply allow speech to live on forever: it essentially embalmed the voice."[72] Even though we would expect her to be the most symbolic of the three performers discussed thus far, given jíbaro music's heavy symbolic associations, she is actually more of a Benjaminian allegory (recalling his magnificent treatment of decadence, nature, and the distinctions between melancholy gazes in "Allegory and *Trauerspiel*").[73] Calandria's vintage recordings sound like they were performed yesterday; sonically speaking, they are not caught in the trap of the old — even though, of course, they belong to the past. This multiple temporality is due in part to her performance and in part to jíbaro music's consistent engagement with contemporaneity, despite being discursively and materially shackled with pastness. A listening public responds to nostalgia, certainly, yet satisfying nostalgia does not fully account for Calandria's continuing relevance. Relatively recent CDs, like *Saludo a mi islita* (A greeting to my island), and older vinyl compilations of oldies or *ecos del pasado* (echoes from the past) have by now become allegorical artifacts as well, transformed into downloads and streaming. Today's listeners respond to Calandria's artistry, the persuasion of her vocal performance, and continue to seek out the jíbaro genre, supposedly dead. This still-relevant icon — with her voice, preserved from the 1950s and 1960s, yet juxtaposed with photographs of the 1970s and 1980s — continues to traverse listening circuits in new formats of circulation, demanding a restitution. She must be restored to cultural memory and receive the critical listening that has long been her due.

FOUR
THE THINKING VOICE

In the brief span of 1952–1968, Puerto Rico sped through its industrialization process. Middle-class residential construction dotted the city of San Juan. Hotels replaced the mansions along its Condado waterfront. The spanking new Medical Center promised health for the sickly, undernourished population, a health that the developmentalist program of the Commonwealth of Puerto Rico — Operation Bootstrap — desperately needed, as it endeavored to offer a cheap, obedient, and presumably bilingual labor force to American capital.[1] The Golden Mile, a name for the financial district established in the area of the sometime royal hacienda, Hato Rey, emerged as the centerpiece of a new downtown. The mythical mall of Plaza Las Américas (formerly a cattle ranch that bred cows for the dairy industry) became the social hub of a polis that increasingly turned to consumerism for its exercise of citizenship. Newspapers and magazines were filled with consumer fantasies of every variety. Along with everything else that was dazzling and new, Puerto Rico consumed a new object for sale, the celebrity pop music star.

Of the various pop artists that came of age in Operation Bootstrap Puerto Rico, Lucecita Benítez was possibly the most musically gifted and the most iconic. She entered the celebrity arena slightly after the peak of developmentalism, exactly before society's steep and painfully obvious fall from its carefully crafted modernization fantasy. Her body's hypervisibility through successive, iconic stages (the dashing auteur of the 1960s, the socially conscious artiste of the 1970s, the hyperfeminine diva of the 1980s) exists in contradistinction to the decline of the country's dream of progress. Yet, also in contradistinction to her mutable, celebrity-dictated image, the constant in her career is the crucible that was her voice in Puerto Rico's social history and music culture.

Lucecita intuited the "thinking voice."[2] The thinking voice is an event that can be apprehended through but is not restricted to music performance. It exceeds notation, musicianship, and fandom, although it partakes of them all. No artist owns the thinking voice; it cannot be marshaled at will or silenced when inconvenient. Its aim is not to dazzle or enthrall, although it may do so. Lucecita lived her long career negotiating the twists and turns of celebrity culture in late colonialism. Yet her endurance as a star does not result merely from successful navigation of celebrity and serendipitous coincidence with historical events. Her vocal phenomenon may be regarded as an unwitting outmaneuvering of celebrity culture whereby something resistant, the thinking in the voice, points to, as Jean-Luc Nancy writes, "participation, sharing, or contagion" versus the "imaginary capture" of the visual, which has dictated the terms of the artist's critical and popular reception.[3] Lucecita opened up the visual register dominant in celebrity culture to Nancy's "resonance" of listening by orienting the listener toward the intangible sense of hearing through her multifold performances across decades of Puerto Rican and Latin American life. This event of music, voice, and listening that is the thinking voice is repeated in other musical celebrity examples through time and space and possibly in nonmusical celebrity contexts where performance, voice, and embodiment are key.

Lucecita's reputation was made on her talent at delivering high melodrama. Her voice's beauty, as well as her youthful good looks, perfectly suited the colonial fantasy of success through increased consumption. Artist lives were favorite consumer objects in the 1960s, and Lucecita became the most appealing such object in mid-1960s Puerto Rico. Her many albums displayed the image of a beautiful woman through a pastiche of European and American models. Playing the vinyls on a portable record player magically conveyed the illusory confidence, even braggadocio, of Puerto Rico's dependent, accelerated modernization. The principal fantasy of this time concerned the magical leap forward of an entire society into the middle class, and middle-class taste reigned and determined print, aural, and visual expressive encodings in the late colony.

Lucecita's first moment of fame was when she starred in a youth show, *El Club del Clan*, a copy of Dick Clark's *American Bandstand*.[4] Its theme song was a Spanish version of "Twist and Shout": "¡Muévanse todos! ¡A bailar! ¡Vengan todos vengan! ¡Este es el Club del Clan!" (Everyone move! Let's all dance! This is the Club del Clan!) Her first chart hit was the Spanish version of Dusty Springfield's "I Only Want to Be with You," titled "Un lugar para los dos" (A place for both of us). Lucecita was modeled after Springfield sonically and, to an extent, visually.[5] This first album featured a mod cover with a composition of several Lucecita snapshots tinted in blue, yellow, and red strips (figure 4.1); the artist is fitted with a beehive wig (albeit not blond like Springfield's but in the style of Martha and the Vandellas and other African American female stars). She is

FIGURE 4.1 Mod album cover, *Lucecita*, Rico-Vox
RVLP 515, 1964.

serially presented as pensive, playful, serious, accessible, and enigmatic. She is photographed with a guitar in three of the frames, showing some skin in the second shot, holding the guitar up in the fifth, and strumming in the eighth. Significantly, none of the photographs feature her singing. The song "El Club del Clan" is the first track of Lucecita's second album, *¡En escena!* (Onstage), which included Spanish versions of "Hello Dolly," "Walk on By" and a track that remained on the Puerto Rican charts for two months in 1965, "Vete con ella," a Spanish version of the Dixie Cups' "Chapel of Love." The Spanish lyrics transformed the song from a happy paean to marriage to a challenge from a jilted lover, daring her lover to go with "the other woman."[6] Lucecita wears a wig, as for her first album, but the visual reference now turns more clearly to early Motown, most obviously the Supremes but also other artists in their stable such as Stevie Wonder, Marvin Gaye, and Tammi Terrell (figure 4.2). As with early Motown records, the frame underscores the subjective view of a listener/viewer, the pleasure of listening punctuated by the artist smiling, and the artist's face framed by her semioutstretched arms, with hands pointing upward. The colors, a blue-green pastel for the background and pink for her dress with ruffles, suggest respectability and pointedly avoid unruliness.

FIGURE 4.2 Motown-style album cover, Lucecita,
¡En escena!, Rico-Vox RVLP 519, 1964.

The visuals contrast with the first track, which was a hit on Puerto Rican radio. Musically, it is delightful to hear the singer in "El Club del Clan" doing her own take on the John Lennon performance classic of "Twist and Shout." Although she did not leave her voice "in shreds," as Lennon famously did, she used vocal rasp throughout the entire track, sounding muscular and masculine. In "Vete con ella," by contrast, Lucecita's performance is touchingly lyrical, with a sweet tone in the middle register interrupted by minor vocal breaks, sprinkling small doses of melodramatic sobbing and whispering. She was essaying a feminine sound, and the effect is markedly different from the Dixie Cups track. Lucecita's version hints at dissolution, not plenitude, not merely because the song's Spanish lyrics were plainly the opposite of the English. Lucecita was sonically trying on melodrama for size. As with many other tracks on her first records, Lucecita is overdubbed harmonizing with herself and is also heard in all background vocals.

The youth female audience was the target audience of *El Club del Clan* and its noon spinoff, *Canta la juventud* (Young people sing), with its catchy groove: "Aquí les canta, les canta la juventud / ye ye / la juventud / ye ye / la juventud / aquí les canta, les canta la juventud / la juventud que viene aquí para gozar"

(The young people of Puerto Rico sing now for you, the young people who are here to have fun). The producers reasoned that there could not be too many male stars, while they needed only a single woman star so she could sell to what was regarded as a limited market for female youth singers. Lucecita quickly eclipsed the other artists in the stable, outselling them all. She was about twenty-five years old when she appeared on the show; however, she was made up, dressed, coiffed, photographed, and otherwise instructed to act as if she were much younger, in her teens ("We outfitted her with wigs because wigs were in fashion then, and we dressed her in simple clothes, so she looked like a girl").[7] Seen mostly in feminine garb, her image suggested innocence and unspoiled or untainted beauty. Her naturalness, of course, was a technology of the self, carefully crafted to match industrial capitalism's notions of the gendered and youth consumers.

Lucecita's voice did not fit as easily into the Club del Clan mold. Other than the superficially linguistic or cultural differences that distinguished these early copies of American youth culture on the island and across Latin America (there were a number of "Clubes del Clan" shows in multiple countries),[8] a more profound difference ensued, less easily mapped but discernible with critical listening, which escaped Lucecita's managers and market demands and ultimately wrested her signification from the entertainment world that was forming in 1960s Puerto Rico.

She had a magnificent vocal instrument, far superior to your run-of-the-mill pop artist. In the liner notes to Lucecita's first album (figure 4.1), her first manager, Alfred D. Herger, had promised:

¡Es Lucecita de Puerto Rico, Lucecita de América!
    The most thrilling female voice to come from Latin America in a long while, Puerto Rico's Lucecita . . . a ballad singer of genuine, vibrant feeling, of direct and honest expression . . . singer, dancer, composer, musician (folk singer, rock and roller . . .) — all that is this girl, and more . . . a multiple personality that belongs to a multitalented artist. . . . Seeing her on stage, or just listening to her records gives you the thrill and sheer emotion of facing a TRULY GREAT artist — you immediately recognize that this young lady has "It," plenty of it. . . . May we present to you a great talent discovery: Lucecita.[9]

Herger's description was not hype. He had been truly impressed with Lucecita's vocal prowess and her capacity to sing multiple genres, all extraordinarily well. He was right: She had "It." Lucecita was a virtuoso singer with sweeping range and extraordinary power. Her diction was flawless. Her timbre was hauntingly beautiful, like a reed instrument, from bassoon to flute, alternatively dusky and bright. Most of all, her deep register was truly wondrous and unique in the constellation of all Latin American and Spanish-speaking singers, not just women.

The album liner notes give the impression that Herger had discovered Lucecita and developed a raw talent out of scratch, but she was a working artist by the time she signed with him. As with other artists hoping to make it, she first competed on the radio show *Buscando estrellas* (Looking for stars), singing the bolero standard "La barca." According to the artist, Piquito Marcano (who had the label Canomar, discussed in chapter 3) also produced shows in New York City in addition to running his record label and working as a musician himself. She recalls her professional debut in the Teatro Puerto Rico in the Bronx:

> I was 15 years old and this guy goes to see my mother, and tells her he wants to take me to New York to sing. My mother said I could not go because I was a minor, and on top of that my father was not around. . . . But since I had an aunt who had lived all her life in New York, my mother thought of saying, "I will let her go if she stays at my sister's house." And so I went. I played guitar; I had no musical accompaniment. Imagine me, all alone in that theater, with thousands and thousands in the audience. . . . Can you believe who I debuted with, without even knowing! Celia Cruz, Rolando Laserie, Marco Antonio Muñiz, and Armando Manzanero when he was still only a pianist.[10]

In figure 4.3, she is seen on this trip with Rolando Laserie, Celia Cruz, and Lucho Gatica, in 1962. "I was the new girl on the show and that's how they presented me, as the new girl. I was referred to as Luz Esther; Lucecita had not yet been born. Consider my debut: a theater filled with five thousand people, with those four monsters. All alone, as a minor, playing my own accompaniment on guitar in four songs. And the audience gave me a standing ovation! It was incredible."[11]

While she scored many melodramatic hits, Lucecita did not record only melodramatic music. One of her greatest hits of this early stage was "Sobrenatural" (Supernatural), and when she performed this song she shimmied after the dance crazes of the 1960s, completely with the times. But this level of comfort with global youth culture does not resolve the disjuncture between

FIGURE 4.3 Group picture of, from left, Rolando
Laserie, Celia Cruz, Lucecita Benítez, and Lucho Gatica,
Teatro Puerto Rico, Bronx, New York, around 1962.
Courtesy of Grego Marcano.

the singer's "girlie" position in iconography of the time and the decidedly
male position of the speaker in "Sobrenatural." This separation is humorously
apparent in the only movie Lucecita has starred in, *El curandero del pueblo*
(The town healer, 1969) alongside Adalberto Rodríguez, "Machuchal," one of
Puerto Rico's best-known comedians (whose persona was based on a comic
interpretation of the Puerto Rican jíbaro as buffoon). Machuchal was always
caught between tradition and modernity. In this movie, he is the town healer
who, in an implausible plot turn, truly the stuff of fantasy, enrolls in a nursing
course in Puerto Rico's newly inaugurated Centro Médico (Medical Center),
one of Operation Bootstrap's measures of progress. Nowadays the Centro
Médico is a symbol of failed bureaucracy and the severe shortage of health
care in Puerto Rico. In the movie, it appeared as awe-inspiring modernity,

Bootstrap's crowning achievement, just like the youth female star, Lucecita Benítez. Both the medical establishment and the modern artist, the movie implies, are hip yet humane. The hospital is so modern it will admit a man and country bumpkin to its nursing program. Lucecita, playing herself, refuses her (fictional) father's desire for his daughter to go to medical school, in his footsteps; a modern woman should make her own choices, and her character pursues her dream to be (of course) a singer. A broken leg momentarily derails her, thus bringing her into contact with Machuchal as his patient in the hospital.

Midway through the movie, Lucecita receives word that her new release, "Sobrenatural," has just hit the stores. Cut to a nurse excitedly delivering the record. Cut to Lucecita barking the order to play the 45 for her fictional, shades-clad boyfriend. Cut to the best scene in the (admittedly mediocre) film as Lucecita lip-syncs and shimmies while the boyfriend character distractedly gazes upon and smiles at the spectacle of a hospital cafeteria full of dancing nurses, smartly dressed in perfectly ironed uniforms and classic nurses' caps. The film offers visual and sonic proof of woman as modernity: the new professional woman, symbolized by the nurses, the attractive yet enigmatic singer shimmying, and the 45 emitting the voice that insists:

Yo quiero, yo quiero saber
Si en la tierra puede haber una mujer
Pues te oí, canturreando una canción
Tarareando una canción
Y tú tienes que ser
Sobrenatural

I want to know, I want to know
If there can possibly be a woman on earth
Because I heard you singing to yourself
Humming a song
You must be
Supernatural

The excerpt shows how the addressee becomes unclear when the gender of the singer goes slightly awry. The speaker is addressing not merely a woman but a woman who is singing. When Lucecita sings these lyrics, she veers toward a forced narcissism, underscored by her framed youth in the mise-en-scène and the societal fantasies of the nymphet that Herger tried to fit Lucecita into.

Lucecita could very well be addressing her own status as a societal fantasy in the track, constructed by various technologies, in the hyperbolic mode of the song presenting as "supernatural." Lucecita's mouthing of the lyrics to "Sobrenatural" intimate a gender ambiguity expressed in sound. Lucecita has remarked, "I was the first rock artist in Puerto Rico,"[12] placing herself ahead of any male counterparts. She simply was peerless. No voice, male or female, was like hers. As the only woman in the Herger stable, she occupied dominant femininity uneasily from the start, occupying various male-dominated formats in music. Finally, her queerness was a source of fascination, without a doubt, despite the repeated attempts to domesticate her image by finding her a boyfriend.[13]

The soundscape in Puerto Rico included a mix of pop songs coming from multiple markets, as seen in the Hit Parade listing of 1967, with "Sobrenatural" coming in at number 9 (figure 4.4). Lucecita's single shares the top spots with five Spanish- and four English-language hits. "Sobrenatural," despite being a Spanish-language hit, is as close to the American and British hits as to the other hits in Spanish, maybe even more so. It belongs squarely to the internationalist pop of the time. A very short recording with plenty of studio sound, it features fast-tempo string embellishments and bass line in the beginning, reminiscent of James Bond movie music. By overdubbing Lucecita harmonizing with herself in the chorus, the track foregrounds advances in recording technology as they became available in Puerto Rico. Although the tune is a short, bouncy, rock-and-roll song, the effect, when compared to tracks recorded at the same time in Puerto Rico by other female pop artists, is a little unsettling. The first glimmerings of a thinking voice surface in this early repertoire.

AUTEUR, ARTISTE

Lucecita's most important track of the 1960s is undoubtedly "Génesis," a ballad that haunts the Puerto Rican collective memory to this day. Under contract to Alfred D. Herger, Lucecita competed in the first edition of the Festival de la Canción Latina (later renamed the Festival OTI), held in 1969 in Mexico. She was a member of the Puerto Rican cohort. Lucecita handily won the first prize for singing, while Guillermo Venegas Lloveras, also Puerto Rican, won first prize for songwriting. Puerto Rico experienced these first prizes as an apotheosis. Throngs greeted the singer at the airport; schoolchildren watched her arrival on televisions brought into the schools; newspapers documented

LOS **10**
PRIMEROS EXITOS
EN EL

HIT PARADE

DE

RADIO WUNO

1. ESTA TARDE VI LLOVER
   ROBERTO YANES

2. QUE SE REPITA ESTA NOCHE
   PAPO ROMAN

3. TO SIR WITH LOVE
   LULU

4. DAY DREAM BELIEVER
   THE MONKEES

5. MI GRAN NOCHE
   RAPHAEL

6. YOU BETTER SIT DOWN, KIT
   CHER

7. SOLO
   LOS MONTEMAR

8. I SAY A LITTLE PRAYER
   DYONE WARWICK

9. SOBRENATURAL
   LUCESITA

10. PERDONAME
    FELIPE PIRELA

RADIO WUNO

1320 Kc
La Emisora del Hit Parade
Llame al 767-1320 y pida
su selección favorita

FIGURE 4.4 The Hit Parade of Puerto Rico as reported by *TeVe Guía*, December 23–29, 1967. Lucecita's hit, "Sobrenatural," comes in at number 9.

a parade for her through downtown San Juan. Lucecita met with the leaders of the two dominant political parties, Governor Luis A. Ferré of the pro-statehood party (the New Progressive Party) and Senator Rafael Hernández Colón (then president of the Senate, he was later elected governor as the candidate of the pro–status quo Popular Democratic Party in 1972, defeating Ferré). Neither politician wasted the opportunity to be photographed with the star nor to appeal directly to the public's heightened affect.

"Génesis" correlated with both the fear of annihilation that the Cold War implanted and Puerto Rico's colonial anxiety over its smallness, which became more intense as the cracks of a failing economic miracle started to show. We sense musical overcompensation in its fully symphonic, semiclassical arrangement and wall-of-sound recording, with bombast to spare. "Génesis" alludes to the destruction of the world from its first verse ("Cuando nada en la tierra quede que tibie el sol" [When nothing is left on Earth to feel the warmth of the sun]) and ends with an image of love's survival, as a flame gently rising from the disaster ("Solo habrá una lumbre y esa será el amor / ¡El amor, el amor! ¡Para empezar!" [There will only be a flame and that flame will be love / Love, Love! To begin again!]). The lyrics' stark portrayal of the immediate future runs head-on into the orchestra's musical embellishments (recalling Hollywood movie music) and the artist's elaborate melodramatic singing. Anyone with access to the Internet can witness the magnificence of the singer's voice and her spectacular performance onstage four decades later, thanks to YouTube (figure 4.5). Lucecita's performance of "Génesis" catapulted her into celebrity status beyond Puerto Rico, providing a blueprint for future Latin American *baladistas* (including the 1970 debut performance of the Mexican pop idol, José José, who, barely a year later, sang "El triste" with similar pomposity and symphonic accompaniment, as well as a Little Prince costume). Lucecita was key in the transition from the bolero's dominance to that of the *balada* starting around this time.

Lucecita's performance struck a disquieting, dissonant chord. The public marveled at her bravura but was shocked by her masculinity; the Mexican press commented on her masculine wear and hairdo, and gossip about her sexuality soon followed in Puerto Rico.[14] After four or five years of pleasing images meant for ready consumption and singular performances that did not strike a nerve in the social fabric, Lucecita's first moment of artistic maturity surprised everyone. This icon clearly did not conform to the well-honed imaginary of the Caribbean woman either visually or sonically, as it had been drawn in campy stereotypes of dancing bodies since the classic Ninón Sevilla

FIGURE 4.5 The auteur. Lucecita Benítez performing "Génesis." Primer Festival de la Canción Latina, Mexico City, 1969. Costume designed by Martin.

vehicle *Aventurera* (1950). Certainly, Lucecita's costume, a native version of the Yves Saint Laurent female tuxedo, helped capture the public's imagination.[15] Lucecita sported a boyish look reminiscent of Italy's Rita Pavone, who was all the rage. Pavone was probably the model for Lucecita's new look, but there are no apt models for her vocal performance. She had spoken of learning to sing by listening to Lucho Gatica's rendition of the classic bolero "El reloj." Contemporaries, in part encouraged by Lucecita's manager, compared her to Olga Guillot, sometimes accusing Lucecita of imitation. She possessed a different instrument with a wider register and rock-stadium power. She had truly let it rip and initiated an auteur phase in which she began to identify with the predominantly masculine position of the songwriter. Part of her transgression involved her incursion into realms of meaning reserved for the male creator.

Lucecita's performance of "Génesis" remains disturbing and nonnormative, despite being her ticket to a celebrity beyond 1960s covers of U.S. and European pop hits, and being remembered as a moment of pride for Puerto Rico. In 1969, Lucecita's star body, already a veritable Deleuzian assemblage, was forever altered by the eruption of a thinking voice and proved capable of truly rattling Latin America's long fascination with queer stars only as the confirmation of naturalized, nationalist gender roles.[16] Lucecita triggered the work voice can make us go through, calling forth what Mladen Dolar invokes when he writes of the voice as a "bodily missile."[17] This voice showed at the moment where bounty of talent coincided with the uncanny alignment of celebrity culture with global danger and colonial and neocolonial shifts, when masculine embodiment erupted through the conventional, fashion-driven vehicle of celebrity in modernity's periphery (with its grossly uneven distribution of capital and its increasing emphasis on commodified symbolic culture).

Lucecita illustrated what happens when a singer embodies meanings and anxieties of the arkhé, sometimes at odds with her individual intentions or desires, due to the crossing of enormous talent, commanding stage presence, and an uncanny capacity to be photographed and visually reproduced that few singers achieve. The contingency of the historical times infused a certain anima or spirit into every object associated with her. This young woman was read in masculine key, but we do not know exactly why. Was it the volume of her voice, or the narrow reading of her costume? Was it her hairdo, which was the global rage but might have read otherwise in Latin America? Or was it the vehicle of the international song festival itself, that 1960s creation for investment and tourism at the peak of the Cold War, catapulting her first persona of the masculine auteur into the world scene with a song that certainly did not resemble the typical feminine fare? On the cover for the single "Génesis," the artist smiles at us, and the print informs us that the song won first prize (figure 4.6). Nothing more. She had arrived at the scene, but she could not be interpreted yet, thrusting her, as a subject unmoored from common social coordinates, into a simulacrum of Americanist unity smack at the apogee of the Cold War. Not only via the lyrics of "Génesis" but also through this simulacrum, she became inextricable from the void — which, far from removing her from meaning, welded her career to meaning making.[18]

Although Alfred D. Herger negotiated the contract that took Lucecita to the Festival de la Canción Latina in 1969, Lucecita signed with a new manager, Paquito Cordero, shortly after.[19] Tomás Figueroa was Cordero's point man for his music artist contracts. Figueroa hired Pedro Rivera Toledo, who had arranged "Génesis," as Lucecita's music director. Rivera Toledo influenced her sound decisively, showing a preference for busy arrangements with plentiful embellishments and many instruments. Several LPs followed vertiginously on the heels of Lucecita's 1969 triumph, that same year, all with suggestive covers fully exploiting the artist's iconic, queer appeal. The records capitalize on the persona of a misunderstood, off-kilter creator. They exploit Lucecita's gender and racial ambiguity to the fullest. They emphasize melodramatic singing.[20]

FIGURE 4.6 Single of "Génesis," 1969. RCA Victor
3-10397. The festival winner was contracted to release
the winning song as a single.

These LPS of her auteur phase would not have worked without the artist's
genius, particularly her vocal pyrotechnics, steering the records away from the
rush to capitalize on her "Génesis" triumph as much as possible. Although her
first records are disdained by many a fan as being inauthentic, light fare, and
although there were problems with management's stifling of Lucecita's gender
difference, their infantilization of her, and what some critics see as a whitening
of the star body, the production values under Alfred D. Herger were higher.
The auteur phase did generate several striking images in album covers.

Lucecita en Acción . . . ! (Lucecita in Action . . . !) portrays her with her eyes
shut and mouth agape, as in a state of corporeal trance (she was well known
for her dramatic gesturing at the time; figure 4.7). The signifier "Lucecita" begins definitively separating itself from the machinery that attempted to simply
manufacture a female youth star (the smiling young woman, suddenly the
pride of her country, poised to attain world fame). The singer is still a surface, a mirror that invites us to share in the moment of vocal plenitude, what
Mladen Dolar calls a *viva voce*, that which cannot be archived.[21] Playing the
record yields diverse tracks that don't necessarily coincide with the singer's

FIGURE 4.7 Album cover, *Lucecita en acción . . !*,
Hit Parade HPST 045, 1970.

visual self-presentation. Her autonomous sonic concept begins to appear in
Lucecita en la intimidad (Intimate Lucecita; figure 4.8). A collector's item, audiophiles esteem this record because they classify it as serious. The cover presents us with an image of docile introspection, tantalizing the viewer with the
chance to reencounter an unadulterated sonority symbolized by the image of
the artist strumming a guitar. The visual plays with prior sartorial signs of the
artist's masculinity, as does the inclusion of the instrument.

As a degree of surveillance started to creep into Puerto Rican social life,
Lucecita's offstage conduct, from her dress, to where she went, to how she
behaved started becoming an object of scrutiny in a far more serious way than
that exhibited at first by overzealous fans. The worry had to do with gender
and racial normativity, obviously. More specifically, the artist symbolized gender and sexuality in an altogether unpredictable way. Vocally, she had begun
to represent voice's "attack," the very possibility of disordering and convulsing
societal desires without containing precise, settled meanings.[22]

Only a few months after her triumph in Mexico, in 1970, Lucecita inaugurated her second iconic moment. Fashion, to which the artist's body so naturally took for the camera lens, probably led her and her team to the African

FIGURE 4.8   Album cover, *Lucecita en la intimidad,*
Hit Parade HPST 040, 1970.

or Afro look, as it was called at the time. In Lucecita's mythology, this change
was about black pride, social justice, and control of her image. It was about
snubbing TV producers and radio's infamous payola.[23] Yet all artists in a celebrity culture must engage in multiple negotiations to stay at the top. We are
not privy to the contents of any such negotiations in Lucecita's career, or to the
artist's interiority. The consensus that Lucecita grew into an enlightened black
identity, discarding an inauthentic 1960s celebrity as a whitened, oppressive
image, may occlude the complexities of Lucecita's career as well as her mercurial personality and star tendency to speak in the terms reserved for divas, a
discourse that can be delightful but is hardly ever transparent.

The Afro and the tux cohabited uneasily during this artiste period. As of
this writing, readers with access to YouTube can see three early 1970s videos of
Lucecita in her tuxedo.[24] Together they exhibit disparate deployments of this
costume. Lucecita appeared on *The Ed Sullivan Show* on December 6, 1970; the
clip is now captioned "Puerto Rican chanteuse croons out tune in Spanish accompanied by her own conga player."[25] (The drummer was not her own player
but the Cuban master Cándido Camero, who worked under separate contract.)
Sullivan announces: "And now, assisted by Latin American drummer Candido,

FIGURE 4.9 Lucecita performs "Todas las mañanas" in the Mexican movie *Tonta tonta pero no tanto* (a vehicle for the Mexican comedy star María Elena Velasco, "La India María"). Lucecita wears a red tuxedo top and her Afro, 1972.

here is one of Puerto Rico's most exciting performers, Lucecita Benítez. . . . So let's have a fine welcome for Lucecita Benítez!" Lucecita cut a handsome figure with her Afro and green Fernando Martin tuxedo outfit.[26] She appeared in *Tonta tonta pero no tanto* (I may be dumb, but not that dumb, 1972), a María Elena Velasco vehicle (the comedian was in character as Mexico's buffoon, La India María). Lucecita performs the same song, the bouncy "Todas las mañanas" (Every morning). This time she dons a red tux jacket and black bow tie, along with her Afro (figure 4.9). The third clip, from 1972 or 1973, shows Lucecita singing "For Once in My Life" with Sammy Davis Jr., probably on the *Toyota Rambler Show* (a Paquito Cordero Productions show, which aired on Telemundo, Paquito Cordero's television station).[27] Lucecita sings a Spanish-language version to Davis's English. Although the artist clearly enjoys her banter with Davis and matches him in cool, she appears Afro-less and slightly more feminine looking, as it was coded at the time.

Reportedly, she left the *Toyota Rambler Show*, which she hosted, because she was dissatisfied with the commercial inclinations of her managers, who injected elements of dissonance when they aided her performance in the market and proceeded to eliminate them at a moment's notice at the slightest hint of a loss of viewers. Lucecita has said that she could not tailor her own image as an artist and was fast becoming weary of recording only for hits and sales. The sartorial tug of war mirrored, to an extent, the sonic pastiche of the records of this second iconic phase, tenuously held together by the artiste pose Lucecita was able to assume thanks to her extraordinary vocal ability and virtuosic dexterity with a plurality of genres. The artiste manifestation allowed her to comply with her manager's demands to appeal to multiple markets. This included adding several English-language songs to her repertoire for her hotel shows, to cater to American tourists as much as the local bourgeoisie. Her manager's tastes and the constant use of polls to gauge market success dictated the production values of the records. At times she sported her Afro, at others not; at times she wore the tuxedo, at others she dressed in ruffles and was heavily made up. She was required to change styles, and her repertoire was, for the most part, mandated.

The LPs Hit Parade numbers 60, 61, and 70 are all titled, simply, *Lucecita*. Their covers feature portraits that directly reference black identity, focusing on her upper body and therefore skirting the issue of the problematic tux. The three LPs were recorded in Spain with mostly Spanish personnel. The second album has a terrific cover that is, in some ways, more unsettling than the other albums that portrayed Lucecita with an Afro. The cover features a single photo of Lucecita (by Gabriel Suau) repeated across the album, guiding the viewer's eye from left to right and down two rows until the eye meets the same photo in negative for a single frame, then to return to the color photo (figure 4.10). It is a close-up of the artist with a faint, knowing smile. While sporting the Afro, her image is not constrained by the imperative to represent; the repetition of the frame, as well as the presence of the single negative frame, emphasizes the image quality of the portrait, its status as an artifact of photography and specifically as a portrait of a pop artist — ideally a changing object, never a monument.

It is perhaps obvious, but needs to be stated, that the cover is playing with the black/white binary, while not resolving it either way. It offers, perhaps, a commentary on the public's by-then obsession with Lucecita as a racial sign. In Benjaminian terms, the cover deflates the image's auratic character, making it equal to the dozens of pretty photos that had by that time been taken of Lucecita, all produced with the speed that the cover itself re-creates in its dizzying repetition of the frame, all for mass consumption. It is a comment on easy iconicity.

FIGURE 4.10 Album cover, *Lucecita*, Hit Parade 61, 1972, showing a repeated color close-up of Lucecita with her Afro, and a single, negative exposure in the second row. Photograph by Gabriel Suau.

The fact that the image is a close-up of the artist plays with the idea that close-ups and a gaze at the camera lens equal sincerity and readability. Close-ups were a standard feature of film and TV melodramas. Here, the close-up is border-line defiant. The image is certainly very distant from the octane-charged, melo-dramatic explosion of *Lucecita en Acción . . . !* or the soft, simple intimacy of the artist strumming a guitar, with her back to the camera, head slightly turned to the side only allowing a partial view of her face, in *Lucecita en la intimidad*.

Lucecita's star body evolved in artistic duress, under fire as various sectors competed for the symbolic space in the increasingly mediatized society of the spectacle.[28] Of the three albums recorded in Spain in Lucecita's artiste phase, with her Afro as main visual signifier, Hit Parade 70, *Lucecita* stands out for both scopic and sonic reasons. The graphic artist Antonio Martorell created an intense album cover, representing Lucecita with her Afro, in the nude, with arms outstretched, using red and blue to create a powerful and alternative image of the star body in a racist, homophobic, sexist, and classist society (figure 4.11). The first track is the hit song "Soy de una raza pura" (I belong to

FIGURE 4.11 The artiste. Cover of the album *Lucecita*, Hit Parade 70, 1973. Cover design by Antonio Martorell.

a pure race) — like "Génesis," a watershed recording and classic of the Puerto Rican late colonial soundtrack.

Television scholar Yeidy Rivero has offered an inaugural analysis of the Afro's social significance and shock element.[29] Rivero focuses on the "Afro look controversy" between 1970 and 1973. Referring to a "televisually constructed whitened body," Rivero posits that the artist was whitened by the use of wigs throughout the 1960s and that up to the moment when she wore the Afro, which Rivero locates on television in April 1970, Lucecita functioned as an acceptable feminine rock-and-roll female star.[30] She writes, "The Afro . . . completely destabilized her — until this point — racially, socially, culturally and somewhat acceptable whitened trigueña/mestiza televisual body. . . . Her Afro also became an emblem of gender, feminine, and even sexual transgressions."[31]

Elements of Rivero's discussion of Lucecita's visuality could be broadened with an inclusion of how the 1960s Lucecita was not merely whitened. Black entrepreneurship models are clearly in evidence on her first covers, as is the ascendancy of the fashion industry, which, while casting the young artist in normative modes, was quite mindful of the market niche emerging from the counterculture. What is undertheorized in Rivero's discussion of Lucecita between 1970 and 1973, and hence in a discussion of race and more specifically blackness, are the sonic and music culture contexts. Granted, Rivero's book is about television, not pop music. Yet in Lucecita's case, the social discussion is, at best, incomplete without a full consideration of her music. The artist's star body, its reception, is unthinkable without taking into account voice's material presence (in the double sense of commodity and event).

Pedro Rivera Toledo arranged "Soy de una raza pura" in Puerto Rico before the artist traveled to Spain with Tomás Figueroa to cut the record. Lucecita works mostly with her head voice, with clear diction and, generally speaking, not much chest voice or low register, which must undeniably have made it less unruly to the middle classes who largely bought records. The song presents what could be thought of as a liberal construction of oppositionality all the way to the song's second half, when, introduced by increased instrumentation and reverb, we hear:

Soy de una raza pura, pura rebelde
Soy tambor y cuerda
Soy bronce de campana

Para llorar a muerte
Pero como soy de bronce también sé gritar
A guerra

I come from a pure race, a rebel race
I am drums and strings
I am the bell's bronze, willing to weep to death
But since I am made of bronze
I also know how to shout
War

This led to the song's most celebrated verse, in which Lucecita, recorded on two tracks spliced together, harmonizes with her own performance:

Soy borincano, negro y gitano
I am Puerto Rican, black, and gypsy

A declaration immediately followed by the ending, a rousing coda:

Soy taíno, y soy lágrimas, y también dolor
Por los siglos que he vivido

Por lo mucho que he sufrido
Soy de una raza pura, pura rebelde
Soy de una raza pura
¡Rebelde!

I am a *Taíno* Indian, and tears, and also pain
Here's to the centuries I have lived
Here's to all that I have suffered
I descend from a pure, pure, rebel race
I descend from a pure race
A rebel race!

"Soy de una raza pura" referenced blackness by enlisting elements of soul. Lucecita worked melodically, with her typically crystalline delivery but without any melodramatic technique. Prior tracks recorded by the artist had serially presented blackness as an alterity loosely aligned with Lucecita's star body. The auteur phase's melodramatic pathos characterized songs like Venegas Lloveras's "Raza negra" (Black race) ("¡Raza que transmite su pena / a través del bongó! [Race that transmits its sorrow / through the bongos!]). In her artiste phase, the stereotypical rhythm section of "Gitanito" (Little gypsy) evoked a tropicalist sound vaguely reminiscent of the blackness that the cover, a profile of the artist with her Afro, colorized in shades of blue and black, virtually guaranteed. "Soy de una raza pura" is superior to either track because of its economy of technique and willful engagement of left-leaning politics. It strives to go beyond the manufactured star body, engaging an artistic cohort she had just met and befriended. This group provided a collective sense to her intuitive vocal disordering of expected sense, her commercialized blackness included. Fred Moten's question, "What is it to be an irreducibly disordering, deformational force while at the same time being absolutely indispensable to normative order, normative form?," is very relevant to Lucecita as a "case of blackness."[32]

"Soy de una raza pura" does advocate for the insertion of racial difference into the unity of the national subject. In this respect, it's not set apart that much from the "three roots theory" Puerto Rican children were learning in school at the time from standard textbooks, such as María Luisa Babín's *Fantasía boricua* (Puerto Rican fantasy). Nevertheless, it struck a new political chord. Audience members waited, some in thrall, others in disgust, until the moment when the artist, performing live on television, raised her left fist on the line "también sé gritar / ¡a guerra!" (I also know how to shout / war!).

She inscribed, via a momentary dissonance in the star body, the proindependence and diffusely leftist gesture forever into the song and collective memory.

One of the finest examples of the rock ballad that Lucecita executed so well is on the same LP (Hit Parade 70), Alberto Carrión's "Camino abandonado" (Forgotten path). The song's reference to "compañero" (which in the original must have been "compañera") is very much in tune with the sexual politics of the period and especially with New Left recastings of the male-female relationship as one of equals. This revised "lovers' discourse" resonates with the Cuban Revolution's adoption of the word "compañero" (comrade) as the socially acceptable form of address, indicating social equality and equal participation in the revolutionary process. Lucecita's recording employed the same arrangement as Carrión's original. The proper place of romantic music in liberation became a hotly debated topic among left artistic circles. In Puerto Rico as elsewhere, love was treated as a laboratory for the revolution, an opportunity to create in microcosm an exemplary space free of the colonial mentality, where equality would function as a seed to move humanity toward a just world. More profoundly, it's clear that romantic music became an uneasy stand-in for aesthetic pursuits and whether they could ever be straightforwardly political: a synecdoche for art, period.

The key to the beauty of Lucecita's interpretation of "Camino abandonado" is, assuredly, the opportunity to hear her singing the entire ballad in the low register, a particularly wondrous experience in live performance. After taking voice lessons in the late 1970s and early 1980s in order to preserve her instrument, by and large a successful effort, she stated, "I am a contralto with a little more tessitura than normal," a designation she likely got from her voice coach, Rina de Toledo.[33] Not only was her voice different from those of her contemporaries, it was also striking in terms of what deep voices in women were taken to represent and the strictures about how women were supposed to sound.[34] Lucecita remarked, "My middle register is the most beautiful" and "folks are amazed that one can reach very high notes," but it's likely that the public associated those high notes with feminine singing, and felt awe much more when she exhibited her capacity to go to the lowest notes.[35] Lucecita managed to suspend the relevance of this expectation, not merely defy it. In her auteur phase, Lucecita had shown her dexterity in usurping the male space of the songwriter and her skill at creating the track, that all-important hallmark of modern musical creativity, often a male preserve. Here, her mighty chest voice belting out the power ballad is an added element of this takeover. Just as important is the claiming of the emptiness or dissolution that the song thematizes:

Cuánto tiempo llevo sola
Necesito un compañero a mi lado
Necesito aquel amor de mi pasado

He vagado sin saber a dónde ir
He intentado recorrer mil senderos que exploré
Y a veces pienso
De qué me sirve rebuscar
Si sé que nada he de encontrar

Oh, I have been alone so long
I need a partner by my side
I need to recover that love from my past

I have wandered aimlessly
I have tried to go back on a thousand paths I have walked on
And sometimes I tell myself
What's the point of all this searching
If I know I will find nothing

Dissolution as a male fear is prevalent in male singer-songwriter (*cantautor*) repertoire (an example might be the later Facundo Cabral and his 1970 hit, "No soy de aquí" [I'm not from here], or Joan Manuel Serrat's 1971 "Vagabundear" [Wandering]). Dissolution is also prominent in the British and American rock ballads Alberto Carrión learned from records and the budding FM radio, and probably favored.[36] Lucecita's vocal power and virtuosity raised this and other ballads above the banality permanently hovering at their edges. Male melancholy ceded space to another code in the making, one with no discursive encasing, like what transpired with her performance of "Génesis." There, she sang, "When nothing is left on Earth to feel the warmth of the sun"; here, she bemoans, "What's the point of all this searching / If I know I will find nothing." These lyrics reflect male melancholy, but Lucecita was not a melancholy star, masculine or feminine. Her vocal performance established the fact. What was she, then? Lucecita's alignment with dissolution or nothing is qualitatively different from that of her male contemporaries, as I explore for the rest of this chapter. Her recoding of melancholy and melodrama suggests

an imbuing of thought into pop song, the existence of a yearning for or orientation to thought.

An extremely interesting, even disturbing, 1973 interview, "Con Lucecita"
(With Lucecita), in the groundbreaking journal *Zona carga y descarga*
(Loading zone), illustrates the artist's loneliness even in the friendliest of
quarters. The first impulse would be to expect Rosario Ferré and Manuel
Ramos Otero, two of Puerto Rico's most important writers of the latter half
of the twentieth century, to grasp Lucecita's singularity fully. Ferré is a path-
breaking feminist writer, and Ramos Otero broke open the literary establishment with his daring, queer short stories of the 1970s. The piece proceeds
along two separate discursive routes: on the one hand, that of the politically
committed artist extraordinaire, virtually a hero, and, on the other, that of the
genius artist who cannot find her interlocution or perhaps exists in another
place altogether, unsymbolizable, possibly the subject position that Giorgio
Agamben has referred to as "contemporary."[37]

Ramos Otero opens the interview praising Lucecita for her just-released
political album (the self-titled *Lucecita*, with the Martorell cover and the track
"Soy de una raza pura"; figure 4.11).

> MANUEL: Lucy, yo quisiera concentrar en tu último disco. Definitiva-
> mente este disco es diferente a los otros hechos anteriormente. Y
> demuestra toda esa unidad en la cuestión del tema de la liberación
> que está presente a través de todo el disco. . . .
>
> LUCY: Pero tú estas entrando políticamente a la música que yo he
> hecho.
>
> MANUEL: No, definitivamente yo creo que la labor que tú acabas de
> realizar en este disco es política.
>
> LUCY: ¿Tú crees que no es artística?
>
> MANUEL: Ah, claro está definitivamente, porque nada que salga de ti no
> podría ser artístico.
>
> LUCY: Indiscutiblemente.

> MANUEL: Lucy, I'd like to concentrate on your last record. Definitely,
> this record is different from the preceding. It demonstrates unity
> in the question of the theme of liberation, present throughout the
> record. . . .
>
> LUCY: But your entry point to my music is political.
>
> MANUEL: No, I definitely think that the work you have produced in this
> album is political.

LUCY: You don't think of it as artistic?

MANUEL: Of course, definitely, because nothing that came out of you cannot but be artistic.

LUCY: Undeniably.[38]

Ramos Otero framed the discussion in a Marcusian politics as liberation at all levels, which addressed personal liberation, self-reflection, self-possession, love equality, and so forth. To be fair, the complete album does respond to these coordinates, being a motley collection of the era's love-and-peace zeitgeist with the exception of the two tracks I have discussed. Lucecita understood those discussions and how they applied to her art, of course. She found it problematic, though, that the first and maybe only appraisal of her work would not be purely artistic. By artistic, she meant perfect. Are the tracks laid out correctly? Is everyone landing the pitches and hitting the notes? Is my diction crystal-clear? In fact, when Ramos Otero asks Lucecita if she has any regrets about the criticism she received upon the album's release, she replies that her only regret was that it "didn't come out perfect," by which she signaled a musician's desire to strive for the aesthetic, for beauty.[39] There was an injunction that the artist represent the social sign, that she be political, when she clearly wanted to be artistic, representing nothing (distinct from her other existence as a private individual, understood as, among other things, a colonial subject). It's not that the political in art did not interest her, but that her execution lacked a corresponding capacity for its symbolization in society, making it hard to sync two diverging senses of what "political" meant: hers and everyone else's.

"Artistic" was also an unclear signifier. I think Lucecita was aware of this, possibly more so than her interviewers, who subscribed to typical left notions of liberation and the role of artists as the vanguard of this liberation. The very notion of beauty was compromised, muddling what "artistic" could mean in this context. In terms of musical taste, the corporatist sound (of which Lucecita's close associate Pedro Rivera Toledo was a main architect as arranger of several pop musicians of the time) had essentially hijacked television and concert life. The memorable, albeit conservative, Festival Casals continued its labor in the symphonic world. Salsa and Afro–Puerto Rican music dueled with American rock and alternative music, pitting two imaginaries in a type of class and race cultural warfare. Puerto Rican pop, in the meantime, was increasingly condemned to middlebrow audiences and its liveness was fast dying out on television. The complete interview includes Lucecita's scathing critique of the entertainment industry. Still, she searched for art's and her own relevance to the times. Pop had become, to put it succinctly, a Baudrillardian simulacrum of a collective existence that did not address the breakdown of society under late colonialism.

As mentioned, Paquito Cordero had Lucecita enter and exit styles and TV shows in rapid succession, never allowing for any one concept to mature and specifically instructing the artist not to express any political sympathies (meaning, to mouth any political opinions). Cordero did not care about a political bent to songs: Her musically inflected oppositionality clearly aided sales (as did her Afro turn and her dissonant, tuxedo-clad femininity). What powerful concerns among the public really resented at this time was her assumption of political speech, such as the well-known raised fist in support of independence. Perhaps more subtly, resentment toward Lucecita's intuitive, yet certainly advanced understanding of the technologies for transmitting the voice, relative to other pop artists in the colony, is discernible too.

Any exercise of a thinking voice in the colony at the close of the 1960s and into the explosive 1970s was dangerous. Lucecita was a celebrity and made money and therefore could defy the expectations of the consumer culture that had made her famous. Her resolute queerness onstage and her capacity to outvocalize anyone in an asphyxiatingly heteronormative society had the potential to be world transforming. In this context, Lucecita and her team's adaptation of black pride iconography must have come as something of a relief to multiple sectors because, however startling the Afro may have been, it was fascinating, readable, containable, deployable, and punishable, while her voice in performance and its queer embodiment demanded a more complicated exercise of thought.

It was, as with "Génesis," the artist's performance and the sedimentation of meanings she had accrued that made "Soy de una raza pura" a classic and touchstone. It climbed the charts and represented an unusual moment when celebrity and the thinking voice coexisted. The artist, however, felt estranged from her recording and image. A closer look at the iconography of 1970–1973 reveals an unexamined tug-of-war between the tuxedo and the Afro — social, mainly sartorial signs that the artist most likely experienced as secondary to the sonorous event of the voice. Having become overdetermined by the social (read mostly visually), Lucecita risked losing her grasp of the thinking voice; she risked merely being consumed as a celebrity, albeit a nonconforming, controversial one. Although as a young artist she had stated she coveted fame, when fame arrived it left her a little cold, perhaps because it became notoriety. It was no longer about the thinking voice. The artist lost interest in celebrity and singing, lamenting in the *Zona* interview on the release of her "Soy de una raza pura," "Yo puedo cantar, pero no hablar" (I can sing, but I cannot speak).[40]

FUGITIVITY

In 1974, finally freed from contractual obligations to her managers and at last the owner of her musical labor, Lucecita was ready to create true artistic trouble with the landmark concert Traigo un pueblo en mi voz (I bring a people in my voice), in which she switched to a cantautor (male singer-songwriter) repertoire. Unfortunately, no recording of the concert is commercially available. The title comes from the 1973 Mercedes Sosa album *Traigo un pueblo en mi voz*; the phrase "I bring a people in my voice" is the second verse of the refrain of "Hermano dame tu mano" (Brother, give me your hand), a New Left song by Jorge Sosa and Damián Gómez. Betzaida "Bebé" López, then married to Danny Rivera, had traveled to Latin America and brought back records that supplied much of Lucecita's political repertoire. Lucecita also turned to Puerto Rican songwriters associated with the left, such as Alberto Carrión and Antonio Cabán Vale, "El Topo."

Politics and affect were coming together in a particularly intense way in Puerto Rico. One of the main economic reasons was the oil crisis of 1973, which affected Puerto Rico severely. Another was homegrown: the failure of the Estado Libre Asociado (Commonwealth of Puerto Rico), which was fast showing its huge cracks, as memorialized in the brilliant Luis Rafael Sánchez novel *Macho Camacho's Beat* and analyzed in a landmark essay by José Luis González, "The Four-Storeyed Country." Writers were coalescing around noted journals like *Zona carga y descarga*, and the group known as "the new historians" was producing a revisionist historiography that yielded many important monographs and changed the writing of Puerto Rican history. And, with the founding of the Partido Socialista Puertorriqueño (Puerto Rican Socialist Party) came one of the decade's most important publications, the newspaper *Claridad* (Clarity), which featured a cultural supplement starting in 1974 called *En Rojo* (In red), announcing, perhaps, its hard-line cultural tendencies. Reportage on politically conscious music and musicians regularly appeared in *En Rojo*. As was to be expected, Lucecita became a regular topic of the supplement. She was as much of a cipher for her left-wing admirers as she was for her mainstream public.

Lucecita sympathized with liberation movements generally and had long been proindependence. Yet she took pains to clarify that she did not "belong to any political party," "was not against any political leader," and "belonged to the people."[41] Mita Torres, who had studied political science at the University of Puerto Rico and had decided to become a political organizer, contacted the artist around 1973. Torres was a member of several small, radical groups, and she joined the Partido Socialista Puertorriqueño upon its founding in 1971. Torres was interested in the cultural promotion of left-wing causes and knew several artists personally: the choreographer Lotti Cordero, the actor Miguel Ángel Suárez, the dance teacher Nana Hudo, and the photographer Gabriel Suau (who was married to the actress Camille Carrión). Through them, she met Lucecita and took up the task of persuading her to sing at a benefit concert for left-wing causes.[42] At that moment the sonic Lucecita, who had poured herself into her recordings, for the most part, and supplemented her output with television appearances as per her contract, turned almost wholly to connecting with large, cross-class live audiences.

The gorgeous program booklet provides a visual trace of this brief but significant attempt to change the terms of Lucecita's celebrity existence, encapsulated in the limpid image of the artist singing, simply emanating sound from an open mouth (figure 4.12). The staff at *Revista Avance*, a short-lived but prescient journalistic venture,[43] keyed into the significance of this image and Lucecita's canny understanding of music production as integrating various elements of the sensorium:

> In all aspects of the concert's publicity: posters, newspaper ads, entry tickets and ticket envelopes, invitations to the press, invitations sent out to guests of honor, the program — beautifully printed with lyrics to some of the songs and sold at a dollar due to printing costs — even in the curtain that falls behind the singer at the end of both parts of the concert, in sum, everything employed a distinctive graphic design created by the artists Felipe Cuchí and Ivonne Torres. This graphic design consisted of a profile of a singing Lucecita, with three variously colored strips emerging from her open mouth, symbolizing musical notes. This proved to be very effective and gave the concert a special touch, being that it is the first time anything of the sort has been done in Puerto Rico.[44]

lucecita·traigo un pueblo en mi voz

FIGURE 4.12 Attempting to exit celebrity. Program cover booklet for Traigo un pueblo en mi voz, May 1974. The cover is printed in black, white, and grays.

The booklet presents lyrics of the concert along with the concert program. It also includes several photographs of the artist away from her celebrity mode, not exactly a star body produced by the machine, but not just any old body, either. She has magnetism and mystique, but put to vastly different ends. She appears carefree and relaxed and is photographed at play and smiling. The first page has a dedication: "Dedicado a mi pueblo y a mi gente" (Dedicated to my people and my folks). The booklet's printed lines are typeset in a clean brown, set against a white background, with no overt nationalist content. There are no Puerto Rican flags or folkloric embellishments anywhere in the program. The politics appear subliminally in the era's typical codes of music as rainbow, music as truth, "my people" as the recipient but not yet categorically defined, and the artist in street clothes. This piece is surely one of the most loaded with meaning of all Lucecita ephemera, precisely because it is simple and understated, yet enormously evocative.

Lucecita was the concert's producer. The photos transmit her ideal of the total artist, involved in every aspect of the production, at the center yet in a group of like-minded individuals, a heterotopia in Michel Foucault's sense.[45] The collective enterprise presaged elements of Nancy's concept of "being-singular-plural," in which singularity and collectivity are not warring existences but comment on each other and remain permanently open ended, open to change.[46] An important detail is the inclusion of a street portrait of Pedro Rivera Toledo, much different from the usual stage persona of highbrow concert director that he is associated with. While posed, it does not respond to leftist ideals of populist authenticity; he is seen bearded and smoking a cigar, in an image reminiscent of contemporary rock aesthetics. The duo Lucecita-Pedro is rendered as one where Lucecita is the source of the art and Pedro an essential artistic soulmate but not the art's creator or administrator, as he would later be seen. The staff at *Avance* wrote, "The basic difference of the Sylvia Rexach [Theater] concert to those of the Hilton is that there will be no songs of the type labeled 'commercial,' only musical compositions with a social content. Along the same line of her latest record, the one with the Martorell cover ('I belong to a pure race . . .')."[47]

Yet this contestatory, scintillating concert appearance soon gave way to a conservative mode featuring a stylized performance of progressive politics, joining middle-class, corporate taste in music with a vaguely left-leaning repertoire. This unlikely marriage structured the 1975 live album *En las manos del pueblo* (In the hands of the people; figure 4.13).[48] Despite its left-leaning name, the album does not feature a political repertoire. Rather, it leans heavily to sentimental song and draws especially on a pop singer-songwriter (cantautor) from Argentina, Alberto Cortez (ten of the nineteen tracks are his). Lucecita returned to costumes, wearing Martin's interpretation of the dashiki, in a vaguely Africanist look with close-cropped hair. Some commentators claimed that Martin had designed this new wear to help Lucecita conceal the fact she had gained weight. More than this sexist appraisal, it's likely that the costume represented the zero of representation, in total opposite to Lucecita's rich iconography up to then. Pedro Rivera Toledo now appeared in the hallowed position of conductor, was called "maestro," and wore a tuxedo. The sound was unabashedly symphonic.

There is a nod to Puerto Rican awareness in Lucecita's performance of "La verdad" (Truth), from the venerable Rafael Cortijo, *Rafael Cortijo and His Time Machine / Y su máquina del tiempo* (1974). It was, significantly, retitled "Le Lo Lai" after Puerto Rico's celebrated phrase of belonging from the jíbaro corpus, which is the song's refrain:

El que me quiera escuchar, que me escuche
Y el que se quiera tapar, que se tape

FIGURE 4.13 Album cover, Lucecita, *En las manos del pueblo*, 1975.

Voy a decir la verdad, caballero
Aunque me parta un rayo

Si usted quiere ser cantante, tiene que aprender primero
A cantar esos cantares que vienen del extranjero
Porque nuestra tradición, caballero,
Rueda por el suelo

Le lo lai, le lo lai, rueda por el suelo

He who wants to listen to me, let him listen
He who wants to hide, let him hide
I'm going to tell the truth, sir
Even if I'm struck by lightning

If you want to be a singer
You first have to learn to sing foreign tunes
Because our tradition, sir
Is going down the drain

Le lo lai, le lo lai, it's going down the drain

FIGURE 4.14 "Lucecita, or frankness in the guise of an artist." Cover of the TV guide, *Telerevista*, of the newspaper *El Mundo*, April 28–May 4, 1974.

Lucecita sang "Le Lo Lai" in Traigo un pueblo en mi voz. The arrangement was copied from Cortijo's recording, including the psychedelic rock guitar line and funky brass blares. It was the perfect cover song for Lucecita, who was on a quest to pursue parrhesia, "speaking truth to power."[49] She had declared just before, in the 1973 *Zona* interview, "When I felt oppressed, when I felt they wanted to reduce me, it wasn't because of my talent, it was over nothing; they tried to stop me because I was telling the truth. . . . I have truth in my hands and if they kill me with it, I will die happy as hell, I prefer to die like that, because I told the truth, not because I kept silent about it."[50] Figure 4.14 is a print drawing of this period that encapsulates Lucecita's noncelebrity persona with the caption: "Lucecita, or frankness in the guise of an artist." Important in this portrayal is her representation in the act of speaking and thinking; it seems she is pausing in the middle of a statement, and she is clearly interpellating a listener via speech, not song. We also notice her out of stage costume, in street clothes, and the visual re-creation of her black identity linked to this frankness. The music and entertainment complex represented this power most immediately; the threat of cultural assimilation figured in the refrain of "Le Lo Lai" represented it more generally, in the context of what was termed at the time "U.S. cultural penetration."

Cortijo is Puerto Rico's most esteemed twentieth-century Afro–Puerto Rican artist and, arguably, the most important. The codes of funk and psychedelic link Cortijo and by extension Lucecita's embroilment with truth to an alternative black modernity, away from the folklorization of blackness that was most familiar to the Puerto Rican audience that clapped and sang with abandon while Lucecita belted out this song live. Rivera Toledo added a cuatro solo at the end of the song (Millito Cruz played the cuatro, which was not featured as an instrument elsewhere in the song performance or the rest of the program), provoking a loud roar of recognition from the audience. While this may be read as a nativist recovery of an otherwise fugitive song, it does not take away from the song's main identity as Afro-diasporic, even if it was not necessarily touted as such.

Lucecita felt just at home with symphonic arrangements. Naturally, these were received as the polar opposite of black music. She could not be read within one matrix, becoming an example of what Daphne Brooks, building on Mae Henderson, refers to as "Afro-sonic feminist noise," "a kind of sound composed of heteroglossic gestures that articulate 'the ability to speak in diverse (musical) languages.'"[51] Brooks goes on to quote Moten: "In 'music' . . . 'blackness indicates chromaticity as a potentially unregulated or profligate internal difference,'" and, further down, Brooks echoes Moten's interest in "radical forms of aurality that upset normative definitions of meaningful speech and conventional musical [structures]."[52] Brooks discusses Nina Simone as paradigmatic of black female vocality in this context of "defamiliarizing sociocultural expectations of where and how black women should *sound* in song."[53] Simone, as is well known, intended to become a classical pianist and, derailed by racism from her life's pursuit, injected this classical affiliation into jazz and pop. Lucecita did not play instruments or desire to become a classical musician ever, but she was undeniably attracted to symphonic sound and used her voice in a virtuosic manner.

Similarly to Simone and others like her, Lucecita had her own logic and simply refused to be confined to any one expectation, whether sentimental or social. This extended to her views on her voice as the vehicle for speech.

She was well aware of her potential to enter the world stage as a spokesperson for Puerto Rico, as multiple commentators had pointed out since her triumph with "Génesis."[54] Studies such as Alexander Weheliye's on sonic Afromodernity might go far to elucidate the extent of Lucecita's transgression as a black musician and allow for a nuanced approach to her concept as a singer and artist, respecting and marshaling the fact that she thought musically. Weheliye rejects the notion of black sound as "an idealized, authentically vernacular, or discrete sphere that distinguishes Afro-diasporic cultural production in/as Western modernity." He argues instead that black sound "creates and re-calibrates" some of modernity's "central topoi, such as the equation of script with reason and humanity, narratives of unmitigated progress, and the configuration of vision as incorporeal and therefore the apex of scientific rationality." Modernity's "discourses are neither erased nor suspended; rather, they are significantly (re)created in their encounter with auditory blackness, which also undergoes substantial shifts in this assemblage."[55] Lucecita's protestation that she needed to reach other audiences than those sympathetic to self-determination might strike some listeners as naive, but it could be read more productively as a refusal to signify easily, to be readily legible as a black artist, which would mean conforming to folkloric protocols of blackness not excluding the easy consumption of oppositionality and sartorial signs such as her own Afro that she had beautifully donned. (Indicatively, the entertainment press discussed her "Afro look" as an assumption of a modern hairdo on more than one occassion.)

Her "incoherent" discourse, much remarked upon but seldom seen in print except for the *Zona* interview, can and perhaps should be read as a refusal to give up the sonic centrality of everything she worked for as an artist. Take, for example, this moment in the 1973 *Zona* interview:

The people who fill the Hilton, etc., they are different from the lefties — those are the ones that need to listen to us. I don't need to convince you, but the fool that sits there, the guy who has money. I have to convince him. Period. That's great, a concert at the University of Puerto Rico, fill the theater, divine, a lot of fist raising and everybody chanting "Long live a free Puerto Rico!" but where I want to instigate the movement is precisely where nothing similar has ever appeared. I'm not with the capitalist, damn it! I believe they utilize and you have to utilize them. They own the medium and well then, you have to go through the medium. I am not proindependence, I am not a nationalist,

I am nothing; I believe that Puerto Rico has to be a free country, period. That's the way it is, good or bad — we have to be free. The only thing you can't allow is to have freedom taken from you, because then you become nothing, nothing, you're nothing, you're nobody, you're a good for nothing.[56]

If we take Lucecita's quest to represent truth at face value, without stopping to verify if she served the protocols of articulateness or codes of conduct of the intellectually inclined singer, we may verify Weheliye's "encounter with auditory blackness" as a "recoloration of topoi."[57] Lucecita's analysis is revealing, its disjointed nature illuminating. In the interview, she severely criticizes right-wing-affiliated singers, pointing out that they are "doing politics too, and don't suffer any retaliation."[58] But perhaps the most telling critique is of the leftist movement in Puerto Rico, and her subtle (although not subtly expressed) appraisal of symbolic culture (of which protest song and the revolutionary ballad partook) as potentially empty gestures that did not significantly alter the status quo of colonialism in Puerto Rico. She raised her left fist in the proindependence gesture during her concerts; however, she felt that performing the gesture in a musical environment among a group of *independentistas* could lapse into a narcissistic self-congratulation or minoritarian plenitude. She wanted no part of that. Hence her frequent declaration that she was not affiliated with any political party but with her conscience or truth.

Troubled with what her own vocalizing had become, Lucecita arrived at the very quandary of vocality, of the human voice: "The voice is sound, not speech. But speech constitutes its essential destination."[59] Vocal performance, as it existed in the colony in the mid-1970s, was possibly curtailing her attempts at speech. She started to mention writing a book about her life. She enrolled in classes at the University of Puerto Rico, where she could be spotted performatively traversing the Río Piedras campus, surrounded by a dancing coterie of hip women. She appeared in political protests, sang in union events and for an array of left-wing groups, and expressed sympathy for the Cuban Revolution, activities that would continue for the rest of the decade.

As part of her exploration of what voice meant, Lucecita embarked on a trip to Cuba in the summer of 1975, just after the concert En las manos del pueblo. There she participated in various consciousness-raising activities and sang at the opening of a school in Matanzas. When she came back she found that her native country had declared her persona non grata, contrary to 1969 and her triumphant return from the Festival de la Canción Latina. Lucecita was blacklisted. She could not record or appear in entertainment venues or on television, and her songs were not played on the radio. Notwithstanding her previous celebrity status, vocal brilliance, and unending supply of "It," she could not find work and became demonized as a leftist extremist. While in 1969 the Cold War had intersected with her performance of "Génesis" and other songs in her repertoire in a putatively positive way, the way her 1975 performances transected world crisis and the Cuban Revolution proved near catastrophic for her career; her celebrity was all but wiped out. The state had succeeded in making her notorious.

For years after Lucecita's political turn, when she attempted to refuse iconography and flout celebrity, she was harassed by the police, who took advantage of every opportunity to either fabricate charges against her or make her into a criminal in the eyes of public opinion, especially as it related to drugs, one of the moral panics created by the new law-and-order state of the 1970s in collaboration with powerful right-wing elements. Artist *carpetas* or FBI dossiers tracked their every move and constructed a narrative of delinquency directly threatening to the state. Archival newsprint items attest to the persecution and demonization of the singer. The front page of the newspaper *El Mundo* on August 25, 1976, shows Lucecita's arrest embedded in local and world events, occupying the center of the page (figure 4.15). Numerous papers ran such images of the singer arrested on drug charges, and she became fodder for all kinds of rumors about her criminal nature. Earlier the same month, on August 1, *El Mundo* had headlined an article dissecting the "political inclinations of artists in Puerto Rico." Lucecita's portrayal is vastly different from that of her colleagues in music and television, with an open mouth (second at the left, under "Pro-Independence") and the caption: "Participates in many Independence Party and Socialist Party festivals." Contextualizing this "mouth" along the lines of Weheliye's sonic Afromodernity necessitates relating it to the mouth Paquito Cordero sought to police.

Most commentators believe that, upon assumption of her Afro, she was liberated from racial shackles and then repressed because of her leftist politics. Yet she clearly did not have this clear-cut trajectory and, moreover, this purely progressive and affirmative trajectory might be an example of a collective wish fulfillment but is not a description of this artist and does little to help us interpret her career and iconic importance. Rather, her various levels of meaning, from social to musical and back, can be read as the disordering and fugitive impulse Brooks, Moten, and Weheliye read as blackness. The artist herself spoke of why she was dangerous in the dominant culture's eyes and at-

FIGURE 4.15 The front page of *El Mundo* shows Lucecita being arrested for possession of drugs, August 25, 1976, in dead center.

tributed this to her orientation toward the true — an orientation that, on more than one occassion, she claimed she did not yet have words or an explanation for (bringing to mind Heideggerian aletheia).

Over the course of her career, her speech conflicted directly with what was legible socially, much as her body was also a zone of contestation between interpretations. Lucecita's statements to Ramos Otero and Ferré could be misinterpreted as an antipathy to the nothing. Yet, in fact, they put into play a very subtle reading of the nothing, showing that there is not a single nothing but several — that the nothing she describes in her *Zona* interview as "no sirve" (it's good for nothing) and rejects is not equal to the rhizomatic nothing that she claims for herself: "I am nothing."[60] The *Zona* interview I have referenced is one of those moments in the archive that allows a glimpse into her uncivil, fugitive speech, with little censorship, self or otherwise. Articles in *Claridad* verify the conflicting way in which her speech was received from the friendly left perspective, which, however, could impose its own set of demands on the artist. For example, in a review of the concert ¡Creceremos! of 1980, Rafael Rodríguez, the paper's music critic, wrote:

> Elsewhere, I have mentioned the difference between Luz Esther — the person — and Lucecita — the singer. Onstage, they become confused with the performer [intérprete] but one of them — Luz Esther — speaks and the other — Lucecita — sings. Luz Esther speaks less, way less. And when she does manage to speak she should always stick to the script she has practiced. The audience doesn't want to hear about "this fucking life. . . . We are screwed. . . . We all shit the same" [la fucking vida . . . , que estamos jodidos . . . , que todos cagamos igual]. All artists belong to their audiences [se debe a su público] and there is no need for that verbal aggression, not to mention the performative aggression [agresión escénica].[61]

Rodríguez mentions Caribe Hilton concerts in June 1977 and July 1978 as examples of good taste, curiously aligning the left project with bourgeois notions of what a pop artist should offer onstage to paying concertgoers. This critic seems quite upset at Lucecita's use of so-called foul language. Anyone who has seen her live can attest to this banter, alarming to some and delightful to others. A different use of obscenity happened out of the earshot of the audience, smack in the middle of a song's performance. She turned her back on her audience in the middle of a searing interpretation of a power ballad (perhaps Carrión's "Camino abandonado" or Alberto Cortez's "Qué tal te va sin mí" [How are you doing without me?]) and mouthed completely unrelated obscenities, addressing her musicians. The dialogue with fellow musicians in performance was more important — in fact, it was the anchor — of putting up a great show for the fans to enjoy. She never cared much for direct contact with fans, disliking the labor that musicians under contract had to perform in order to cultivate the fan base back then (such as greeting fans after a concert). These obligations were out of sync with her understanding of voice. Indeed, since her days as a youth star, she entertained an ambivalent relationship with fans and their relationship of identification with her — their demand that she be their "all."[62] This correlates with the type of reaction she sought to elicit, geared toward truth rather than emotionality or adoration, which in turn correlates with her relationship to technology and aligns her with Weheliye's constellation of the Afro-diasporic.

Since her career began, she had shown a propensity to create the track, that hallmark of musical modernity, possibly in a superior way compared to her contemporaries in pop music. From various interviews, I gathered that the artist's approach to laying down tracks was all business, in the best sense of the word. She understood what was at stake for each and every instrument when encountering the technological medium, and famously demanded perfection (as seen in the *Zona* interview when she said that her only regret was that it "didn't come out perfect"). During the 1970s, and not coincidentally after she ended her contract with Cordero, she explored amplification, particularly the microphone, essential to live performances. Around this time, multiple images, such as the album cover for *En las manos del pueblo*, display a good-sized microphone very close to her mouth. Steven Connor writes of the "touched sound" of the microphone. Against the easy interpretation of the microphone as phallic, he suggests, instead, "The grippings, bendings, brandishings, and more violent repertoire of 'tactations' effected upon the microphone seem to enact the determination that the production of sound should be not so much highly and spectacularly visible as visibly tangible, a plastic work of hands and mouth combined, an exteriorization of the minor agon of sound production in the mouth."[63] Connor makes it possible to understand Lucecita's filiation with the microphone as a way to focus on her music and not on her image.[64]

Mita Torres recounted how the artist routinely blew out microphones while she was testing them on trips to New York.[65] She needed a mike that could carry her volume, that would not fail technically during the moment of delivery and leave her in the nothing she deplored, in the state of "no sirve," of being "good for nothing." Musically, Lucecita transmitted her vocality in a very substantive way and targeted that "telephone receiver" that was the listener's ear which, as Freud commented, was connected to the "telephone" of the unconscious.[66] She did not want to evoke emotions or contribute to affects traditionally associated with music fandom, which stem from identification and plenitude. She wanted people to think, to pursue truth. Truth for her was not the social-realist message of protest songs, or the simple lyrics of equality between men and women in love ballads, much discussed in the pages of *En Rojo*.[67] Truth was transport, a moment of suspension when the listener was completely keyed into her voice, subordinating the social content, the symphonic arrangement, the conductor's authority, everything to that moment of transmission and reception, creating a fugitive subjectivity.[68] Her quest resonates with 1970s advances in media theory. Lucecita wanted to contribute to "an emergent structure of listening" "as a gateway to a new collectivity,"[69] one she did not recognize in the formations she witnessed around her and that competed to enlist her voice.

Nevertheless, she had to mine the Latin American political and sentimental repertoires for her live concerts. Seeking to assume a noncelebrity persona, Lucecita borrowed from the Latin American cantautor, the singer-songwriter embodied in various figures of the times, from Atahualpa Yupanqui and Facundo Cabral to Alberto Cortez and, although not Latin American, the Catalan with an important Latin American exile period, Joan Manuel Serrat. This is a notable and not sufficiently studied aspect of her innovation: how she crossed gender lines to claim a space and repertoire that was invariably gendered male. One of the critical elements in the performances of these singer-songwriters was, in fact, their use of declamatory song and their frequent mingling of spoken and sung stanzas, making it possible to address her statement, "I can sing, but I cannot speak."

As of this writing, readers with YouTube access can find a clip of Lucecita singing in the watershed *Siete días con el pueblo* (Seven days with the people), a weeklong series of concerts held in the Dominican Republic in 1974, at the time under the despotic rule of Joaquín Balaguer.[70] As in Puerto Rico, Dominican dissident singers were routinely followed and harassed and many were simply prohibited from performing in certain venues, especially outside of the capital city of Santo Domingo. The near seven-minute performance of Atahualpa Yupanqui's "Coplas del payador" (Folk verses) shows Lucecita's positioning in absolute artistic control and her quest for musical perfection; she is listening to her accompaniment, correcting the tempo, and tuning Pedro Rivera Toledo's guitar. (Somehow, she was able to hear the pitch over and above the noise in the wide open space.) The live footage is a rare opportunity to listen to her combining spoken and sung stanzas and witness her relationship to the mike as an expression of fugitivity, a play with the relative nothing she had taken care to assume by then. The ending minute and a half, with the simple, three-chord guitar accompaniment of the *milonga*, is:

Una canción sale fácil
Cuando se sabe cantar
Cuestión de ver y pensar
Sobre esas cosas del mundo
Si el río es ancho y profundo
Cruza quien sabe nadar

Cantor que cante a los pobres
Ni muerto se ha de callar
Pues donde vaya a parar
El canto de ese cristiano
No ha de faltar el paisano
Que lo haga resuscitar

Yo no soy jíbaro malo
Defiendo la honestidad
Una sola es mi maldad
Y se la voy a decir
Con todito mi sentir
Me gusta la libertad

[Recited] A song comes easy
If you know how to sing
It merely requires seeing and thinking
About life's things
If the river runs deep and wide
Only those who know how to swim can hope to cross [chuckle]

[Sung] Singer, you who sing to the poor
Not even death can silence you
Wherever the song
Of the faithful goes
There will be a fellow countryman
Who will bring it back to life

I am not a bad jíbaro
I simply defend honesty
I have but one flaw
Which I'm going to tell you about
With all my feeling
I like freedom

Lucecita adapted Yupanqui's *criollismo* by inserting the Puerto Rican phrase "jíbaro malo" right before the song aligns the first-person speaker with honesty and freedom. The apparent transparency of this discourse, its pared-down arrangement and bare-bones instrumentation, might make us forget that she is singing in a huge stadium in front of thousands of people and depending on the agon of her mouth meeting the microphone. Additionally, we may miss the fact that even in leftist circles of protest and social music, Lucecita's body is a far cry from the accepted feminine embodiment, and that her employ of the Latin Americanist repertoire points to an identification with meaning making more than it does with the relatively simple male fantasies of detachment and unmooring evident in the song "Coplas del payador" and other classics of the era that she performed and some of which she recorded. Listening to her today, in the tracks she created then, without factoring in this gender crossing yields an incomplete appraisal of her feat as an artist. Part of it is not noticing the conceptual density of her relationship to technology, exemplified by the microphone, in particular.

Her participation in events such as Una semana para el pueblo or her performances of "Traigo un pueblo en mi voz" and "La verdad" ("Le Lo Lai") in the 1970s are much different from the more familiar and, in historical terms, more recent delivery of "Oubao Moin" as her concert finale, taken from Juan Antonio Corretjer's fifth canto from the longer *Alabanza en la Torre de Ciales* (A song of praise in the Ciales Tower), a 1950 nationalist poem of protest and rebellion. The Puerto Rican singer-songwriter Roy Brown had recorded "Oubao Moin" as part of his 1977 record *Distancias* (Distances), in which he set to music ten Corretjer poems. Lucecita used "Oubao Moin" to end her concerts from the 1980s onward. This finale can be heard in the 1987 reprise of Traigo un pueblo en mi voz, which deployed the New Left repertoire when it was becoming archival. Mercedes Sosa herself had by then returned to Argentina and sought to record new songwriters, many working in *rock en español* and pop. The original finale, the song "Traigo un pueblo en mi voz," became a recycled curiosity as the signifier "pueblo" was fast being recoded. In 1987

Puerto Rico, the song was a symbol of the cultural nationalism historian Carlos Pabón meticulously and brilliantly deconstructed in *Nación postmortem* (Nation, postmortem), not necessarily of self-determination. Musically, the performance was a throwback to the New Left reverence for the male space of the Great National Poet, and the pop mythology of "authochthony" (in the song, the subjects of the so-called three roots of Puerto Rico — white, black, and indigenous — are celebrated in turn as examples of the revolutionary subject: "¡Gloria a esas manos indias porque trabajaban! / ¡Gloria a esas manos negras porque trabajaban! / ¡Gloria a esas manos blancas porque trabajaban!" [Glory to those indigenous hands because they toiled! / Glory to those black hands because they toiled! / Glory to those white hands because they toiled!]).

A generation of Puerto Ricans were acquiring Taíno names in the 1980s: Guananí, Urayoán, Bayrex, Bayoán, Ataveyra, Guarionex, Loaíza, Yoaíza, Yabanex, and several other chieftains and damsels in distress were recalled with awe by new parents who were professors, former activists of the 1970s, sympathizers of social justice causes, leftovers from the radical fringe of the 1970s, believers in Puerto Rican independence, and the new segment of folks who were "Puerto Ricanist" but not necessarily and often not leftist. Many fans of the 1970s patiently suffered through the middling repertoires of the late 1980s just to be able to hear the singer perform "Oubao Moin" one more time, with the bombastic, martial instrumentation Pedro Rivera Toledo created for the song (complete with bugle clarion call at the end), leading to the moment when Lucecita raised her left fist and sang: "¡Alabanza! ¡Alabanza! ¡Para ellos y para su patria, alabanza!" (Praise! Praise! Praise be to them and their motherland!). The listener had to extract Lucecita's voice from the inferior, shrill background vocalists that inexplicably worked with her through two decades, hampering her concerts and many recordings. And yet, through it all, the singer held the audience in thrall. Whether it was due to the waning of oppositional politics, or to her sound and execution, to nostalgia, or a combination, the footage of those performances today demands a reading separated from the exercise of personal memory. It should take very seriously the clash between the song's content and arrangement and the multilayered differences of the star body performing the song: By the 1980s, the singer had changed her persona completely. While the reasons were, in part, commercial, there may be others at play too. Her perfect execution (pitch, diction, and so forth) finally could coexist on stage with the obscene, street, and queer that had been repressed before. The political repertoire she became notorious for is inseparable from these truly scandalous elements, even if they were written out of discourse and directly censored (the Luz Esther / Lucecita dichotomy quoted above from *Claridad* is exemplary, but by no means the only instance; other characterizations were more extreme and directly insulting). By the same token, her romantic repertoire, long her specialty, should not be summarily dismissed as apolitical.

THE DIVA

Despite continual harassment and difficulty landing any gigs, Lucecita remained steadfast in her commitment to independence and to social justice. She thus became intrinsically related to meaning and truth beyond the realm of celebrity. Through the Socialist Party's annual Festival de Claridad and other such open-air events, principally Puerto Rico's numerous *fiestas patronales*, or patron saint town festivals, she retained a live connection with an audience. Left circles, looking to the futurity of the "new man," continued to have a hard time with sentimental song, deeming it an instance of false consciousness unless it straightforwardly represented equality between a man and a woman. Indeed, the topic recurred in the Socialist Party's newspaper's estimable cultural supplement, *En Rojo*, in which a wide array of articles dissected the *nueva canción* and *nueva trova* movements and the potential harm sentimental songs could portend for "the masses."[71] The left's support of Lucecita was important but partial. It ultimately did not know what to make of her and continued to be patriarchal and normative, homophobic and sexist, thereby reducing thought.

Eventually, because of her dire financial situation, she accepted somewhat perverse but well-paid invitations to appear at exclusive private parties of wealthy liberals, where she was invariably requested to perform "Génesis," a song she had outgrown.[72] For these occasions, she was outfitted after this elite's taste, in designer gowns evoking a normative femininity that was the polar opposite of the 1969 caped tux. Thus elites manipulated the artist through their twisted and privatized exercise of memory and their acquisition of power. They purchased a memory of the elusive moment when Puerto Rico broke into world fame but stripped this performance of thought and reformatted it to comply with heteronormativity.

It is incorrect to blame the artist's so-called difficult personality or her alleged personal afflictions or her political turn for the derailment of her career, as many commentators, fans, and associates have done. Several social actors — right, left, and center — had a share, in part through damaged or absent listening and a refusal to think voice. The right was the most problematic, since it aimed for outright suffocation of the voice. Imitating repressive regimes in South America and Spain, the state promoted what Daniel Party terms the *placer culpable* (shameful pleasure) of the 1970s balada, supporting artists who worked in this dominant, presumptively apolitical, and certifiable celebrity music.[73] The singer really had little choice but to return to the more normative realm of celebrity as it was expressed in music culture in the aftermath of the 1970s.

Lucecita's third and final iconic moment happened with her turn to hyperfemininity in the 1980s. It began with *¡Creceremos!* (1981), her first foray into recording after her six-year forced hiatus. Although mixed in terms of its concept, it is in tune with Lucecita's working-class, socialist sympathies while remaining faithful to her core, the ballad. The album art is vastly different from that of preceding years, reflecting a more limited budget for packaging and a virtually nonexistent budget or network for marketing, a recurring headache in the artist's career. Nearly all of these records had a companion concert, which was often the only marketing resource available and also the singer's chief way of making a living. Lucecita, much feminized, is portrayed holding a baby on the cover (Danny Rivera's daughter Soldanela). *¡Creceremos!* was her attempt to renovate her concept to appeal to dominant market taste while remaining faithful to her pursuit of artistic truth.

In 1981, coming out of a period of blacklisting, during which the artist maintained a full work schedule of local, live performances at political festivals, private parties, and especially fiestas patronales, the singer knew that she had to respond to market changes in Puerto Rico and tried to create a record that would respond to her left-leaning (though not militant) proindependence stance and her clear attraction to the melodramatic music she executed so well. *¡Creceremos!* (We shall grow together!) is, of course, an echo of *¡Venceremos!* (We shall win!), the celebrated phrase of the New Left and in the Puerto Rican context immediately connected to the Cuban Revolution. The eponymous title track opens with a fast, unrelenting tempo, unchanging high key, and uninterrupted crescendo. The lyrics herald an unspecified new order that will not be derailed by a series of subjects, from animals to social actors. The political "we" of the song is likewise unspecified.

¡Creceremos! includes two of Benítez's shining recorded performances. The first is "El aumento" (The raise), which became a hit on the Puerto Rican pop charts in 1981, serving notice that the singer still had her audience and that her voice was in prime form. Tite Curet Alonso, a giant of Latin American

songwriting (known for scores of salsa classics and for having written La Lupe's most memorable songs) wrote "El aumento" (although he is not officially billed as the songwriter).[74] Curet was a genius at writing for singers whom he regarded as unique, matching songs specifically to their temperament. Curet correctly identified that Lucecita was not a *sonera* (something the singer recognized, while stating, correctly also, "Yo tengo la clave" [I can sing with the beat]).[75] He wrote a salsa song laid out before the recording, requiring no improvisation from the singer or *descargas* (improvs) from the instruments. "El aumento" is not a *montuno* with a break followed by call and response. It is a virtuosic series of vocal leaps into progressively higher notes. "Tite says: 'Lucy has a fabulous lower register' and he writes something for me that starts low, goes to the mid-register and ends in a crescendo toward the high notes, the song's denouement."[76] "El aumento" alludes to salsa compositions as discourse, particularly referencing 1970s salsa's strong social content. The song allowed Lucecita to make use of her wide register, low, middle, and high, to surprise listeners with her seemingly effortless, rapid switches between notes, always perfectly on pitch.

"El aumento" sought to capture the moment of unrest happening in Puerto Rico after the long-term effects of the failed Estado Libre Asociado and the oil crisis of 1973 became the daily routine and could no longer be considered passing crises. During the 1970s, the headlines steadily reported increases in prices from basic food staples (like locally produced coffee) to electricity and water rates, to gas, among many other essentials. The 1981 UTIER (Unión de Trabajadores de la Industria Eléctrica y el Riego) strike pitted labor against the government and filled the newspaper headlines. The song's last section dramatizes a scene of repression, specifically a police arrest of a brown-skinned union leader, in obvious sympathy with the strikers from the utility company. The ending featured her friends, the actor Miguel Angel Suárez and noted broadcast personality Pedro Zervigón, reviving the heterotopia of the mid-1970s they had belonged to. The dramatization fades out to Lucecita's ending improv, also in fadeout:

Ya se llevaron al mulato Juan Barriento
Trabaja negro trabaja y nunca llega el aumento
Aumenta la gasolina, pero no aumenta mi sueldo

They just arrested the mulato, Juan Barriento
The black man works and works and the raise never happens
They raise the prices on gasoline, but they don't raise my wages

The other shining recording of *¡Creceremos!* is the medley "Romántica Luz, romántica voz" (Romantic Luz, romantic voice), a thirteen-plus-minute rendition of classic boleros. Political and sentimental still coexisted as Lucecita's two authentic natures that she refused to choose from.

"Luz" is Lucecita's given name and the name by which she was known in her inner circles. Lucecita scored a radio hit with the abridged version. "Romántica Luz, romántica voz" represented an attempt to move her away from the associations of her political repertoire by positing a mature, intimate Luz to the social Lucecita. As Arnaldo Cruz-Malavé points out, Lucecita's use of volume for creating intimacy and softness has gone unnoticed.[77] Proper music criticism, especially among cultured listeners, often remarked that she should only sing with small ensembles and not larger orchestras, that she should forgo excess instrumentation and especially loud accompaniment and focus, instead, on the softer singing associated with the artiste and that such listeners recall from her years as a regular in the Caribe Hilton hotel. "Romántica Luz, romántica voz" is a brilliant example of her vocal strategy, where volume serves to cement the bond between the listener's ear and the discursive register of intimacy. Volume relates to the "signal," in Douglas Kahn's initial sense, later developed by multiple theorists of transmission.[78] Essentially, volume and signal are interconnected; a signal tries to accommodate as much volume as possible in transmission. Lucecita clearly produced a reaction that short-circuited the conceptual apparatus and aimed straight at transmission, initially expressed through her love of the microphone. Transport is the success of transmission.

Further, by working through the theatricality of the repertoire, there is no room for the illusion of identification; it is, strictly, a drama, an experience of the moment without pretense of a future. This maneuver keeps the performance focused on the execution, with the goal of centering the bond between the performer and the listener on the transmission-transport dyad that the singer had made synonymous with truth. In a recent interview, the older Lucecita made her approach plain: "I'm selling you a love story, with characters and dialogues, and through the song I thread together a complete person for you. . . . You see them, there comes a moment when this creation materializes in your mind. When I touch you that way, a very intimate sensibility transpires."[79] The vocal performance Lucecita achieved in the medley "Romántica Luz, romántica voz" should be counted among the era's classic performances of intimate music, foregrounding both vocal power and vocal intelligence.

After *¡Creceremos!*, Lucecita resorted to producing her own records, eventually releasing albums under her own label, Lobo. The recording label name is an homage to Isla de Lobos, an island off the eastern coast where the group I alluded to as a heterotopia — the one that had been responsible for the famed political concerts of the 1970s and had supported the artist though her period of blacklisting — often spent time together.[80] "Lobo" is associated with self-determination, at this point, and of necessity, of the more individual variety as the artist now struggled as a working musician. Lobo's first release is *Criollo Folklore* (1983), Lucecita's first attempt to time a release for the Christmas season to ensure sales, catering to the upper-middle-class fondness for the nativist repertoire during these festivities only. *Criollo Folklore* is a jíbaro music recording. The title is not the catchiest; it has a ring of what was named *música de arte* at the time, that is, music that was partially financed by the state because it illustrated the "cultural storehouse," the legacy or *patrimonio*. While one can say that *Criollo Folklore* is musically proficient (with the exception of terrible background vocals), it suffers from an overly pedagogical approach to the problem of recovery, hinging on the basic nostalgic ploy of resurrecting jíbaro music while not addressing society's debt to jíbaro musicians and even the genre itself (chapter 3). It forgets that a true revival reconceptualizes the source and keys it into contemporary listening. Lucecita's renditions are flawless, but the album's calculus makes it sound detached.

The cover is its best feature, embodying Lucecita's call to a new cohort of fans. The album's insertion of the singer into the nativist music of Puerto Rico, signifying authenticity, clashes with this visual content. Jochi Melero's cover portrait of Lucecita encapsulates her 1980s diva embodiment: Lucecita looks arresting with big hair, heavy makeup, large earrings, and necklace (figure 4.16). While she had always dressed onstage and for the television camera in outfits tailored to her artistic needs, her deployment of high fashion in the 1980s was qualitatively different from earlier iterations. The glam creations targeted the upper bourgeoisie and carried with them social meanings that directly referenced social segregation and gender normativity. While this is a fact, it must be pointed out that this new costuming created horror too, particularly among those who looked upon Lucecita with disgust as a cross-dressing *marimacha* (tomboy) and did not mince words when expressing their homophobic hatred of the singer. The artist went on to develop this persona into the 1990s and revel in it.

FIGURE 4.16 The diva. Cover of the album *Criollo Folklore*, Grabaciones Lobo 001, 1983. Photograph by Jochi Melero.

The second Lobo release, *Éxitos callejeros* (1984), was apolitical, but the singer's deployment of a thinking voice resurfaced at the intersection where fans across classes, many women, many queer, met as nomads outside of the political deadlock in the island nation.[81] It is, perhaps, the most successful of Lucecita's 1980s albums in terms of a complete concept and widespread reception. Different from the abstract appeal of "Génesis" in the Cold War and from the liberal-to-left recourse to the people or the nation during the debacle of the 1970s, the call of this music was to the *calle* (street). The meeting ground proposed was abjection, a sort of bottom power, a sentimental politics.

"Éxitos callejeros" is, according to Pedro Rivera Toledo, an adaptation of a musician's term for a repertoire played live in street festivals and other such events ("tocados en la calle"), from which most of the working musician's income derives.[82] This repertoire, in theory, diverges from the songs chosen for recording on an album. Therefore, in a way the title alludes to the work that Lucecita had done, toiling through years of downfall and then relative obscurity, performing for left-wing, independence, and social justice causes in Puerto Rico. Indeed, the concerts and continued appearances in open-air events kept alive, so to speak, the artist's symbolic representation of such causes, even if her performance motifs were almost completely altered from the 1960s and 1970s and the politicized voice had ostensibly disappeared.[83]

All the tracks re-create very conservative portrayals of heterosexual love, sometimes in the moment of sex, sometimes unrequited love, relating to the mass fascination with illicit sexual behavior, ravenous sexual desire, and complicated triangles. Most of the songs are about sex; examples include the Lucecita concert staples "Cabalgata" (Horse ride), "Qué tal te va sin mí" (How are you doing without me), and "Decisión" (Decision). The repertoire belonged to established balada stars, like Roberto Carlos, Raphael Martos, Ángela Carrasco, and Rocío Dúrcal. It is probable that the Spanish singer Rocío Dúrcal was the primary visual model for Lucecita's new look. In the album's signature track, "Fruta verde" (Unripe fruit), copied with few modifications from Dúrcal's 1983 recording, her performance works saucy content into a melodramatic tour de force targeting the "feminine" listener and injecting pathos into a casual song. It is a departure from the more abstract versions of love that Lucecita had represented until then and a vast improvement over Dúrcal's rather bloodless interpretation. She gleefully unleashed kitsch, her main 1980s code, inciting the jouissance of soap opera in her listeners. (In fact, both versions were soap opera themes: Dúrcal's was used in Spain, Lucecita's in Argentina.) Low budget and low tech, the song was recorded in a makeshift studio, in the home of her former artistic director and the "Génesis" arranger, Pedro Rivera Toledo, who played most of the instruments. Rivera Toledo plays a sax solo during the song, referencing sensuality and carnal knowledge. It was squarely aimed at lowbrow taste, constructed as women's preference. As such, the recording went against the grain of Lucecita's more typical masculine identifications.

Fans responded with near frenzy at her encapsulation of hurt yet soulful feeling in this virtuosic power ballad. Bafflingly, Lucecita is not regularly included in lists of Spanish-language pop divas of the time, although arguably she executed the full melodramatic form in a more masterly way than the singers on such lists. Virtuosic vocal breaks, pitch contrast, and climaxes, delivered in a haunting lower register, distinguished her from other pop stars, male and female, with their thinner, higher voices and monotonous renditions. Her delivery overcame the clichés that abounded in the songs, as all the while she cut an imposing figure in full-length feminine gowns or elegant suits, salon hair, and sequins or star-studded jewelry. Despite the accoutrements, she was as strikingly butch visually as were her performances musi-cally, doling out pianissimos and fortissimos in equal measure.[84] Possibly her butchness is the reason she is excluded from diva lists. Compare her perfor-mances to those of her counterparts across the Spanish-speaking world, and she emerges as unmistakably, arrestingly queer in a voice that thinks.

Nostalgia (1986) would be Lucecita's last record pressed in vinyl. Like much of her late career, the record is conflicted. After several shattering events that rent the social fabric in the 1970s (the assassinations of Santiago Mari Pesquera and Carlos Muñiz Varela, and the Cerro Maravilla murders come immedi-ately to mind), the right wing had effectively severed the artist from the enter-tainment circuits and the press because she was identified with left causes.[85] *Nostalgia* was, to a degree, a ploy to regain footing in this powerful sector and access to the important Miami market. The album's tracks offer a mé-lange of Cuban sones, Puerto Rican rumbas and guarachas by Rafael Hernán-dez, Mexican standards by Agustín Lara, and one or two regional classics of the Latin American repertoire. The arrangements are fairly conventional copies of earlier 1950s recordings, intended to sound like ballroom music. Some critics referred to this repertoire as *bohemio* (bohemian), but this use signified much differently than the bohemian circle Ernestina Reyes frequented (chapter 3). It was class inflected as refined and superior. The back cover features photos clearly meant to evoke the golden age. Because of copyright disputes, the flip side was not reproduced on the CD. However, it must be recalled in order to re-create *Nostalgia*'s attempt to earn market forgiveness.

Nostalgia's portrait of Lucecita made up as a Madame Butterfly character, taken by Gabriel Suau, the same photographer (and friend) who produced her iconic Afro images of the early 1970s, can be read as a defiant rejoinder to those who would classify her diva, hyperfeminine incarnation as grotesque. Lucecita boldly displayed her looks, her rare relationship to the camera, and her singular truth as a quintessential star body. The operatic framing resonates with the virtuosity of her singing voice and reframes her angle of speech and expression into her third pop avatar, that of diva.

The success of "Fruta verde" combined with her new persona of diva led to records where Lucecita exploited fans' desire to hear her performance of *can-ciones cortavenas* (literally, "slit-your-wrists songs"), exaggerated, sentimen-tal songs about unrequited love that re-create a depressed affect ("Mujer sin tiempo" [A timeless woman], "Gaviota del aire" [A seagull of the wind]). Such songs were often featured in the soap opera programming of the Argentinian Alberto Migré, creating an audience that still follows the singer faithfully whenever she plays in Buenos Aires, screaming out their requests for various late 1980s hits. For several years she gave concerts with this concept with relative success. She enjoyed a solid following in the Southern Cone countries and often would threaten her Puerto Rican audiences by saying, "¡Me voy a la Argentina!" (I'm leaving you and going to Argentina!). Many fans believe she actually relocated to Argentina and visited Puerto Rico for professional purposes, and not the other way around.

Her fandom divided into two camps. One delighted at the artist's change and presumptive end of the long political song nightmare. Another experienced something akin to a loss of meaning, a cultural melancholia. Full disclosure: I was one of those forlorn fans who continued attending concerts throughout the 1980s waiting for the real Lucecita to come back. Like all fans worth their salt, I was convinced I knew what she should sing. I did not like the repertoire, costume, affect, or anything else of this 1980s incarnation. With time and study and critical listening, I've realized that a thinking voice lurks also in that last iconic moment of her career.

Now in her seventies, Lucecita is still singing and occupying her role, however emptied, as La Voz Nacional de Puerto Rico (Puerto Rico's national voice). Yet no renewed iconicity emerged after the 1980s. Instead, she regularly recycled her three prior avatars into concerts appealing to the nostalgia market and released disparate records with wildly differing concepts, none of which took. In the neoliberal 1990s, anything could be consumed, and everything was flattened to suit consumption, so that her live appearances, CD releases, and rereleases of her old records all became the same cultural nationalist product, drained of a thinking voice.[86]

In terms of community, something she clearly cared about since she was young, the artist was left with a trite insistence on love and an unresolved demand for restitution. "Puerto Rico doesn't love me," Lucecita repeated insistently through the 1990s. Yet, as listeners today, we can orient our sense of hearing to what is allegorical in the voice, to its pastness, tuning into the artist's call to restitution by listening to "the contemporaneity of the audible."[87] More than most artists of her time, Lucecita embodied and stood by voice's desire to articulate truth and speech in unjust late colonial modernity and its celebrity culture. As an object culled from recordings, footage, recollections, archive of images, and print, through which she lives in a celebrity afterlife, she continues to compel us to think voice. "I have always preferred to sing. Each place has its ambiance, its folks, its music. Of course, people in stadiums want to dance and they're not interested in thinking. They don't want to be stopped in order to pause. When you sing in front of multitudes, it's very difficult to create silences. But you can accomplish it. . . . I have."[88]

EPILOGUE
NOTHING IS SOMETHING

Myrta Silva's signature song, "Nada," became an albatross after the 1950s. Silva was expected to perform the song well after her interest in it had waned. In footage of the early 1970s, Silva forgets the lyrics to "Nada" during a tribute to Rafael Hernández at the Institute of Puerto Rican Culture. She finally blurts out, "I forgot the words. What was it, something about getting a divorce? I think I have sung this so many times my brain doesn't want me to sing it again."[1] Silva is intentionally deceptive. She had performed forgetting and changing the lyrics to the same song before. In fact, her entire recitative had been filmed in the Banco Popular 1965 tribute to Hernández. Silva was not forgetful; she was stating the musical need to move on. But the 1970s did not allow her to; the *pista* (canned musical accompaniment) ruled and she was reduced to lip-syncing her own songs and changing her aesthetics to suit the increasingly corporate taste that television demanded. Vocal performance on television was no longer live, the meat and potatoes of Myrta.

As with any entity, the nothing had an afterlife. While distinct from Silva's marvelous play with her figure as a void, Lucecita Benítez, from "Génesis" on, created a rhizomatic nothing that updated Silva's version. From queer masculinity (the auteur of "Génesis"), through Puerto Rico's "wild transfer-ence" in the political sign in the 1970s (the artiste of "Soy de una raza pura"), to hyperfeminine yet very butch normativity (the diva of "Fruta verde"), she showed remarkable dexterity as an artist reluctantly immersed in celebrity culture and paradoxically constrained precisely by her innate star quality and capacity to transmute visually.[2] Against any demand on the artist to confess to salacious truths that would settle and confine her voice's meaning, throughout her career her reticence — her desire to signify only her persona and keep her person to herself — stands out. Unwittingly or not, she danced around celebrity's strictures and kept the focus on vocal performance, impelling her public toward an exercise of thought through the sense of hearing and the act of listening. This is, in Heideggerian terms, the "gift" of the thinking voice.

Along this book's way, Ruth Fernández seemed distant from this gesture of "full emptiness" that renders the Thing as "both present and absent."[3] If Myrta Silva embodied the lewd and obscene in the face of bourgeois morality, mobilizing the ethnic against the grain of dominant culture, Fernández chose to represent a vision aligned with the dominant classes and social normativity. One interpretation of her decision is to see it as a product of having few options. Society and the music industry impinged heavily on Fernández because of their racist interpretation of her voice. She stressed respectability, indeed, and yet the goal of attaining respectability does not suffice to explain how, in retrospect, Fernández presented her career and indeed entire life as the successful product of populism in Puerto Rico and specifically as a success story of the Popular Democratic Party. As she stated on a Mexican television show of the early 1980s, *Desnudo total* (Stripped bare; a show that purported to understand the strange island in order to present its reality to the rest of Latin America), "I got ahead in Puerto Rico thanks to the Popular Party. As a woman. As the first black woman to sing. The first black woman to be able to sing in a first-class hotel. The first black woman who could attend school. The first black woman who was elected to any senate in the world."[4] Clearly, she was well aware of her symbolic power, scoping out what kind of femininity she could assume from the nonfemininity the dominant gaze and listening imposed. Thought around this figure revolves around a particularly difficult question: Was this merely a trickster strategy or did she in fact fill her emptiness with this societal meaning, even as elite society spewed hateful racist remarks about her (out of earshot, of course)?

Ernestina Reyes, as we saw, was very neatly cataloged as the greatest of all the singers working in her genre of jíbaro music. Although by all accounts she was very far from being a melancholy self, she was easily slotted into this nothing required by nationalist affect because the entire genre was formatted and packaged as a music of evanescence. Of the genres studied, guaracha, bolero, bomba, plena, and balada, country music was put the most at governmentality's service and understood the most in terms of a biopolitics of the nation, going as far as to classify the entirety of jíbaro as white and Hispanophile, in an example of Foucault's "state racism."[5] Women appear in close to misogynistic terms, whether because of morals, lack of talent at decimar (improvisation), or as nonexistent social subjects. Out of this anonymity and near-total oblivion, out of this intense polarity between adoration and derision if not hatred, the figure speaks most loudly.

It should have become clear by now that I do not believe in the ideology of the great woman singer, the specificity of the female voice, the logic of women's resistance, or the inherent beauty of feminine music. If I have studied the great woman singer, if I have put her to the test, it has been to perform a critical listening that will help undo these practices. I have taken my cue from the four singers I have studied, not as champions of anything but rather as placeholders of the nothing.

I have, so to speak, played variations on this nothing throughout the book. Myrta Silva had the greatest conceptual separation from, and therefore the most theoretical understanding of, her voice. She also executed voice in many more capacities than singing, yet her various manifestations were masterfully connected through parlando and the extimate. Mocking fantasies about female vocalists, directly concerning herself with a radical negativity, she is truly the template for the entire book. She knew she was a phobogenic object — causing anxiety — and incorporated the anxiety she provoked into her act, aligning it perfectly with her vocal performance. The position of woman as doll, being surveilled constantly by the male gaze, was re-created in the refrain from an early hit, predating her persona, penned by Rafael Hernández. Silva sang, "Mujeres, no se duerman / que los hombres las están velando" (Women, don't be caught unawares / Men are watching you). Her cadence transformed the doll into a ferocious boomerang returning a quite different entity after "Nada," fully owning the acousmatism of the part-object.

Ruth Fernández, as a black woman singer who did not meet society's criteria for its preferred myths about black women as sexual objects, also had to establish a separation from the nothing she was threatened with being since her birth. She constructed a public musicality out of the void created by racist conceptions of black contralto voices. She did not relate to singing as conceptually as Silva, and her manifestations of voice outside of her own musical career lacked Silva's unsettling capacity. She was unsettling to multiple quarters simply because her great voice existed and labored in a world that was not welcoming and that did not care to really listen. Hortense Spillers writes, "Frantz Fanon spoke of the 'Negro of the Antilles' [and by association, any Negro] as a 'phobogenic object, a stimulus to anxiety.' It would be useful to know, however, how bodies in general, respond to bodies not like our own, and what it is that 'sees' — in other words, do we look with eyes, or with the psyche?"[6]

Fernández allows us to factor in the sonic as a source of anxiety when "it is no like our own" and continue the discussion of the acousmatic part-object of voice by drawing on racial theory and its treatment of acousmatic blackness. Do we hear with ears, or with the psyche?

Ernestina Reyes's thought process regarding her voice is opaque to us, thanks to the nature of dominant print sources, which ignored jíbaro music or any cultural expression that was not middle- or highbrow. I could not find any reportage on her performances, or interviews with the artist in any venue I consulted. A valuable trove of recordings enchants but is also, oddly enough, hard to crack open as a signifying system of the always already past, a mandate exacerbated in the case of women. Jíbaro singers faced a dilemma of existing different from that of individuals like Ruth Fernández, who could at least aspire to be exceptions, hateful as the suppositions surrounding exceptions were. Country music singers were seen as cogs in a collective subject and were expected to represent the past, not to inhabit the modernizing present. To add insult to injury, they were expelled from the home that much of their singing celebrated. And they barely could make a living on music. Such was their particular nothing to bear, from which they created their lasting corpus, Ernestina Reyes among them at the hallowed top.

Lucecita Benítez directly refuted any injunction to represent anything, and continues to do so. She navigated through circumstances of naked profit making, first, and life-stifling persecution of dissidence, second. Uncannily perfect in song, she searched for silence and thought in her audiences, which she extracted through pure manipulation of vocal sound. Contrary to the "lyrics to listen to" with which I began, verbal content was truly secondary. The relationship to reception was real, but abstracted, happening in another realm. In a way, her temperament is Nietzschean, philosophical to the end, uninterested in common ideas of what one says and how. She was the beginning of the book, when I invoked her "I am nothing," and she is the end of the book, its arrival at the thinking voice. After the mid-1970s, she spoke of having encountered "poets" (songwriters she could relate to) and "serious poetry" or simply "poetry" (referring to stanzas that compelled her to sing them). I often wondered at her use of the poetic as a descriptor of a certain synchronicity that had eluded her in her prior repertoire and that she began to encounter in the 1970s. Giorgio Agamben wrote a treatise on the relationship of poets to their times, basing his thoughts on Nietzsche: "Contemporariness is, then, a singular relationship with one's own time, which adheres to it and, at the same time, keeps a distance from it. More precisely, it is *that relationship with*

adheres to it through a disjunction and an anachronism. Those who
)o well with the epoch, those who are perfectly tied to it in every re-
lot contemporaries, precisely because they do not manage to see it;
)t able to firmly hold their gaze on it." Lucecita's synchronicity was
nchrony," which, as Agamben helps clarify, does not mean she was
nostalgic or living in another time.[7]

What ties these chapters together is their variations on a common theme of
nothingness, gender, and song. Clearly, there should never be a great woman
singer, just singers; one should not have to practice defamiliarization in order
to listen to women; one should merely react to the unmediated voice and
decide on its significance, merits, or value. I have heard versions of this ob-
jection to a study of gender and voice, and these unfriendly statements have
helped me grasp just how difficult the attempt to "change listening itself" (to
recall Barthes) is. There are a great many prejudices directed at, as well as
received ideas about, women singers. Many are unconscious. All are problematic. I selected these four women specifically because, in their figures, the
impossibility of this business as usual is embedded a priori. It is in this sense
that I consider their careers as feats, not because they succeeded as symbols,
but rather because they never ceased to be allegories.

By insisting on their allegorical nature, in the Benjaminian sense, it should
be clear that I do not advocate a utopia when singers such as these will be freed
from limited to nonexistent listening. Why not listen to women as the social
subjects they are? Can we really envision, within our horizon, a time when
voice will not be grasped through gender? Should this be a goal? These are
questions for other books. What I've pursued in this one is a reckoning with
a sonorous past. I have set in motion a call that these particular existences,
belonging to that past covered by gender (here I'm riffing once more on
Hortense Spillers's discussion of the subject "covered" by race),[8] be listened to
with their historicity in mind.

Voice is a cultural artifact, a product of culture, at the same time that singular manifestations of voice ask "big questions about their cultural moments and
the crises and problems of their time."[9] These "big questions" are sometimes posed directly, in immediately recognizable form. At others, the
questions may be more latent or implicit, slower to come to the fore. I have
employed Giorgio Agamben's archaeological method to offer a particular
variant of reconstruction and a particular mode of archival work.[10] Instead
of elegiac and nostalgic, lamenting the obsolescence of so many objects and

experiences — or, conversely, trying to animate or resurrect them to restore the archive to its plenitude — I aimed for getting as close as possible to the arkhé in order to unsettle protocols of listening and challenge the distribution of the sensible that kept — and possibly still keeps — a whole class of subjects on the outside it demarcates.[11]

NOTES

INTRODUCTION

All translations from Spanish are my own.

1. Venegas Lloveras, *Marzo dos*, 215.

2. Diego Manso, "Lucecita Benítez: 'Yo no canto tonterías.'" *Revista Ñ*, June 14, 2013.

3. Foucault, *The History of Sexuality*, vol. 1.

4. *Le partage du sensible*, the distribution of the sensible, is Jacques Rancière's well-known concept. See Rancière, *The Politics of Aesthetics*.

5. Feminist scholars have considerably complicated this narrative. Farah Jasmine Griffin (*If You Can't Be Free*) on Billie Holiday, Judith Halberstam (*Gaga Feminism*) on Lady Gaga, Gayle Wald (*Shout, Sister, Shout!*) on Sister Rosetta Tharpe, Laura Gutiérrez (*Performing* Mexicanidad) on Mexican cabaret stars, Deborah R. Vargas (*Dissonant Divas in Chicana Music*) on the "dissonant divas" of the Texas border, Alexandra T. Vazquez (*Listening in Detail*) on Cuban music, and Shane Vogel (*The Scene of Harlem Cabaret*) on Harlem cabaret come to mind as examples of how the study of female stars is at a much different place than when I began this book a decade ago. These scholars debunk dominant narratives, in which female stars don't have complex histories or put a great deal of intelligence into their performances.

6. Many works have discussed this problem of listening critically. See, for example, Kun, *Audiotopia*, who takes his cue from his objects of study, in a move that is similar to mine in this book: "Kafka's dog performs the same kind of critical listening that Los Tigres [del Norte] do, the same kind of listening that all of the subjects in this book do — a critical listening that does not necessarily reject consensus or harmony, but questions its default functionality as an apparatus of obligatory group belonging and nationalist solidarity" (16). In this book, I privilege dissonance over harmony, following Vargas, *Dissonant Divas*, but do not discourage and, when called for, document the positive affects that may be created by liberating "spaces of music" (Kun, *Audiotopia*, 22). I do, however, query any "sanctioned citizenship as women members" within nationalist formations (Vargas, *Dissonant Divas*, ix).

7. "The individual in the collective traversed by 'race' — and there are no known exceptions, as far as I can tell — is covered by it before language and its differential laws take hold." Spillers, "'All the Things You Could Be by Now,'" 378.

8. Monsiváis, "'Los que tenemos unas manos que no nos pertenecen,'" 50.

9. Agamben, "Philosophical Archaeology," 230.

10. Rubén Torres, "En PR al igual que en todo el mundo, la música busca la libertad" [In Puerto Rico and elsewhere, music searches for freedom], clipping found in the Oscar Hernández Scrapbook, Fundación Nacional para la Cultura Popular, San Juan, Puerto Rico; source and exact date not available, circa 1968 or 1969.

11. Benjamin, "Allegory and *Trauerspiel*," 166, translation modified.

12. "My method is to read patterns of adjustment in specific aesthetic and social contexts to derive what's collective about specific modes of sensual activity toward and beyond survival. Each chapter focuses on dynamic relations of hypervigilance, unreliable agency, and dissipated subjectivity under contemporary capitalism; but what 'capitalism' means varies a lot, as each case makes its own singular claim for staging the general forces that dominate the production of the historical sensorium that's busy making sense of and staying attached to whatever there is to work with, for life.... [Affect's] activity saturates the corporeal, intimate, and political performances of adjustment that make a shared atmosphere something palpable and, in its patterning, releases to view a poetics, a theory-in-practice of how a world works." Berlant, *Cruel Optimism*, 9, 16.

13. Lacan, "Subversion of the Subject," 693. Lacan discussed the voice as a part-object in *Anxiety*. Mladen Dolar has brilliantly glossed Lacan's contributions to the study of the voice (extending their application in multiple manifestations as objet a) in *A Voice and Nothing More*.

14. Molloy, "La flexión del género en el texto cultural latinoamericano," 54.

15. Freud, "Recommendations to Physicians," 357, 360.

16. Szendy, *Listen*, 122.

17. Glasser, *My Music Is My Flag*, 168.

18. Carpentier, "Del folklorismo musical," 44.

19. "One day Ogilvy observed that the program for industrial development was going well, with hundreds of new factories, but if they were not careful, they would turn that lovely island into an industrial park. What do you suggest? asked [Teodoro] Moscoso. 'Well, my native island Scotland was always regarded as a barbarous place until Rudolph Bing went to Edinburgh and started the Edinburgh Festival. Why don't you start a festival?' Moscoso made a note in his little diary. Three months later, he persuaded the cellist Pablo Casals to come to live in Puerto Rico and start the Casals Festival of Music. In one ad, instead of showing Pablo Casals just sitting there, playing the cello, which Ogilvy said would have been a 'visual bromide,' the photograph showed an empty room, with a cello leaning against a chair. The evocative scene, described by a creative man as 'lit by Vermeer,' became a classic." Roman, *The King of Madison Avenue*, 94–95. Although Moscoso was put in charge of the Festival, as head of the Compañía de Fomento Industrial, the official invitation came directly from the governor, Luis Muñoz Marín, acting on the advice of Abe Fortas, in 1955.

20. Berlant, "On the Case," 665.

ONE GETTING OFF . . . THE NATION

1. *"I'm a winner.* Yo nunca he fracasado en mi vida. Mis fracasos fueron en los primeros años . . . desde que yo me hice figura, ya más nunca fracasé." Myrta Silva, interview by Gilbert Mamery, Mayagüez, Puerto Rico, February 10, 1973, Díaz Ayala Collection of Latin American and Cuban Music, Florida International University, Miami.

2. Silva's exact date of birth is a bit of a mystery. Accounts vary, from 1922 from 1927. Silva herself gave the date as 1925; she says she arrived in New York City just shy of turning thirteen, in 1938. Myrta Silva, "Gran serie 1: Esta es mi vida" [Great series 1: This is my life], as told to Elsa Fernández Miralles, *El Nuevo Día,* February 25, 1975, 25. This self-narrative appeared in five parts on five consecutive days.

3. See Glasser, *My Music Is My Flag,* 129–168. On the guaracha, see Moore, *Nationalizing Blackness,* 54–56. Arcadio Díaz-Quiñones offers a useful discussion in his "Introducción" to Luis Rafael Sánchez, *La guaracha del Macho Camacho.*

4. Silva, "Gran serie 1," 25.

5. *TV Radio Mirror,* August 1966, 66–67.

6. Jerónimo Berenguer, "Por labor en TV, Myrta Silva recibe premio de revista" [For her TV work, Myrta Silva receives magazine prize], *El Mundo,* July 6, 1967, 54.

7. Sullivan later apologized. See Arturo Díaz Rivero, "Myrta Silva: Yo no creo ni en Ed Sullivan" [Myrta Silva: I believe in nothing, not even Ed Sullivan], *TV Guía,* November 9–15, 1968, 26.

8. *Myrta Silva, los compositores, su música y anécdotas* [Myrta Silva, songwriters, their music, and their anecdotes], episode on María Grever, exact date of broadcast unknown, 1981, archives of TuTV, San Juan, Puerto Rico.

9. See Muñoz, *Cruising Utopia,* 169–183.

10. Silva, "Gran serie 1," 27.

11. Glasser, *My Music Is My Flag,* 116.

12. Silva, interview by Mamery.

13. Silva, interview by Mamery.

14. Pedro Malavet Vega quotes newspaper accounts of the young Silva triumphantly arriving in Puerto Rico with Rafael Hernández and the Cuarteto Victoria in 1939: "She is a fan of the bongo and one of the best maraca players around." "Música popular en Cuba y Puerto Rico," 132.

15. Silva's trademark headscarf, which would become part of her Chencha costume, comes from this pose a la guarachera. See Robreño, quoted in Moore, *Nationalizing Blackness,* 53.

16. Laura Gutiérrez, *Rumberas in Motion (Pictures),* unpublished manuscript.

17. Available on DVD as *La música de Rafael Hernández.*

18. I thank her friends and colleagues, the late Mariano Artau, Velda González de Modestti, and Helen Monroig, for sharing their affectionate recollections of Silva. I also thank Glenn Monroig, who characterized Silva memorably as "a power dyke in an

age of men" (Monroig, interview by Licia Fiol-Matta, San Juan, Puerto Rico, March 8, 2007), and Miguel Ángel Hernández.

19. On the polymorphously perverse, see Freud, "The Archaic Features and Infantilism of Dreams."

20. Myrta Silva, performing live in a tribute to Rafael Hernández, Instituto de Cultura Puertorriqueña. The exact date is unknown, possibly mid-1970s. Edgardo Huertas, personal collection. With thanks to Tristana Rivera.

21. Enrique Rosado, a prominent Mexican radio pioneer, recounted how Silva's recording of "Mis tres novios" was indelibly marked in his memory of attending the circus as a small child in Mérida (Personal communication, January 19, 2007). Silva recalled how her songs were played on street organs in the cities she visited (Silva, "Gran serie 1," 26).

22. In "Musical Personae," Philip Auslander defines musical persona as "the version of a self that a musician performs qua musician" (104) and speaks of the musician's "front" as "a point in which performances intersect with larger social contexts" (108). Further, he writes that "musical persona varies with the performance situation, and may reflect the definition of that situation more than the musicians' individual personalities" (110). In Auslander's definition of musical persona, audience and genre play as large a part in the emergence of persona as does the musician's individual temperament. Auslander indicates that the audience and genre framing might tilt the balance of a persona and that audiences are heavily invested "in the performance personae they help to create" (115).

23. Nancy, *Listening*, 40.

24. See Auslander's discussion of music and other recordings as performance in *Liveness*.

25. The "quilting point" is "the point at which the signifier stops the otherwise endless movement of the signification" (Jacques Lacan, quoted in Dylan Evans, *An Introductory Dictionary of Lacanian Psychoanalysis*, 149).

26. It is next to impossible to translate this refrain: "Aw shucks, shucks, shucks, this rumba is driving me crazy, I'm fed up with this rumba."

27. The early Silva correlates with the three characteristics that Donald R. Dudley identifies with the cynical life: "Cynicism was really a phenomenon which presented itself in three not inseparable aspects — a vagrant ascetic life, an assault on all established values, and a body of literary genres particularly well adapted to satire and popular philosophical propaganda" (*A History of Cynicism*, xi–xii). The *guaracha picaresca* provided more than enough stock characters and situations to stand in for the literary genres Dudley speaks of. With thanks to Noel Luna for the reference.

28. Silverman, *The Acoustic Mirror*; Felman, *The Scandal of the Speaking Body*.

29. Sigfredo Ariel, interview by Licia Fiol-Matta, Havana, Cuba, December 22, 2006.

30. Manuel Villar, interview by Licia Fiol-Matta, Havana, Cuba, December 23, 2006.

31. The reference is to Jean-Paul Sartre, *Saint Genet*. Pozo is one of Cuba's most important musical geniuses. Tragically and mysteriously, Pozo had multiple run-ins with the law and reportedly suffered from a violent nature.

32. René Espí, interview by Licia Fiol-Matta, Havana, Cuba, December 23, 2006.

33. "In the present, yes, there is 'someone.' The 'someone' that perhaps will make me feel, at long last, and that in reality, true love is knocking on my door. The love I have been seeking, a full, absolute, generous love, the kind that asks for nothing and gives it all. Will I remarry? I don't know. I'm married to my career and the bond is too strong. Not everybody can share it." "Myrta y el amor" [Myrta's love life], *Revista Estrellas* 18, no. 228 (1987?): 63. Special issue with a forty-three-page spread commemorating Myrta Silva upon her death; the magazine reprinted an earlier, commemorative edition, which was vol. 4, no. 37 (1973): *Myrta: ¿retiro definitivo?* [Is Myrta retiring for good?] In the 1960s, Silva began to mention a one and only, doomed love that "she preferred not to remember," and in the 1970s the tale had developed into a pregnancy lost to an accident and a tale of sacrifice to pursue her supreme object, music. When I tried to fact check this marriage and pregnancy, I could not find a single mention of it in the Mexican press during the year it had supposedly transpired, when David Silva was enjoying his peak success after the film *Campeón sin corona* and spent some time in Hollywood attempting a crossover. None of Silva's associates that I interviewed recalled any such marriage or pregnancy or period of distress. This is not to say it absolutely could not have happened, but that Silva's discursive turn toward explaining her musical output in terms of symptoms, suffering, and splitting, as compensations for the lack of heteronormative sexuality so in evidence in her life, as well as the relative absence of suffering, strike me as typical maneuvers on the part of commercially successful artists to protect their careers. I would, at the very least, urge caution when approaching self-discourse of this melodramatic and highly subjective variety when it comes to examining an artist's life. I would also avoid making individuals wholly responsible for their discursivity and instead regard it as a shared and self-conscious enterprise pointing to a problematic homophobia, sexism, and moral panic around artistic representations and the collective subject.

34. "Through her irreverent humor, singing style, and physical overendowment, she self-parodically subverted popular expectations of the delicate, fragile, and even sexy female singer. Although matronly, she was not at all a maternal figure but rather more of an androgynous image on television, her body and voice a social space of conflicting gender expectations." Aparicio, *Listening to Salsa*, 177.

35. Ngai, *Ugly Feelings*, 335–336.

36. Dolar, *A Voice and Nothing More*, 106. Also see Evans, *A Dictionary of Lacanian Psychoanalysis*, 58–59.

37. I employ "signifierness" after Jacques Lacan: "it is that which has a meaning effect" (*Encore*, 19).

38. Lacan elucidates the structure of the letter in the "Seminar on 'The Purloined Letter,'" demonstrating how meaning solidifies in the letter's endless passing from hand to hand, without ever containing a settled meaning.

39. Thanks to Lena Burgos-Lafuente for calling my attention to this song.

40. Silva, "Gran serie 4: Esta es mi vida" [Great series 4: This is my life], February 28, 1975, 28.

41. Nancy, *Listening*, 16.

42. Lacan makes multiple references to emptiness, fullness, the void, and the gap in his work. See Evans, *An Introductory Dictionary of Lacanian Psychoanalysis*, 71–72; Lacan, *The Seminar of Jacques Lacan, Book XI*, 20–23; and Lacan, *The Seminar of Jacques Lacan, Book I*, 108.

43. "'Chencha' tuvo la culpa" [It's 'Chencha's' fault], *Bohemia* (Havana, Cuba), July 27, 1947, 41.

44. "'Chencha' tuvo la culpa," 42.

45. "'Chencha' tuvo la culpa," 42.

46. See Yeidy Rivero, "Spectacles of Decency: Morality as a Matter of the Industry and the State," *Broadcasting Modernity*, 75–101. She discusses censorship in the radio as well as the preoccupation with decency in television. Also thanks to Yeidy for clarifying matters of censorship in Cuba as well as the fate of early Puerto Rican television footage (Rivero, personal communication, March 31, 2007).

47. "Yo le daba las inspiraciones, y él componía los números" [I conceived of the sketch, and he wrote the songs]. Silva, "Gran serie 2: Esta es mi vida" [Great series 2: This is my life] February 26, 1975, 50.

48. Silva, "Gran serie 1," 27. In an interview, the composer stated that "Chencha la gambá" was his most popular guaracha, and that it had broken all sales records. Don Galaor, "La musa traviesa de Ñico Saquito" [Ñico Saquito's playful muse], *Bohemia*, April 6, 1949, 102.

49. See Moore's discussion of the stage mulata in the Cuban *teatro vernáculo* in *Nationalizing Blackness*, 49–50. Moore writes, "In the guaracha and related genres, the *mulata* appears above all as the object of sexual desire, the epitome of wanton carnal pleasure. . . . The *guaracha* transforms the socially oppressed and marginal condition of black and mulatto women at the turn of the century, suggesting that they were only interested in sex" (50).

50. Moore, *Nationalizing Blackness*, 130.

51. Silva, "Gran serie 1," 27.

52. Szendy, *Listen*.

53. Lacan listed the nothing as a part-object along with the voice in "The Subversion of the Subject."

54. Jacques-Alain Miller writes: "The term *extimacy* is constructed on *intimacy*. It's not intimacy's opposite, becuse the extimate is precisely the intimate, even the most intimate — since *intimus* in Latin is already a superlative. This word indicates, how-

ever, that the intimate lies in the exterior, that it is like a foreign body." *Extimidad*, 14 (my translation).

55. Silva, "Gran serie 4," 29.

56. Velda González de Modestti, interview by Licia Fiol-Matta, San Juan, Puerto Rico, March 9, 2007; Helen Monroig, interview by Licia Fiol-Matta, Carolina, Puerto Rico, March 9, 2007.

57. The delirious subject is theorized across the writings of Gilles Deleuze and Félix Guattari; see *Anti-Oedipus* and *A Thousand Plateaus*.

58. I take "methexic" from Jean-Luc Nancy's well-known argument in *Listening*: "the sonorous [is] tendentially methexic (having to do with participation, sharing, or contagion)," (10).

59. With thanks to Chiara Medina for providing me a copy of the LP and information about its genesis.

60. Foucault describes the "care of the self" in *History of Sexuality*, vol. 3. His phrase "speaking truth to power" is eloquently discussed in *Fearless Speech*.

61. Lazo, "Three Facets of Pau Casals' Musical Legacy."

62. Heartfelt thanks to Patricia Vega for locating a copy of *Las canciones unidas*.

63. Silva, "Gran serie 1," 29.

64. "Myrta Silva, artista polifacética" [Myrta Silva, a multitalented artist], *Bohemia libre*, May 2, 1962, 78.

65. Lauren Berlant, in *The Female Complaint*, discusses how to love the conventionality of women's culture "is not to love something that constrains someone or some condition of possibility, it is another way of negotiating belonging to a world" (3). Berlant discusses sentimentality as an "intimate public" created "when a market opens up to a bloc of consumers" and makes these consumers feel that the commodity expresses their most intimate feelings. Berlant's articulation is useful because it allows us to comprehend Silva's self-discourse and her attachment to a conventional vehicle as in tune with her demand for social inclusion, not a pathological split based on speculations about her private life. Much before, the Mexican writer Carlos Monsiváis had discussed melodrama as an intimate public and feminine genre created for consuming publics, especially women, especially working-class women, throughout Latin America at midcentury. In this context, the bolero as commodity, as he has brilliantly written, is one of Latin America's most forceful records and vehicles of collective affect, cross-class relationships, and cultural belonging. See Monsiváis, "Bolero."

66. Silva, quoted in "Dualidad artística" [Artistic duality], *Revista Estrellas* 18, no. 228 (1987?): 57.

67. The tale of theft found its way to late-twentieth-century mass culture. In 1992, Angela Meyer, a well-known Puerto Rican actress, produced the six-part miniseries *Sylvia Rexach: Hasta el fondo del dolor* (Sylvia Rexach: Into the deepest well of pain). This soap opera re-creates the cultural accusation. Myrta Silva, played by the Puerto Rican soap opera and comedy star Gladys Rodríguez, is shown in a bar in New York

talking to Sylvia Rexach, played by Rexach's real-life daughter, also a soap opera staple of 1970s and 1980s Puerto Rico, Sharon Riley. The character Rexach tells the character Silva she is in New York to see what she can do to "get her son out of drug trouble." Rodríguez, playing Silva with an unconvincing, booming voice, asks the sobbing, hunched-over and drunk Rexach character, "Do you need money?" Cut to the next scene, when Rexach, back from New York, still drunk and crying, confesses to her daughter, the character Sharon Riley, "I sold two of my daughters." Bizarrely, Riley's participation in this mini-*telenovela* about her mother's life, starring as her mother (whom she uncannily resembles), is at odds with her appearance as the sole invited guest on Silva's 1981 program, *Myrta Silva, los compositores, sus canciones y anécdotas*, in an episode that Silva devoted to Rexach's oeuvre. Riley was warm toward Silva. Undeniably, the mini-telenovela of 1992 showed crass taste given that Silva had died a death five years before that her associate, Mariano Artau, poignantly described to me as "one she did not deserve" (Artau, interview by Licia Fiol-Matta, Río Piedras, Puerto Rico, March 8, 2007). Thanks to Perry Miranda for directing me to this miniseries, and to Carlos Andres Pérez, Sección Audiovisual, Universidad del Sagrado Corazón, for providing me with a copy for research purposes.

68. On Sylvia Rexach, see Rosaura Vega Santana, "Una canción llamada Sylvia."

69. "Fue el público latino de Nueva York quien me hizo a mí" [The New York Latino audience made me a star], Myrta Silva, "Tira y tápate" [Dodgeball], *Bohemia libre puertorriqueña*, January 28, 1962, A-32.

70. *The Myrta Silva Show*, Channel 47, exact date unknown, 1966 or 1967, YouTube, posted July 7, 2011, https://www.youtube.com/watch?v=vQtdwHhEIwk.

71. Dolar, *A Voice and Nothing More*, 13.

72. Myrta Silva, tape of *El Show de Myrta Silva*, Telecadena Pérez Perry, Channel 11, WKBM-TV, exact date of broadcast unknown, early 1970s. Edgardo Huertas, personal collection. With thanks to Tristana Rivera.

73. Žižek, "The Undergrowth of Enjoyment," 14.

74. Artau, interview by Fiol-Matta; González de Modestti, interview by Fiol-Matta; Monroig, interview by Fiol-Matta.

75. "The three main types of of parrhesiastic practice utilized by the Cynics were: 1) critical preaching; 2) scandalous behavior; 3) what I shall call the 'provocative dialogue.'" Foucault, *Fearless Speech*, 119. Lacan discussed ethics as a subject's relationship to their desire ("not giving ground on one's desire," in his famous formulation), in *The Seminar of Jaques Lacan, Book VII*.

76. "Every utopian fantasy construction needs a 'scapegoat' in order to constitute itself. . . . Every utopian fantasy produces its reverse and calls for its elimination. Put another way, the beatific side of fantasy is coupled in utopian constructions with a horrific side, a paranoid need for a stigmatized scapegoat." Stavrakakis, *Lacan and the Political*, 100.

77. I reference Jean Baudrillard, "Simulacra and Simulations": "It is the generation by models of a real without an origin or reality, a hyperreal" (166).

78. Baudrillard, "Simulacra and Simulations."

79. Silva, live performance in Teatro Colón de Mayagüez, Mayagüez, Puerto Rico, February 10, 1973, recorded by Gilbert Mamery, Díaz-Ayala Collection of Latin American and Cuban Music, Florida International University, Miami. Audiocassette.

80. "¿Qué hace este niño encaramado en la cabeza de este? Miren que Mayagüez tiene una fama media rara por ahí sabe . . . bájate . . . que se baje, que baje . . . bueno nene, si a ti te gusta la posición y él te aguanta, que sean felices . . . ¡festejen!"

81. *Myrta Silva, los compositores, su música, y anécdotas*, episode on Myrta Silva, exact date of broadcast unkown, 1981, archives of TuTV, San Juan, Puerto Rico. Related to the sinthome and queer life, see Lee Edelman's discussion of "sinthomosexuality" in *No Future*.

TWO SO WHAT IF SHE'S BLACK?

1. Pedro Malavet Vega gives the date as probably October 16, 1937. "Ruth Fernández," 4.

2. Ruth Fernández, interview by Marvette Pérez, June 20–21, 1999. Latino Music Oral History Project, National Museum of American History, Smithsonian Institution. I feel deep gratitude to Marvette Pérez for providing me a copy. A second part was recorded on April 3, 2001.

3. Costa, "Ruth Fernández," 30.

4. Fernández, interview by Pérez, 1999.

5. Díaz-Ayala, typescript, Cristóbal Díaz-Ayala Collection of Cuban and Latin American Music, Florida International University, Miami, undated.

6. The invitation from Rudolph Bing is recounted in multiple sources; see, for example, Sylvia M. Lamoutte, "Alma amable de la canción" [The kind soul of song], *El Nuevo Día*, September 18, 1988, 7. Glenn Sauls as intermediary for Rudolph Bing also appears in multiple sources; see, for example, Marilya Agostini, "Ruth Fernández llevará nuestro folklore al Metropolitan Opera House" [Ruth Fernández will take our folklore all the way to the Metropolitan Opera House], *Bohemia de Puerto Rico*, July 11, 1965, 4-A.

7. Fernández, interview by Licia Fiol-Matta, Bayamón, Puerto Rico, March 9, 2007.

8. Fernández, interview by Pérez, 1999.

9. Eric Hobsbawm coined the phrase "the short twentieth century" in *The Age of Extremes* to refer to the period 1914–1991, from the First World War to the fall of the Soviet Union.

10. In 1992, Vernon Boggs observed, "One of the enigmas of Afro-Hispanic music is the role of women. While women occupy center stage in terms of the lyrics, in person

they are usually relegated to the backstage of the music's production and its execution. . . . It can be argued that the world of music is similar to private clubs; all-male with exclusionary policies." Boggs, "Latin Ladies and Afro-Hispanic Music," 109, 118.

11. For brief accounts of her career, see Malavet Vega, "Ruth Fernández," and Alfredo Romero Bravo, "Ruth Fernández: Una leyenda viviente de la música popular."

12. I have attempted to listen to and view episodes of these shows but have thus far been unable to obtain any of this material.

13. As an older Fernández confided, "Everyone in Puerto Rico calls me Titi [Auntie] Ruth." Fernández, interview by Fiol-Matta.

14. Lacan, "Seminar on 'The Purloined Letter,'" 10.

15. Fernández, interview by Fiol-Matta.

16. Dolar, A Voice and Nothing More, 14.

17. See Freud's "Mourning and Melancholia," for an introduction to the discussion of identification.

18. Moore, Nationalizing Blackness, 130.

19. Mendi Obadike, quoted in Eidsheim, "Marian Anderson and 'Sonic Blackness,'" 646 ("Sound may summon the presence of blackness even without the attendance of black bodies").

20. "The tall, heavy-set Negro [sic] says she is a mixture of Spanish nobility and African slave. However, she does not recall having any identity conflicts. 'I'm just Ruth Fernández, Puerto Rican,' she said." Peggy Ann Bliss, "Singer as Senator: Ruth Fernández: I'd Put Humanity in Politics," San Juan Star, October 16, 1971, 33. See Fernández, interview by Pérez, 1999, for a detailed exposition of this self-narrative.

21. I'm following Benjamin, "The Work of Art in the Age of Its Technological Reproducibility" and "Little History of Photography," for the concept of "looking back at us."

22. Glissant, Caribbean Discourse, 120.

23. The three roots theory would become dogma in the ELA. For a view that both defends and seeks to explain the dominant "three roots" theory, see Babín, "The Inhabitants," 27–66.

24. Babín, "The Inhabitants," 123. "I was well aware that their reception was like they had a little piece of Puerto Rico." Fernández, interview by Pérez, 1999.

25. The political arm is Operation Commonwealth; the economic arm is Operation Bootstrap; and the cultural arm is Operation Serenity. Of the three, Serenity is the most vague. It never became law but nevertheless guided cultural policy. See Serra Collazo, ed., Explorando la Operación Serenidad, for an introduction to this critically important aspect of muñocismo (the name given to the time period as well as the policies of Luis Muñoz Marín, foremost figure of the PPD, main architect of the ELA, and elected governor of Puerto Rico for four successive terms, from 1948–1964).

26. I'm following Jodi Melamed's analysis in Represent and Destroy.

27. "This obedient type is the rhythmical type. . . . Any musical experience of this type is based upon the underlying, unabating time unit of the music—its 'beat.' To

play rhythmically means, to these people, to play in such a way that even if pseudo-individualizations—counter-accents and other 'differentiations'—occur, the relation to the ground meter is preserved. . . . The standardized meter of dance music and of marching suggests the coordinated battalions of a mechanical collectivity." Adorno, "On Popular Music," 460–461.

28. Costa, "Ruth Fernández," 29.

29. Fernández, interview by Pérez, 1999.

30. The architect Enrique Vivoni writes, "But material prosperity was not the only concern of the Ponce elite. The establishment and preservation of prestige as an index of 'belonging' and as a commodity that could, at given moments, remedy financial shortcomings, was a preoccupation of families throughout this period in which significant changes in the cultural and social scene were taking place." He speaks of an "urban Brahmin class" with a "compulsion for prestige." Vivoni Farage and Álvarez Curbelo, *Hispanofilia*, 222. Fernández clearly became affiliated with this class and identified with its cultural project. I thank Silvia Álvarez Curbelo for providing me with the reference. Álvarez Curbelo adds, "There is a junction at which various musical elements meet, both Creole and Afro-Caribbean, within musically European formats. It opens up possibilities in the wide spectrum of socio-economic positions that the audience represented. One could speak of a certain mobility through music" (Silvia Álvarez Curbelo, interview by Licia Fiol-Matta, San Juan, Puerto Rico, October 6, 2007). Álvarez Curbelo's argument implicitly leads to the pivotal role of listening in cross-class contact zones.

31. Abelardo Díaz Alfaro, "Ruth la negra, Ruth la blanca: En el homenaje a Ruth Fernández en Nueva York," *El Mundo*, February 16, 1963, S-10. This article is a reprint of a speech Díaz Alfaro gave on the occasion of Fernández's tribute in New York City for her twenty-five-years singing career, organized by the Centro Cultural y Recreativo, Inc., a local Puerto Rican club.

32. Fernández, interview by Fiol-Matta. This assertion appears in many of her interviews.

33. See Findlay's fascinating account of turn-of-the-century Ponce and the raced variations of decency and how various subjects responded to this injunction. Findlay, *Imposing Decency*.

34. Ruth Fernández, interview in *Raíces* (Banco Popular, 2001), documentary.

35. Álvarez Curbelo, interview by Fiol-Matta.

36. The first time she appears in the news record, she is not mentioned by name. In the society column in *El Imparcial*, under the title, "Comentarios sobre el último baile sabatino en El Escambrón" (Comments about last Saturday's dance at El Escambrón), we read: "La 'Whoopie Kids' trajo una innovación: una cantante de sones y blues" [The Whoopie Kids introduced an innovation: a blues and son singer], October 19, 1937, 28.

37. See López's groundbreaking chapter on Eusebia Cosme: "Re/Citing Eusebia Cosme," in *Unbecoming Blackness*, 63–111.

38. For Eidsheim's complex argument, see "Marian Anderson and 'Sonic Blackness' in American Opera." She speaks of "timbral blackness" as "not the resonance of a particular type of body; instead *it resonates in the listener's ear*" (646).

39. See Cristóbal Díaz-Ayala's account in *Música cubana: del areyto a la Nueva Trova*, 241.

40. *Ñáñigo: El espíritu afro-cubano de la música* (Ñáñigo: The Afro-Cuban spirit of music) was first released in 1955 as Montilla FM-54, with two different covers, one with the additional title, *Ruth Fernández Sings*. It was reprinted in Spain (1956) and France (1959).

41. Lamoutte, "Alma amable de la canción," 70.

42. See Carpentier's disquisitions on Amadeo Roldán and Alejandro García Caturla as examples. *La música en Cuba*, 464, 467.

43. "The conflicting tendencies of racism and cultural nationalism were resolved through a process of stylization. . . . Composers used many terms to describe the process of transforming Afro-Cuban expression commercially including 'purify' (*depurar*), 'make sophisticated' (*sofisticar*), 'dress with elegance' (*vestir con elegancia*), and 'universalize' (*universalizar*). They accepted as given the idea that street music did not constitute valid expression in its own right and needed to be altered in order to increase its mass appeal." Moore, *Nationalizing Blackness*, 134, 135.

44. Fernández, interview by Pérez.

45. See Ochoa Gautier, *Aurality*.

46. Ruth Fernández, "Candilejas: Del brazo con Ruth Fernández" [From the footlights: Guided by Ruth Fernández], *Alma Latina*, September 15, 1962, 75.

47. "Afrocuban imagery from the past seems to have been viewed both as more picturesque and as less controversial than contemporary expression. It could be freely reinvented on the stage with little or no regard for sociohistorical authenticity since it had never been carefully documented in its day. It had the additional advantage of avoiding sensitive issues such as contemporary racial conflict, discrimination, and black urban poverty that otherwise might have surfaced in the dialogue of the libretto. With the abolition of slavery in the 1880s, depiction of the suffering of Afrocubans under colonial authorities became a relatively noncontroversial means of incorporating 'serious' themes into the *zarzuela*." Moore, *Nationalizing Blackness*, 138–139.

48. Díaz-Ayala, *Música cubana*, 245.

49. Leticia Stella-Serra, personal communication, October 10, 2005.

50. Orovio, *Cuban Music from A to Z*, 4.

51. Ruth Fernández, with Obdulio Morales con su Orquesta Típica Cubana y Coros, *Ñáñigo: El espíritu afro-cubano de la música* (including "Mi Ochún," "Facundo," "Macongo," and "Chivo que rompe tambó"), *Vintage Cuba* no. 40, June 3, 1958.

52. Fernández, interview by Fiol-Matta.

53. Álvarez Curbelo explains that around this time "political marketing" started to coalesce and that the PPD, in particular, became interested in artists for propaganda purposes. Álvarez Curbelo, interview by Fiol-Matta.

54. Álvarez Curbelo, interview by Fiol-Matta.

55. "I am certain that someone of Ruth Fernández's stature received all kinds of news regarding entertainment and music, news about what Cubans were doing in variety theater, about vaudeville, the Harlem Renaissance. . . . All these influences are there. There is a sophistication in this sense to Ruth. A figure like her must be understood within this dense web. After singing jazz at the Casa Cabassa, she would switch to something else, a weepy bolero popular in those days or an Afro-Caribbean rhythm." Álvarez Curbelo, interview by Fiol-Matta.

56. Fernández, interview by Fiol-Matta.

57. Agostini, "Ruth Fernández llevará nuestro folklore," 4-A. "Some of the words in the letter were erased by Ruth's tears, when, undone by the surprise, she started to weep."

58. Rosario Guiscafré, "Hablando con Ruth Fernández: Imposible Separar a la Cantante de la Mujer" [A conversation with Ruth Fernández: It is impossible to separate the singer from the woman], *El Mundo*, April 13, 1963, S-10.

59. Blanco, *Elogio de la plena*, 45. The original Spanish reads: "Por todo lo demás la *plena* es — plenamente — blanca."

60. Carmen Reyes Padró, "La fiesta jíbara de Ruth" [Ruth's jíbaro party], *El Mundo*, November 1, 1972, 11-A.

61. Bliss, "Singer as Senator," 33.

62. Alberto González, "Habla Ruth Fernández: Llegar, llega cualquiera" [Ruth Fernández speaks: Anyone can make it], *Bohemia* 58, no. 201 (3rd series), February 5, 1967, 52.

63. Jerónimo Berenguer, "Unos 20,000 aclaman en N.Y. a Ruth Fernández, Aída Pujol" [Twenty thousand people give their acclaim to Ruth Fernández, Aída Pujol], *El Mundo*, July 19, 1965, 15.

64. I am indebted to John Pennino, archivist of the Metropolitan Opera House, for sending me a copy of the original program sheet. The program did not include notes.

65. Agostini, "Ruth Fernández llevará nuestro folklore," 4-A. "Poder llevar nuestra música a un sitio así, no era otra cosa que vestir a nuestro folklore de etiqueta" [To be able to take our music to a place like that is nothing less than dressing up our folklore in a tuxedo]; "Ruth Fernández y Bienvenido Bustamante tienen ahora en sus manos imponer nuestra música" [Ruth Fernández and Bienvenido Bustamante now shoulder the responsibility of making our music heard], (6-A). In the same article, Fernández is compared to Marian Anderson (6-A).

66. Richard D. Freed, "Music: Latin Rhythms at the Lewisohn," *New York Times*, July 19, 1965, 30.

67. Louis Snyder, "Latin-American Night at the Lewisohn," *New York Herald Tribune*, July 18, 1965, 8.

68. Pancho Cristal, liner notes, Ruth Fernández, *Yo soy la que soy* [(S) LP 1132], Tico, 1966.

69. "'I would be foolish to want Puerto Rico to be a state after traveling through the south of the United States and being treated as a second class citizen,' she said." Bliss, "Singer as Senator," 33.

70. Álvarez Curbelo, interview by Fiol-Matta.

71. Santiago-Díaz, *Escritura afropuertorriqueña*, 65–67, 71.

72. I have in mind Scott's discussion of infrapolitics in *Domination and the Arts of Resistance*. See also Lipsitz, *Footsteps in the Dark*, on the concept of "hidden histories."

73. The Institute for Puerto Rican Culture was founded in 1955. On the Libres de Música, María Luisa Muñoz Santaella writes, "Thanks to Law #365, submitted in the House of Representatives by its President, Ernesto Ramos Antonini, Esq., three Escuelas Libres de Música were founded, with the objective of attaining 'a methodical learning plan for our people's music education and of creating a favorable environment in which to foster music's development, which will culminate in the emergence of music bands that will inordinately assist in the elevation and the ennoblement of our everyday life [vida popular].' This bill, approved on April 20, 1946, was signed by the Interim Governor, Manuel A. Pérez." Muñoz Santaella, *La música en Puerto Rico*, 142. Muñoz Santaella adds that the Libres were transferred to the purview of the Institute for Puerto Rican Culture in 1950, that the conservatory was founded in 1960, and that the Libres became the conservatory's feeder schools. The Puerto Rican Symphony Orchestra was founded in 1958: "This entity was organized to comply with the dispositions of another bill submitted by the President of the House of Representatives, Ernesto Ramos Antonini, Esq., and was approved by the insular legislature and signed into law by the Governor of Puerto Rico, Luis Muñoz Marín, in 1957" (146).

74. The Casals Festival began in 1957. Jaime Benítez, then Chancellor of the University of Puerto Rico, first invited Casals to Puerto Rico in 1952. According to Reina Pérez, in 1955, the governor, Luis Muñoz Marín, heeding the advice of Abe Fortas, formally invited Casals to inaugurate a festival of classical music bearing his name. Roman states it was Teodoro Moscoso, on the advice of David Ogilvy, in 1957, shortly before the festival was inaugurated.

Interested readers should not miss the spirited discussion that played out over decades between Donald Thompson and Francis Schwartz on the pages of the *San Juan Star*, now collected in Thompson and Schwartz, *Concert Life in Puerto Rico*. "This festival was first conceived in 1956, to serve a number of symbolic and practical purposes. Symbolically, this was a means by which musicians and music lovers from the four corners of the world could assemble to honor Don Pablo Casals and the music with which he had become very closely associated. It was also spoken of as a symbolic gesture on Casals' own part: a means by which he could honor Puerto Rico, his mother's birthplace. But legislatures are seldom moved to vote heavy appropriations by sentiment alone (we hope). On the practical level of money and politics, the prime purposes were to open a previously untapped field of tourism by placing Puerto Rico on the international music festival circuit and to improve Puerto Rico's cultural image abroad, which would have a healthy effect on general tourism and other aspects of the island's economic development." Donald Thompson, "The Casals Festival," *San Juan Star*, May 30, 1971 (rpt., *Concert Life in Puerto Rico*, 119–120). Thompson points out, correctly, that the performing arts were never part of the Institute of Puerto Rican Culture's mandate or interest; rather, it was mandated by law to concentrate on the arts and crafts of the island's folklore, preservation of historic buildings, publications with particular mention of history and biography related to Puerto Rico, and other such endeavors. Donald Thompson, "The Culture Bills," *San Juan Star*, June 14, 1980 (rpt., *Concert Life in Puerto Rico*, 292–293).

75. "Casals was a special person in my life. He stated that popular music deserved respect and seriousness. He pointed out that people thought popular music was vulgar, but that wasn't so. There is good music and bad music. I have always felt proud, and have gotten great satisfaction out of being able to sing." Lamoutte, "Alma amable de la canción," 70.

76. Irma Iris García, "Insiste inclusión de artistas de isla en espectáculos" [She insists on the inclusion of local artists in all productions], *El Imparcial*, January 18, 1969, 27. "In between bouts of applause, she expressed her opinion that it is a shame that tourists who visit the island hardly have opportunities to become acquainted with our folklore, that they should come here to see the same shows they can find in their own country, while our talent has to migrate in search of opportunities. She clarified that she was not reducing anyone's talents and is not against anyone from abroad. She just wanted to express that she was in favor of our local people."

77. Fernández's political platform in the 1970s, as she geared up for her Senate nomination, is fairly well encapsulated in Elia G. Ramos, "Soy incapaz de pedirle a mi pueblo que vote por mí" [I wouldn't dream of asking my people to vote for me], *Bohemia de Puerto Rico,* June 26–July 2, 1972, 19–21.

78. Darcia Moretti, "Ruth Fernández: Talento y corazón" [Ruth Fernández: Talent and heart], *Revista Sábado, El Nuevo Día*, March 31, 1973, 8. In another source, we read, "The 52-year old singing dynamo said in an interview that being black is no handicap to elective office on an island as 'color blind' as Puerto Rico. Even being a woman, she believes is not much of a barrier as old prejudices crumble in this male, dominates [*sic*] Latin society." Bliss, "Singer as Senator," 33.

79. Costa, "Ruth Fernández," 28.

80. Fernández, interview by Pérez, 1999.

81. Pérez, "La Negra de Ponce," 63–64; Costa, "Ruth Fernández," 28–29.

82. Quoted from Fernández, interview by Pérez, 1999. Appears also in Costa, "Ruth Fernández"; Lamoutte, "Alma amable de la canción"; *Raíces*; and Patricia Vargas, "Negra, ¿y qué?" [So what if I'm black?], *El Nuevo Día*, October 12, 2000, 112, among others. Fernández does not indicate the exact date of this event; she tells Pérez she was

not yet out of high school and recalls being around seventeen years old. She tells Costa it was between 1936 and 1937 (Costa, "Ruth Fernández," 31). These facts have not been confirmed, to my knowledge. In Moretti, "Ruth Fernández," Fernández mentions the childhood incident (8) but not the episode at the Condado Vanderbilt she later reported, which was re-created, docudrama style, for the TV special *Raíces* (Roots, 2001). This would indicate a change in her representation of racial prejudice, away from the prior insistence on racial harmony and toward an ethos of heroic individuality.

83. For an account of the operatic diva self-narrative, see Koestenbaum, *The Queen's Throat*.

84. Fernández, interview by Pérez, 1999.

85. As Koestenbaum observes, "The diva's will to power culminates in a scene of vindication" (91).

86. Fernández, interview by Pérez, 1999.

87. "Her collection of Rafaela Santos dresses is legendary." Álvarez Curbelo, interview by Fiol-Matta.

88. Lamoutte, "Alma amable de la canción," 71.

89. Fernández, interview by Pérez, 1999.

90. I take this term from Eidsheim's discussion of Marian Anderson, "Marian Anderson and 'Sonic Blackness' in American Opera."

91. See Santiago-Díaz's brief but illuminating discussion of this album in light of "double consciousness" and the "toning down" of blackness, 55–58. "Just as with the musical expression of other black and brown artists, Fernández's renditions illustrate pretty clearly the need for Afro–Puerto Rican artists to downplay any affirmations of their African identity, through a parallel allegiance to dominant discourse's postulates and formulations of national identity" (65).

92. Findlay brilliantly analyzes Ponce's raced femininity in *Imposing Decency*.

93. Griffin, "When Malindy Sings," 103.

94. "El alma de Puerto Rico Hecha Canción, Ruth Fernández, de llegar a ocupar un escaño legislativo, será la 'Senadora que canta'" [If she is elected to a Senate seat, Puerto Rico's Singing Soul, Ruth Fernández, will be the 'singing senator']." Sonia Vallés, "Ruth Fernández tiene fe en humanidad, cree escaño en el Senado la hará darse más" [Ruth Fernández has faith in humanity; she believes that a Senate seat will make her give more of herself], *El Mundo*, October 22, 1972, 3-B.

95. Alfredo Margenat, "Doña Inés ataca el PAC en Mitín de Carolina" [Doña Inés attacks the Christian Action Party in Carolina], *El Mundo*, August 31, 1964, 17.

96. Vallés, "Ruth Fernández tiene fe en humanidad," 3-B.

97. Vallés, "Ruth Fernández tiene fe en humanidad," 3-B.

98. Ramos, "Soy incapaz de pedirle a mi pueblo que vote por mí," 19–21. Fernández told Marvette Pérez that Luis Muñoz Marín and Felisa Rincón de Gautier had approached her to ask her if "she had ever been interested in politics." Fernández, interview by Marvette Pérez, 2001.

99. Fernández, interview by Pérez, 2001.

100. Thanks to Yvonne Rivera Picorelli, librarian, Comisión Estatal de Elecciones (State Elections Commission), for the copies of the ballots and for explaining electoral procedures and history to me. I discussed music as grid of Puerto Rican identity with Álvarez Curbelo (interview by Fiol-Matta).

101. *Desnudo total* (Stripped bare). Television broadcast. Channel 13 of Mexico, circa 1980. Archivo General de Puerto Rico. Filmed in Puerto Rico.

102. *Desnudo total.*

103. Jaime Torres Torres, "Ruth la eterna" [The eternal Ruth], *El Nuevo Día*, October 17, 1999, 124.

104. I use "auratic" in the Benjaminian sense. An object has aura when it manages to retain a certain inscrutability of the past and does not merely become recycled as a commodity in its technological reproduction. See "The Work of Art in the Age of its Technological Reproducibility" and "Little History of Photography." I'm extrapolating here, perhaps going against the grain of Benjamin's singling out of visual media, to incorporate the concept into music as also indexical and technologically reproduced at the advent of industrial capitalism.

105. Griffin reminds us that this description of the black woman's voice has been recorded since the times of slavery and into jazz: "In all these cases the voice is unfamiliar, uncanny, almost otherwordly" ("When Malindy Sings," 107).

THREE TECHNE AND THE LADY

1. Naturally, I disagree with any hierarchical renderings, whether it be those subordinating women to men or among women. I encourage readers to listen to Priscilla Flores, Anatalia Rivera (Natalia), María Esther Acevedo, Luz Celenia Tirado, Adela Hernández, Matilde Narváez, and Irma Rodríguez, among other outstanding jíbara singers.

2. Viguié News, *Un amigo en New York*, 1952, 16 mm film; Viguié News, *Un amigo en Chicago*, 1956, 16 mm film. These shorts advertised the services offered by the Migration Division office, including assistance in employment, social services, free physical examinations, identification, and education. The Chicago office, opened later, served Puerto Rican communities in several states in the Midwest. The Migration Division was established in 1947 by Public Law 25 and began operations in 1948 under the Puerto Rico Department of Labor. Its stated mission was "to provide the proper guidance with respect to opportunities for employment and the problem of adjustment usually encountered in environments which are ethnologically alien."

3. Carmen Ortiz, interview by Licia Fiol-Matta, Carolina, Puerto Rico, October 5, 2007. Heartfelt thanks to Doña Carmen for this most illuminating interview, and to Roberto Silva for putting me in touch with Mrs. Ortiz. "Sin bandera" is a bolero by Pedro Flores; "Campanitas de cristal" is one of the most famous boleros of the Latin

American repertoire, penned by Rafael Hernández. Pedro Albizu Campos, a Harvard-trained lawyer, was the revered leader of the Nationalist Party of Puerto Rico. He suffered through multiple, cruel, and dangerous imprisonments upon the rise of Luis Muñoz Marín and the ELA.

4. Accounts of her age at first pregnancy vary. I am following the facts as recounted by Ernestina's sister, Carmen, during our conversation.

5. Ortiz, interview by Fiol-Matta.

6. A décima is a ten-verse lyric with octosyllabic verses and usually a *rima consonante* (a rhyme scheme in which both vowels and consonants are identical). This ancient style is shared across Latin America in literary and song forms. Its origins date from Spain in the fifteenth century. In Puerto Rico, there are two trends in the décima, referred to as "culta" (literary) and "popular" (folk). For the history of the literary form, see Lluch Vélez, *La décima culta en la literatura puertorriqueña*: "In Puerto Rico, the décima, of courtly origins and a rigorously classical poetic form, became the foremost expression of the popular muse, practically substituting the *romance*, which had been the favorite form of popular expression in the Iberian peninsula" (15). For an overview of the sung décima, see Escabí and Escabí, *La décima*. Prisco Hernández offers an excellent explanation of the art of *decimar*, as well as the principal kinds of seises (the traditional song form of this music), the instruments that form the *conjunto típico*, the characteristics of singing and playing, and the importance of the audience-singer connection in his article, "Décima, Seis, and the Art of the Puerto Rican Trovador." See also Quintero Rivera, *Salsa, sabor y control*; and Bofill-Calero, "Improvisation in Jíbaro Music." A wealth of information is available at the Cuatro Project (www.cuatro-pr.org).

7. There are other accounts of where her name came from. See Calandria's biography on the Fundación Nacional para la Cultura Popular (National Foundation for Popular Culture) website (www.prpop.org).

8. Jaime Torres Torres, "Trovadoras: inolvidable y sufrida La Calandria" [Female singers: Calandria, an unforgettable sufferer], *Por Dentro, El Nuevo Día*, December 26, 2004, 8.

9. I take the phrase from Bartra, *The Cage of Melancholy*.

10. Agamben discusses bare life in *Homo Sacer*.

11. An important migrant community was in Chicago. Gilberto Almenas recalled the Teatro San Juan on Division Street, La Conga on Fullerton, La Concha on North Avenue, and bars La Buruquena and El Tropical. Personal communication, July 21, 2008.

12. Joaquín Mouliert "El Pitirre de Fajardo," interview by Licia Fiol-Matta. Naguabo, Puerto Rico, January 19, 2009. With thanks to Roberto Silva for putting me in touch with Mr. Mouliert.

13. "Educate consent" refers to Gramsci's (*Prison Notebooks*) theory of hegemony as a successful manufacture of consent.

14. "Lettered city" is Ángel Rama's groundbreaking concept; see *The Lettered City*.

15. In *La actualidad del jíbaro*, Antonio S. Pedreira wrote, for instance, "Without taking into account certain variations, and at a glance, we can say that every Puerto Rican shelters a hidden jíbaro and that this jíbaro possesses the fundamental features that define a criollo, regardless of whether he lives in the countryside or in the towns. . . . He is an amateur musician and composes décimas off the top of his head" (16, 19). For an anthology of the literary canon cementing the jíbaro mythology, see Laguerre and Melón, eds., *El jíbaro de Puerto Rico: Símbolo y figura*, one in a series documenting Puerto Rican cultural identity that was published in the 1960s, Puerto Rico, realidad y anhelo (Puerto Rico, reality and hope).

16. Burgos, *Desde la Escuela del Aire*, 37–38.

17. According to Luis Rosario Albert ("*Wonderful Island of Puerto Rico*"), the state radio station name was derived from the phrase "Wonderful Island of Puerto Rico." Jíbaro music was the first Puerto Rican music heard over its airwaves.

18. Abelardo Díaz Alfaro, "Estampas de la vida de Teyo Gracia" (Scenes from the life of Teyo Gracia), *Alma Latina*, November 15, 1962, 7.

19. We cannot expect Díaz Alfaro to have been a music critic or historian, but it is absolutely stunning that this interpretation survives to this day and that contemporary critics remain uninterested in the jíbaro genre. Quintero Rivera railed against this paucity in *Salsa, sabor y control*, 217–251. More recently, Bofill-Calero ("Improvisation in Jíbaro Music") also laments this paucity and summarizes the scant and mostly ethnomusicological bibliography on jíbaro music.

20. The original lyrics read (to a tune that sounds like a children's school hour march):

Jalda arriba va cantando el popular
Jalda arriba siempre alegre va riendo
Va cantando porque sabe que tendrá
La confianza que ha de tenerlo contento

Jalda arriba con su líder marchará
Con el vate que es nuestro gobernador
Jalda arriba va triunfante va subiendo
Jalda abajo van los de la oposición

The *popular* (member of party faithful) sings while he goes uphill
Uphill, but always cheerful, always laughing
He sings because he knows he will have
The confidence that will keep him happy

Uphill with his leader he marches on
With our bard, our governor

Uphill he is always triumphant, always climbing
Downhill goes the opposition

21. See Nazario Velasco, *El paisaje y el poder*, for an in-depth analysis of Muñoz's complex ideology and politics of land.

22. As mentioned in chapter 2, Serenity was never formalized in law. Muñoz referred to "serenity" and only occasionally to "Operation Serenity" in various speeches.

23. Monod, " 'Ev'rybody's Crazy 'Bout the Doggone Blues,' " 184.

24. Similarly to Monod's analysis, Marybeth Hamilton's revision of the myths surrounding the Delta as the birthplace of the blues provide a comparative counterpoint to the construction of the Puerto Rican countryside as a pure space sheltered from history, allowing for transformations in jíbaro music that do respond to the changes an accelerated modernization wrought. Hamilton discusses the impact of the 1960s revival of the Delta and the extent to which this revival birthed the myth of the originary delta in the first place. Hamilton writes that "there is another story to be told about blues music," one not dependent on magic or mystery; the exact same can be said about jíbaro music. Hamilton, *In Search of the Blues*, 29.

25. Critics could follow Jeffrey T. Manuel, for instance, who has questioned the creation of the "sound of plain white folk" through intellectual exegeses and recording industry market niches. On reassessing U.S. southern country music, Manuel writes, "A close reading of country music history and the folklore, anthropology, and ethnomusicology from which it was derived, with a particular attention to the implicit and explicit racial assumptions built into the literature, suggests that such studies go beyond analysis of the past and may be understood as attempts at the racial classification of something as inherently fluid and hybrid as sound. Working concurrently with the commercial construction of racialized genres aimed at particular market segments, country music scholarship inscribed whiteness back onto the history of the genre. . . . Building on recent scholarship that has questioned the nature of 'social' claims, this article returns to a genre's founding moments not only to make an argument about country music, but in the hopes of making strange the connection between musical form and social category inherent in the work of identifying a genre's 'social origins.' " Manuel, "The Sound of the Plain White Folk?," 418.

26. Regarding Hawaiian Puerto Ricans, Ted Solís informs us, "Beginning in the 1950s, New York- or Puerto Rico-recorded LPs featuring popular jíbaro singers such as Ramito and Chuíto began to find their way into Hawai'i. Many had flamboyant jackets foregrounding stereotypical jíbaro symbols such as machetes, straw hats, cockfights, sugar cane fields, and the like. For many Hawai'i Puerto Ricans, the albums became a foundation for subsequent re-contact with contemporary Puerto Rico. The recordings included most of the traditional jíbaro musical genres . . . many of which had not been heard or specifically named (apart from the fading memories of the oldest in the community) for decades. While they formed the basis for a resurgence of musical tradi-

tionalism, this new mediation has made it increasingly difficult to distinguish pieces 'learned from the parents' from those acquired through later contact with visiting musicians from Puerto Rico and their recordings." Solís, "'You Shake Your Hips Too Much,'" 98. Calandria's great musical coconspirator, Ramito, traveled twice to Hawai'i, and Calandria appears in one of the photographs gracing the flip cover of *Ramito en Hawaii* (suggesting that she also performed, despite not being given billing or being included in the record). Solís's account illustrates how the era's recordings and performances came to stand in as the authentic and originary jíbaro forms and how the elements of persona assisted the musicians in their portrayal as the purveyors of folk music in places far and wide.

27. Tom Wolfe, "Ramito! Jíbaro Hero," *New York: The Sunday Herald Tribune Magazine*, July 4, 1965, 12. Wolfe notes that Ramito's single, "Yo no cambio a Puerto Rico por quinientos Nueva Yores" (I would not exchange my Puerto Rico for five hundred New York Cities), sold 200,000 copies. His description of Las Villas is memorable: "One is in *Las Villas*, a cluster of 15 or 20 Latin resorts in the hills and dells of the Platteskills [*sic*]. The Spanish Alps, as many Puerto Ricans call them — suddenly you are tooling through the huckleberry vistas and bambambambambim you hear the conga drums from one place and then the whole conjunto band as you drive by the main entrance, and you are still hearing the drums from one place when you come upon the next, the trumpets, the drums, guiros, the mambos, merengues, and it seems like you are driving up and down the dells of the Plattskills with Caribbean music rising up around the bend every time you get there. The *villas* — literally, country estates — look at first glance like road houses. Most of them have simple one-story construction, with a lot of cinderblock and plate-glass and electric signs, but six of them have hotel or motel accommodations, and taken together they are the big summer resort for New York's 900,000 Latin-Americans. Thousands come up in buses, the old Otis buses go yawling through the hills and dells, and thousands more come up by car, and everybody goes around from *villa* to *villa* — Villa Clara, Villa García, Villa Nueva, Sunny Acres, Casa Pérez, Villa Galicia, Toto's, Los Tres Argentinos, Villa San Juan, Villa — yet an American comes up on all of this like . . . Rip Van Winkle: the travel books, the guide books never heard of it all" (12).

28. Trigo, "Anemia, Witches, and Vampires: Figures to Govern the Colony," 70.

29. Findlay, *Imposing Decency*.

30. Rodríguez-Santana, "Conquests of Death." On women as measures of progress and objects of social policy measures in the context of moral panics, see Briggs, *Reproducing Empire*.

31. "This everyday violence, that wreaks havoc with our tried and true images of the past, sustains the *machista* outlook on life. You can't walk the streets of Utuado without a knife in hand; you attend the country dances with a machete; gatherings feature clubs, sticks, and German-issue guns. Some folks attend wakes so as to look for a fight. Three Kings Eve is not that saccharin image our writers have burdened us with. Sure,

there is verse, cadence and beat, but it is also ruckus, rape, and spite. The tough guys fondle the new crop of females; the guitar is brandished like a weapon; and altars are overturned in the midst of the uproar." Picó, *Los gallos peleados*, 29.

32. Gilberto Almenas, personal communication. Mike Amadeo, interview by Licia Fiol-Matta, Bronx, New York, August 7, 2008. Amadeo made an interesting observation: "Everything that was said about men, that's who she was, in woman."

33. Scholars have touched upon the fact that the signifier "jíbaro" carries the traces of racial ambiguity and anxieties about the jíbaro's presumed whiteness, a mythical creation of the intelligentsia. In *Undoing Empire*, José Buscaglia-Salgado traces the "mulatto" as a metaphoric subject by considering its origins not only in the plight of Africans brought to the Caribbean in bondage but also in the always already suspect purity of the Spaniards who colonized Puerto Rico, Cuba, and the Dominican Republic. Although the jíbaro is not his focus in his book, Buscaglia offers an interesting twist on the standard interpretation of the jíbaro's whiteness. This critic maintains that "in the context of the plantation the *jíbaro* and the *guajiro* were irrevocably unstable, as was the mulatto, and according to the dictates of protocol in the socioracial annals of the viceroyalty, they were white only to the degree that they were spotted with 'white stains'" (195). Also commenting on the jíbaro's gendered whiteness, Arlene Dávila, an anthropologist, writes, "the *jíbaro* is usually portrayed as a white male whose main influence comes from his Spanish predecessors although he has a tinge of Indian heritage. An African contribution to the *jíbaro* is never acknowledged or emphasized, as neither is a female gender identity" (*Sponsored Identities*, 71–72). In a related vein, see Quintero Rivera's excellent discussion of the genre in terms of its complex hybridity and his refutation of jíbaro music as merely "mountain music" (and, therefore, white) in *Salsa, sabor y control*, 217–251.

34. Silvia Álvarez Curbelo, interview by Licia Fiol-Matta, San Juan, Puerto Rico, October 6, 2007.

35. Recalling Melamed in *Represent and Destroy*, the PPD marks a noticeable change in the racial regime in Puerto Rico toward what she terms "a formally antiracist liberal capitalist modernity" (1). See chapter 2.

36. Nazario Velasco includes a fascinating account of the bohío's conflicted status among intellectuals as a symbol of the Puerto Rican countryside in early modernity. He usefully details how, in this contemporary moment, it was fast being replaced in practice and discourse by the *casa* (house) the PPD promised the jíbaro, a suburban-style dwelling made of concrete. See Nazario Velasco, "Pan, casa, libertad," in *El paisaje y el poder*, 271–310. His chapter title riffs on the PPD slogan of "Pan, tierra, libertad" (Bread, land, liberty), which appears as part of its logo, a clean profile of a man with a straw hat representing the jíbaro.

37. The cuatro, the most important musical element in the ensemble, plays the distinguishing melodic line of the wide variety of lines, called *seises*, that serve to categorize the musical corpus. The cuatro establishes the tempo and provides melodic

embellishments that complement the singer at every turn, often seeming to respond to the singing with a voice of its own. Cuatro players, called *maestros*, are revered. Up until very recently, women *cuatristas* (cuatro players) were rare; it was absolutely a male preserve. Hernández offers a concise description of the seis that cuatristas play: "The music to which the *trovador* improvises his lyrics is known as the *seis*. There are many varieties of *seis*, over eighty have been identified. The faster types are suitable for dancing, such as the *seis zapateo* and the *seis chorreao*, while the slower varieties are preferred by the trovadores for their improvisations. The most popular of these slower *seises* are the *seis celinés*, the *seis Andino* and the *seis mapeyé*. Another favorite is the *seis con décima* (the *seis* with a *décima*), the standard from of improvised poetry. The various *seises* consist of an introduction and a basic harmonic pattern that is repeated indefinitely until the trovador ends his improvisation. There are *seises* in both the major and the minor chords. For example, the lively *seis chorreao* and the melodious *seis de Andino* are in the major, while the highly chromatic *seis celinés* and the *seis mapeyé* are in the minor mode. The very popular *seis con décima* may be taken as an example of a *seis* in the Phrygian mode since it consists essentially of an elaboration of the Andalusian cadence" ("Décima, Seis, and the Art of the Puerto Rican Trovador," 22). Peter Manuel writes of the seis, "The backbone of *jíbaro* repertoire consists of the purely local *seis* and *aguinaldo*. Both the *seis* and the *aguinaldo* have several subvarieties, distinguished by stock melodies and harmonic progressions. They are named variously after places of origin (*seis fajardeño, aguinaldo orocoveño*), musicians (*seis andino*), or formal features (*seis con décimas*)" (*Caribbean Currents*, 54–55). See López Cruz, *Método para la enseñanza del cuatro puertorriqueño*, for musical examples. See also Quintero Rivera, *Salsa, sabor, y control*, 217–251. The name seis most likely came from its dance origins, referring to six couples dancing together in a choreographed manner (Manuel Alonso, quoted in López Cruz, *La música folklórica de Puerto Rico*, 4). Most jíbaro music was actually played for dancing until the 1960s, in *terrazas*, large outdoor makeshift dance spaces common in the countryside, now as extinct as the countryside itself.

38. The DIVEDCO was founded by decree of law in 1949. The American documentary filmmaker Edwin Rosskam was its first director. This ambitious project explicitly called for graphic and visual artists, composers, and writers to come together to produce a series of educational films, booklets, and silkscreen posters to promote literacy, health campaigns, and self-initiative projects in the peasantry. Some of Puerto Rico's most noted filmmakers were schooled in the DIVEDCO, and silkscreens produced by graphic artists working for the DIVEDCO are now expensive, prized artworks. The program constituted one of the most important cultural and communitarian enterprises in twentieth-century Puerto Rico and the Caribbean. Music was also an area of profound achievement, in terms of both original compositions and also films documenting Puerto Rican popular music. Surprisingly little has been written on the DIVEDCO. On graphic art, see Tió Fernández, *El cartel en Puerto Rico*. On music, see Thompson,

"Film Music and Community Development in Rural Puerto Rico." On the role of intellectuals in film productions and print materials, see Marsh Kennerley's excellent *Negociaciones culturales*.

39. With thanks to Catherine Marsh Kennerley for copies of this booklet.

40. Richard Bauman and Charles L. Briggs, *Voices of Modernity*, 5, quoted in Ochoa Gautier, "Sonic Transculturation, Epistemologies of Purification, and the Aural Public Sphere," 210.

41. Sterne, "The Theology of Sound," 220.

42. Fox, *Real Country*. Fox elucidates a similar working-class practice in American country music. See especially chapter 6, "'Bring Me Up in a Beer Joint': The Poetics of Speech and Song." "Speech saturates song, and song saturates speech and in between speech and song lies an enormous and frequently traversed zone of verbal art" (230).

43. Barthes, "The Grain of the Voice," 181.

44. Mouliert, interview by Fiol-Matta. Inquiries regarding details about how she obtained her recording contract, musicians employed in recording sessions, and location of sessions proved, unfortunately, unfruitful. My interviewees did not recall much about the specifics of Calandria's recording career. Interestingly, all described her voice as sweet.

45. It is believed that Ramito, despite his mythology, did not write all the compositions with which he is credited and that a good part belong to songwriters whose names we are likely to never know, people he became acquainted with over the course of his career. As with other folk musics, the notion of authorship was blurry, and the question of songwriting credits was often not pursued to the letter. Musicians believed they had credit if they recorded something first.

46. Canino, "Trovadores, improvisadores, versificadores y cantadores," 115 (emphasis added).

47. The lyrics read: "No conformes con la historia / los padres de la menor / escogen a Nueva York / de escuela reformatoria / mandan a la chica notoria / en este panal de colmenas / y aunque aquí la vida es buena / seis años ella vivió / pero cuando regresó / ya llevaba una docena." (They couldn't just leave it there / The child's parents / selected New York / as a reformatory school / They sent the troublesome girl / to this beehive / and, even though life here is delightful / she lived here for six years / and by the time she returned to Puerto Rico, / she had had a dozen kids.)

48. See Rodríguez-Santana, "Conquests of Death."

49. See López Cruz, *La música folklórica de Puerto Rico*, 36–37, on the mapeyé. He believes "mapeyé" is short for "brother Peyé" (hermano Peyé). The name for the seis mapeyé itself might allude to this male-male bond.

50. "Porque el jíbaro o es ruiseñor o es pitirre . . ." (Because the jíbaro is either a nightingale or a kingbird). Díaz Alfaro, "Estampas," 7.

51. For "distribution of the sensible," see Rancière, *The Politics of Aesthetics*.

52. Luis Miranda "El Pico de Oro," interview by Licia Fiol-Matta, San Lorenzo, Puerto Rico, January 16, 2009. With thanks to Roberto Silva for putting me in touch with Mr. Miranda. Matilde Narváez, "La Jíbara de Toa Alta," also remarked that "tenía un tono muy bello" (she had a beautiful timbre). Narváez, personal communication, January 12, 2005. With thanks to Roberto Silva for the contact.

53. Ortiz, interview by Fiol-Matta.

54. With thanks to Arturo Butler, who clarified matters to me in a conversation during which he discussed his personal collection of Calandria recordings. Thanks also to Mr. Butler for being so generous with his collection, enabling my access to a great number of Calandria's tracks from the 1950s. Finally, thanks to David Morales of the Cuatro Project for putting me in touch with Mr. Butler.

55. I queried the ethnomusicologist and professor of music Jaime Bofill-Calero about Calandria's voice. He took my question to students in a course he was teaching at the Conservatory of Music in Puerto Rico and e-mailed me with some conclusions of their discussion. The students had used the following technical, descriptive language: "Voz nasal, ronca en el registro agudo, chillona, ligeramente nasal, sonido abierto, sonido de garganta, vibrato" (A nasal voice, hoarse in the high register, shrill, slightly nasal, open sound, throaty sound, vibratos). He volunteered that the group had noticed a change from her younger voice, "Aguda y finita aun un poco inocente pero mañosa" (high-pitched and thin, innocent-sounding but a little crafty), and what they characterized as the voice she developed later, "Con más cuerpo, más swing, más ronca" (With more body, more swing, hoarser). Bofill, e-mail communication, September 22, 2014. Thanks to Bofill-Calero and his students for sharing their descriptions.

56. The reference is to Bourdieu's classic, *Distinction*.

57. Mercedes Pérez Glass, interview by Cristóbal Díaz-Ayala, 1991. Cristóbal Díaz Ayala Collection of Cuban and Latin American Music, Florida State University Libraries, Cassette 1514.

58. Ray Brack, "Money Programming: All-Alike Music in Latin Locations Is Loco," *Billboard*, July 16, 1966, 77, 86.

59. The track's cuatro player, Nieves Quintero, once remarked, "I put something new into cuatro playing, something Americanized." Nieves Quintero, "The Cuatro Project interview with Nieves Quintero," by Juan Sotomayor, Cuatro Project, http://www.cuatro-pr.org/es/node/326.

60. Moncho Osorio had returned from living in New York during the 1950s. Before that, he had served in the army. His lifelong pursuit became music. He is also rumored to have been involved in forms of armed struggle, although this remains unrecorded and as such is unverifiable. Miranda, interview by Fiol-Matta; Egberto Almenas, e-mail communication, April 8, 2008; Gilberto Almenas, personal communication. The Caguas Historical Archive received the contents of Osorio's personal collection and is in the process of cataloguing it.

61. Thanks to Liza Fiol-Matta for helping me with the translations of "La Peluya" and "La infortunada," and to Lena Burgos-Lafuente.

62. Ortiz, interview by Fiol-Matta.

63. Torres Torres, "Trovadoras."

64. To listen to musical examples, see Cuatro Project (www.cuatro-pr.org).

65. Mouliert, interview by Fiol-Matta.

66. Ochoa Gautier, "Disencounters between Music's Allure," 20.

67. Ochoa Gautier, "Disencounters between Music's Allure," 20. In the full article, Ochoa discusses the Colombian virtuoso vocalist Laura Pulido and the *champeta* musicians of the black neighborhoods of Cartagena. Regarding champeta, an "urban, self-produced, electronic dance music" (20), Ochoa mentions jíbaro music as part of its generative sounds (21).

68. Irma Morales "La Jíbara de Salinas," personal communication, January 12, 2005. With thanks to Roberto Silva for the contact.

69. Thanks to the Archivo Histórico de Caguas, where I was able to consult these LPS.

70. Mario Ortiz Jr., "Mario Ortiz and His All-Star Band Revival: A Conversation with John Child," Descarga.com, September 6, 2009, http://www.descarga.com/cgi-bin/db/archives/Interview60.

71. Sterne, "A Resonant Tomb," 287–332.

72. Sterne, "A Resonant Tomb," 298.

73. "Whereas in the symbol destruction is idealized and the transfigured face of nature is fleetingly revealed in the light of redemption, in allegory the observer is confronted with the *facies hippocratica* of history as a petrified, primordial landscape. Everything about history that, from the very beginning, has been untimely, sorrowful, unsuccessful, is expressed in a face — or rather, in a skull. . . . If nature has always been subject to the power of death, it is also true that it has always been allegorical." Benjamin, "Allegory and *Trauerspiel*," 166 (translation modified).

FOUR THE THINKING VOICE

1. Operation Bootstrap, as discussed in preceding chapters, is the English term for Manos a la Obra, in Spanish literally "put your hands to work," the 1947 economic program intended to spur the accelerated modernization of Puerto Rico through the replacement of a rural with an industrial economy. It was the centerpiece of the 1952 founding of the current status quo, the Estado Libre Asociado (Commonwealth of Puerto Rico). The program relied heavily on a corporate tax exemption for U.S. companies to operate in Puerto Rico; providing cheap labor costs to U.S. companies; and state-sponsored mass migration to the United States. The heyday of Bootstrap occurred roughly between 1955 and 1970.

2. I employ "thinking" after Heidegger, *What Is Called Thinking?*: "Everything thought-provoking *gives* us to think. But it always gives that gift just so far as the thought-provoking matter already *is* intrinsically what must be thought about" (4).

3. "The visual is on the side of an imaginary capture (which does not imply that it is reduced to that), while the sonorous is on the side of referral/*renvoi* (which does not imply that it exhausts its amplitude). In still other words, the visual is tendentially mimetic, and the sonorous tendentially methexic (that is, having to do with participation, sharing, or contagion), which does not mean that the two tendencies do not intersect." Nancy, *Listening*, 10.

4. See Santiago, *Nueva ola portoricensis*, for wonderful documentation of this youth movement, and the two-part TV documentary, *Prohibido Olvidar: La Nueva Ola* [Forgetting is forbidden: The new wave], dir. Roberto "Tito" Otero and Luis Rafael Trelles Hernández, Unidad de Cine y Televisión de la Universidad de Puerto Rico, Río Piedras, and TuTV Canales 6 y 3, 2003.

5. In *Dusty!*, Annie J. Randall discusses British pop's Dusty Springfield as the greatest exponent of what Randall calls the "pop aria": "Each pop aria does its work in a slightly different way, using the orchestra to create a mood and an atmosphere appropriate to its particular conceits, yet they all share a melodramatic structure in three parts: an introduction saturated with devices that fix our emotional location and point of view; at least one modal shift and/or modulation to a higher key, which leads inexorably toward the final payoff: the singer's vocal breaking point" (84). These descriptions fit early Lucecita hits perfectly. Surely she should be counted as one of the 1960s pop aria's foremost exponents. A splendid early example is her rendition of Pino Donaggio's "La vita" ("La vida," known to English-language speakers in Shirley Bassey's masterly version of "This Is My Life"). It could be argued that these hits in the internationalist festival style of the 1960s, which came from Europe, laid the necessary groundwork for Lucecita's watershed performance of "Génesis."

6. During her years as a youth star, part of the marketing narrative used to sell records and promote *El Club del Clan* involved a romance between Lucecita and her costar, Chucho Avellanet, followed by heated accounts of a tempestuous romantic triangle in which Lucecita was cast as the rival of the daughter of Cuban exiles escaping communism, Lissette Álvarez. As fans of the period remember, a number of contests were held on the radio where fans daily voted via telephone for their favorite stars. Much journalistic coverage of the time claimed that Lucecita had hit the top of the charts with "Vete con ella" because the song faithfully revealed her emotional state, due to her rejection by her male costar, Chucho.

7. Alfred D. Herger, interview in *Prohibido olvidar*.

8. For an example, see Varela, *La televisión criolla*, on Argentina's *El Club del Clan*. Herger claims he had Clark's blessing to copy his show wholesale as long as he did not use any of the show's registered trademarks. Herger recounted that he traveled to

Philadelphia and that he had realized that the show was quite simple. If it was about enlisting young people to dance for free, he figured, it would be an easy sell and a cinch to produce. Herger, interview in *Prohibido olvidar*.

9. Liner notes, RVLP 515. The album is unnamed. Rico-Vox, 1964.

10. Diego Manso, "Lucecita Benítez: 'Yo no canto tonterías'" [I don't sing nonsense], *Revista Ñ*, June 14, 2013.

11. Guadalupe Treibel, "Soy lo prohibido" [I'm what's forbidden], *Página 12*, September 28, 2012. She gives her birth year as 1948; other accounts state it was 1942.

12. Lucecita Benítez, interview in *Prohibido olvidar*.

13. This boyfriend was very phantasmatic. See, for example, the *Bohemia* cover of February 19, 1967, with a picture of the young artist and the caption, "Lucecita tiene novio" (Lucecita has a boyfriend). Inside, the article title reads: "He encontrado al hombre que me adora" (I have found a man who adores me). The reporter, Rosario Guiscafré, writes, "About him, we can tell you that he is a young man, but a few years older than her, very handsome, six feet tall, has a bright future, is very serious-minded, is responsible, and has a lot in common with her. He is wise enough to have laughed along at *all the stories that have been fabricated about her*. He understands that they are typical of the entertainment industry, which takes advantage of all kinds of publicity stunts, and because of this they enjoy their sweet secret of three years since they met at a party even more" (42, emphasis added).

14. "La cancionista puertorriqueña Lucecita, vistiendo ropa masculina y corte de pelo a la usanza varonil, pero con personalidad muy femenina, interpretó de forma muy impresionante la canción 'Génesis,' en representación de Puerto Rico para obtener la mayor puntuación" (The Puerto Rican singer Lucecita, wearing masculine dress and hairdo, but with a very feminine personality, was impressive in her performance of the song "Génesis," representing Puerto Rico and obtaining the highest score in the competition). Ramón Inclán, "'Génesis,' canción de Puerto Rico, arriba en el Festival" ["Génesis," a Puerto Rican song, comes out on top in the festival], *El heraldo de México*, May 11, 1969. As stipulated in the contract, the winning artists were required to record their song as a 45 single and their trophy became contingent upon achieving specified sales numbers. Upon winning, Lucecita recorded "Génesis" in Mexico City and released the LP *Lucecita en México*, a collector's item. The cover features Lucecita posing in the suit she wore for the competition; on the flip side, she is using the suit's jacket like a toreador in a bullfight, certainly an interesting pose no doubt meant to underscore how the Mexican press received her costume as suspiciously masculine.

15. Designed by Fernando Martín, known as the designer "Martín."

16. "An assemblage is precisely this increase in the dimensions of a multiplicity that necessarily changes in nature as it expands its connections." Deleuze and Guattari, *A Thousand Plateaus*, 8.

17. "In a curious bodily topology, it is like a bodily missile which separates itself from the body and spreads around, but on the other hand it points to a bodily interior,

an intimate partition of the body which cannot be disclosed—as if the voice were the very principle of division into exterior and interior." Dolar, *A Voice and Nothing More*, 70–71.

18. "It is the silent voice of an appeal, a call, an appeal to respond, to assume one's stance as the subject. . . . It is the voice in which the linguistic, the ethical, and the political voice join forces, coinciding in what was the dimension of pure enunciation in them. They are knotted together around that pivotal kernel of the object voice, of its void, and in response to it our fate as linguistic, ethical, political subjects has to be pulled to pieces and reassembled, traversed, and assumed." Dolar, *A Voice and Nothing More*, 124.

19. In 2013, Lucecita, interviewed in Argentina, spoke of the contradictory affordances of her isolation at this time. On the one hand, she felt free, because she associated freedom with being able to pursue a career in music. On the other, she spoke of the manager's absolute control over her as a commodity. "They forbade me to have friends. They forbade everything. When you make it big you don't belong to yourself. You belong to the management office, Alfred in this case. Then he sold my contract to Paquito Cordero, a *capo* from over there in Puerto Rico. Herger sold me like peanuts. Then it got worse; they isolated me from everyone. I didn't have a life. If I had not followed the rules of the game then, I would not be the Lucecita I am today. I would've gotten lost on the way." She recounts, as in multiple interviews, that this period ended when she "ran into her conscience" shortly after. Manso, "Lucecita Benítez."

20. In *Vocal Tracks*, Jacob Smith discusses some of the characteristics of the melodramatic voice, all of which Lucecita deployed. He covers whispering, talking, sobbing, overacting, and, in singers, pitch contrast, stretching the range of timbre, and abrupt changes in inflection. Smith comments on how "the voice is an instrument of timbre par excellence" (120) and discusses the undertheorized question of timbre in music (117).

21. Dolar, *A Voice and Nothing More*, 107–112.

22. I'm riffing on Nancy in *Listening*: "[sonorous] presence *arrives*—it entails an *attack*, as musicians and acousticians say" (14).

23. For examples of Lucecita's self-discourse at this time, see the interviews by Magali García Ramis, "La transformación de Lucecita," *Avance*, August 6, 1973, 20–25; Luz Raquel Ávila, "Lucecita en el Coliseo: 'A mí no me controla nadie,'" *Avance*, November 11, 1974, 54–57; and Manuel Ramos Otero and Rosario Ferré, "Con Lucecita," *Zona carga y descarga* 1, no. 6 (1973): 22–23.

24. Lucecita on *The Ed Sullivan Show*: YouTube, posted May 13, 2016, https://www.youtube.com/watch?v=4I_xytWdFIE; Lucecita in *Tonta tonta pero no tanto*: YouTube, posted December 12, 2011, https://www.youtube.com/watch?v=e8dd6sdbSzM; Lucecita on the *Toyota Rambler Show*, with Sammy Davis, Jr., YouTube, posted August 2, 2007, https://www.youtube.com/watch?v=C8XiSgkIHoQ.

25. I received this information from Mary Sherwood, SOFA Entertainment, e-mail communication, February 26, 2007.

26. Lucecita's managers sent five song choices for Lucecita. Javier Santiago recalls four of the five: "Génesis," "You've Lost That Loving Feeling," "Day by Day," and the eventual selection, the *rumba gitana* "Todas las mañanas" (Javier Santiago, interview by Licia Fiol-Matta, San Juan, Puerto Rico, October 9, 2007). Ed Sullivan's sister had some kind of role in the Casita María in the Bronx, a helping nonprofit agency, and contacted the artist to perform at a benefit. According to Lucecita, Paquito Cordero would allow it only on the condition that she perform on *The Ed Sullivan Show*. Sullivan wanted her to lip sync to taped music, and she refused, insisting on the live orchestra accompaniment (Treibel, "Soy lo prohibido"). Pedro Rivera Toledo confirms that the contact was Sullivan's sister. He also recalled that once she performed, Sullivan was amazed (Rivera Toledo, interview by Licia Fiol-Matta, October 9, 2009). Cándido worked under separate contract. A few years before, Myrta Silva had led a protest against Ed Sullivan's bigoted remarks about Puerto Rican women; one wonders if there was any connection.

27. "He was my great teacher. Sammy, for me, is the altar. He wanted to buy out my contract from my manager to take me with him to the United States, but my manager replied I was not for sale. It has not been easy to fly to the heights." Treibel, "Soy lo prohibido."

28. The reference, naturally, is to Debord, *Society of the Spectacle*.

29. Rivero, *Tuning Out Blackness*, 72–85.

30. Rivero, *Tuning Out Blackness*, 73.

31. Rivero, *Tuning Out Blackness*, 73.

32. Moten, "The Case of Blackness," 180.

33. Rafael Rodríguez, "Luz Esther habla de Lucecita" [Luz Esther talks about Lucecita], *Suplemento En Rojo*, *Claridad*, August 21–27, 1981, 3.

34. We can think of Daphne Brooks's suggestion in "Afro-Sonic Feminist Praxis": "These women of the lower registers . . . push our imaginations, our desires; our quotidian needs to engage with the traces of suffering by challenging us through sound to go to (other) extremes and border regions to tarry in the boundaries of the elsewhere. By way of their location on these 'lower frequencies,' they 'speak for' us" (220).

35. Rodríguez, "Luz Esther habla de Lucecita," 3.

36. As Mita Torres reminded me, "De hecho, es rockero" (In fact, he is into rock). Torres, interview by Licia Fiol-Matta, Hato Rey, Puerto Rico, January 14, 2009.

37. Agamben, "What Is the Contemporary?"

38. Ramos Otero and Ferré, "Con Lucecita," 22.

39. Ramos Otero and Ferré, "Con Lucecita," 22.

40. Ramos Otero and Ferré, "Con Lucecita," 23.

41. No author, no title, *Claridad*, October 15, 1974, 20.

42. Torres, interview by Fiol-Matta.

43. It is worth consulting Díaz, *Huele a bomba*.

44. P. Z. [Pedro Zervigón?], "Concierto 'Traigo un pueblo en mi voz' en el Sylvia Rexach," *Avance*, May 13, 1974, 60.

45. "There are also, probably in every culture, in every civilization, real places . . . which are something like counter-sites, a kind of effectively enacted utopia in which the real sites, all the other real sites that can be found within the culture, are simultaneously represented, contested, and inverted. Places of this kind are outside all places, even though it may seem possible to indicate their location in reality. Because these places all are absolutely different from all the sites they reflect and speak about, I shall call them, by way of contrast to utopias, heterotopias." Foucault, "Of Other Spaces," 24.

46. See Nancy, *Being Singular Plural*. "Creation takes place everywhere and always — but it is this unique event, or advent, only on the condition of being each time what it is, or being what it is only 'at each time,' each time appearing singularly" (16).

47. "Su primer concierto en vivo" [Her first live concert] *Avance*, April 22, 1974, 55.

48. Also presented in hotels, which may help explain its quite different packaging. She presented this concert at the Hotel Helio Isla Verde in April 1975, with thirty-two musicians. Luz Raquel Ávila, "Lucesita quiere ser madre" (Lucecita wants to be a mother), *Avance*, April 7, 1975, 17. The turn toward a repertoire dominated by Alberto Cortez songs might have been motivated by financial concerns, as it could be fitted into the hotel mold and also employed for love-themed events, such as Valentine's Day 1975 (Luz Raquel Ávila, "Lucecita interpreta a Alberto Cortés [*sic*] o la fuerza omnipotente del amor," *Avance*, February 10, 1975, 52–53). The show was recorded for television.

49. The concept appears throughout Foucault's work but is succinctly captured in the discussion of ancient parrhesia: "a verbal activity in which a speaker expresses his personal relationship to truth, and risks his life because he recognizes truth-telling as a duty to improve or help other people (as well as himself). In parrhesia, the speaker uses his freedom and chooses frankness instead of persuasion, truth instead of falsehood and silence, the risk of death instead of life and security, criticism instead of flattery, and moral duty instead of self-interest and moral apathy" (*Fearless Speech*, 19–20).

50. Ramos Otero and Ferré, "Con Lucecita," 24.

51. Brooks, "Afro-Sonic Feminist Praxis," 207.

52. Moten, "Chromatic Saturation," quoted in Brooks, "Afro-Sonic Feminist Praxis," 208.

53. Brooks, "Afro-Sonic Feminist Praxis," 209.

54. "For its full development, Puerto Rico needs, among other things, not only minoritarian artists enrolling in universities, but pop artists who reach universality itself from pop music. I think Lucecita Benítez, if she minds her art only (and not the superficial stuff that surrounds it) can become a unique, world-class pop singer of Latin pop songs with social relevance." "El maravilloso arte de Lucecita Benítez" [Lucecita Benítez's marvelous art], *El Mundo*, November 14, 1971, 8.

55. Weheliye, *Phonographies*, 45.

56. Ramos Otero and Ferré, "Con Lucecita," 24.

57. Weheliye, *Phonographies*, 45.

58. Ramos Otero and Ferré, "Con Lucecita," 23.

59. Cavarero, *For More Than One Voice*, 12.

60. "Any point of a rhizome can be connected to anything other and must be . . . a rhizome ceaselessly establishes connections"; "the point is that a rhizome or multiplicity can never be overcoded." Deleuze and Guattari, *A Thousand Plateaus*, 7, 9.

61. Rafael Rodríguez, "¿Creceremos?" [We shall grow?], *En Rojo*, August 21–27, 1981, 6.

62. "I have been asked more than once to write an open letter to my fans, because many fans complain that I do not look after them like I should, that I ignore them, don't love them or give the impression I really don't need them in my life at all." The letter apologizes to fans for having been "brusque," "awkward," and "even insulting [*grosera*] to some" and cites as a reason the "tensions to which we artists are subject before, during, and after each performance." Lucecita states that dealing with these "tensions" is the artist's responsibility, that she had to "control herself better," and that the artist should be more available to the fans. She accepts being the model for "la generación a go go" although not without relatively pointed jabs at negative gossip about her. "Open Letter to All of Lucecita's Benítez's Fans," November 1967. Oscar Hernández Papers, Fundación Nacional para la Cultura Popular, San Juan, Puerto Rico. As with several sources about the artist's life, the fan letter, interviews in less than reputable journalistic venues, and opinions proffered in public have to be carefully vetted for their truth claims. It is unknown whether Lucecita herself penned this letter. However, as discourse, fan letters such as these reflect the mass circulation of diva prose, and this letter certainly sounds much like interviews and live sound bites the artist has delivered through the decades. Ephemera reflect the public's obsession with knowing all about "their" artist, and the entertainment press reflects the sometimes irresponsible attitude of reporters in search of the scoop. These various modalities of pop discourse represent struggles around the interpretation of culture in the pop realm where, it seems, authority constantly shifts and the artist has to strenuously negotiate privacy and publicity, art and market taste.

63. Connor, "Edison's Teeth," 165.

64. Curiously, in one interview, she recounted, "While other kids were playing with dolls and other things, I was already playing with microphones." Rosario Guiscafré, "He encontrado al hombre que me adora" [I have found a man who adores me], *Bohemia*, February 19, 1967, 42.

65. Torres, interview by Fiol-Matta. Torres explained that at around this time, wireless microphones started to hit the market, but that Lucecita refused to use them because they could not withstand her volume.

66. "It consists simply in not directing one's notice to anything in particular and in maintaining the same 'evenly suspended attention' . . . in the face of all that one

hears. . . . To put it in a formula: [The analyst] must turn his own unconscious like a receptive organ toward the transmitting unconscious of the patient. He must adjust himself to the patient as a telephone receiver is adjusted to the transmitting microphone." Freud, "Recommendations to Physicians Practicing Psycho-Analysis," 357, 360.

67. See, for example, Roy Brown, "¿La canción protesta?" [The protest song?], *Suplemento En Rojo, Claridad*, April 12, 1975, 12–13, where the esteemed singer-songwriter states that part of the revolution's mission is to liberate love (between men and women, it goes without saying).

68. I take the concept of the fugitive and its intervention into theories of blackness from Fred Moten. He writes, "What's at stake is fugitive movement in and out of the frame, bar, or whatever externally imposed social logic—a movement of escape, the stealth of the stolen that can be said, since it inheres in every closed circle, to break every enclosure. This fugitive movement is stolen life, and its relation to law is reducible neither to simple interdiction nor bare transgression." Moten, "The Case of Blackness," 179. See also Harney and Moten, *The Undercommons*.

69. I quote from Mowitt's classic, "The Sound of Music in the Era of Its Electronic Reproducibility," 193, albeit out of order: "[Perhaps] contemporary music can be seen as a gateway to a new collectivity, since it situates subjects within an emergent structure of listening which offers experiential confirmation of a social confirmation."

70. YouTube, posted September 29, 2012, https://www.youtube.com/watch?v=ony TquV-jBM.

71. *Nueva canción* and *nueva trova* refer to late 1960s–early 1970s musical movements in Chile and Cuba respectively, with a wide continental appeal. These were leftwing, anticommercial, often revivalist movements aligned particularly with Salvador Allende's Popular Unity Front and the Cuban Revolution, respectively.

72. Torres, interview by Fiol-Matta. Edna Rivera was also present and confirmed this account. She is the wife of Pedro Rivera Toledo and was part of the group of artist-activists I characterized earlier as a "heterotopia." A profound thank you to both Torres and Rivera for such an interesting and clarifying interview. Thanks also to Ida de Jesús, who put me in touch with Torres.

73. See Party's excellent discussion of balada's association with repressive regimes in "*Placer Culpable*," 72–78.

74. Rodríguez, "Luz Esther habla de Lucecita," 2–3.

75. "Yo soy de barrio, tengo la clave y he bailado salsa con mis hermanos y amigos" [I come from the barrio. I can follow the beat and have danced salsa with my brothers and friends]. Rodríguez, "Luz Esther habla de Lucecita," 2.

76. Rodríguez, "Luz Esther habla de Lucecita," 3.

77. Cruz-Malavé, personal communication, April 16, 2015.

78. Kahn, "Art and Sound," discusses the avant-garde as the first to consider sound in art as more expansive than merely music: "The theory of the avant-garde can be described with relative ease when pegged to the familiar figure and functioning of the

phonograph, or of any technology for that matter. Beyond that, we can detect three figures of a more abstract character — vibration, inscription, transmission — that begin to account for how sounds are located or dislocated, contained or released, recorded or generated" (43). He continues, "The most pronounced impression produced by figures of vibration was that of spatiality, whereas inscription reduced space into impressions on a surface. . . . Figures of transmission combined aspects of both vibration and inscription, fusing the spatial features of vibration with the objecthood and corporeality of inscription, but exceeding them both in terms of complexity. . . . Vibrational space that had existed only in representation was given breadth and depth once again by a *signal* silently crisscrossing space, bearing both sonic content and the objects that had been demobilized by inscription in a variety of manners. . . . Transmission was basically the return and invigoration of objects and bodies that had been fixed by inscription to the space implied by vibration" (45).

79. Treibel, "Soy lo prohibido."

80. Speaking of this location, she says, during the live 1987 concert, Traigo un pueblo en mi voz: "Yo me suelo perder en esos lugares con mis amigos" [I often get lost in those places with my friends].

81. Deleuze and Guattari discuss the nomad throughout *A Thousand Plateaus*.

82. "Musicians call it 'playing in the street.' It comes from the hotel era. Musicians who did not play in hotels were said to play in the street." According to Rivera Toledo, Lucecita came up with the title and concept. Rivera Toledo, interview by Fiol-Matta. Heartfelt thanks for an illuminating conversation. Edna Rivera and Mita Torres were also present.

83. Mita Torres clarified that, even in her flush years, Lucecita depended on *fiestas patronales* for her income. Torres, interview by Fiol-Matta.

84. See Colón Zayas, "Imagen discográfica e identidades" [The album cover image and identities], for a perceptive analysis of Lucecita's album covers and the semiotic codes through which to discern her 1980s visual butchness. Colón follows Richard Dyer's influential, semiotic analysis of lesbian stars. Colón writes, "Lucecita's image, her representational form, creates an aesthetics of instability. We behold a series of photographic images that show us a diva who has transformed her mood and physicality. Lucecita, the star, the persona, constructed and thought-out, works her spectacularity from an excess of photographic images, that, in the context of a normalized society such as the Puerto Rico of the time, goes from the conformity of the first pictures, to the rejection of norms and rebelliousness of the second moment, to finally arrive at a regime where she balances those first initial moments, equalizing them, with photos that echo the nostalgia industry and apparently neutralize the combative euphoria of her second stage. However, as we can observe, there is more to it than compliance. The third stage does preserve the combative, secure gesture of the great diva" (92).

85. Santiago Mari Pesquera, the son of the Socialist candidate for governor, Juan Mari Bras, was assassinated in 1976. Carlos Muñiz Varela, a young Cuban man and San

Juan resident interested in bypassing the era's hardline politics and sponsoring youth trips to Cuba from Puerto Rico, was assassinated in 1979. The 1978 Cerro Maravilla murders of Carlos Soto Arriví and Arnaldo Rosado Torres, two pro-independence activists, is one of the darkest chapters in Puerto Rican history.

86. There are, of course, peaks and valleys in her concert and recording life in the two decades I do not discuss here. Her best recording of the period, by far, is the Christmas classic *Un regalo de alegría* [A gift of joy], a terrific CD that shows revivalism at work in a supremely effective way and that, compared to *Criollo Folklore*, renounces didacticism and transmits exuberance and the joy of the title. It showcases Lucecita's natural gift for power genres (in this case, songs with a salsa tempo and sound). Her CD *Live from Carnegie Hall*, from 2000, is also of note. Lucecita's live performances continued through the 1990s, including memorable presentations in the Teatro Puerto Rico in the Bronx, with a reduced jazz ensemble, along with her appearances at the Festival de Claridad. In recognition of her extraordinary contributions to *Claridad* over the years and her political importance and steadfastness, *Claridad* named her the honoree of its festival in 2010. Those interested in her later career should consult her serial appearances on the Banco Popular Christmas specials, beginning with the 1993 *Un pueblo que canta* (A people who sing).

As of this writing, her latest recording is *Luz en Julia* (2015), a tribute album to the Afro–Puerto Rican poet and icon Julia de Burgos. It includes ten poems set to music by Alberto Carrión. The CD features artwork from Antonio Martorell, the artist who created the landmark *Lucecita* (Hit Parade #70) album cover in 1973, associated with the track "Soy de una raza pura" and since renamed with this title after its reissue in CD. The artwork is a composite of Lucecita's and Burgos's portraits and reflects a sharp turn from Martorell's earlier gesture. Interestingly, the two icons are linked by race and gender, but the end result is an ordering of either one's fugitivity. The actual recording happened over a decade earlier, in Havana, with members of the Cuban National Symphony. The arrangements proceed along a generic, symphonic accompaniment to Lucecita's vocals, reminiscent of Pedro Rivera Toledo's earlier arrangements. The artist, naturally, is several decades older than in her signal concerts in the 1970s and 1980s, but still capable of producing a mesmerizing performance.

87. Nancy, *Listening*, 16.

88. Treibel, "Soy lo prohibido."

EPILOGUE

1. Silva, live performance, tribute to Rafael Hernández, Institute of Puerto Rican Culture, exact date unknown, possibly mid-1970s. Edgardo Huertas, personal collection. With thanks to Tristana Rivera.

2. Speaking of the Lacanian term "acting out," Evans writes: "such acting out can be considered 'transference without analysis' or 'wild transference'. He quotes Lacan's

seminar of January 23, 1963. Evans, *An Introductory Dictionary of Lacanian Psychoanalysis*, 3.

3. Lacan, *The Seminar of Jacques Lacan, Book VII*, 141. "For Lacan, the *Thing* is the empty space of thought, the suturing with which the drive imagines that it fills the black hole that always bounces back from the surface of the signifier." Ríos Ávila, *La raza cómica*, 178.

4. *Desnudo total* [Stripped bare] (television broadcast), exact date unknown, circa 1980. Channel 13 of Mexico. The episode was filmed in San Juan. Archivo General de Puerto Rico.

5. Foucault, *"Society Must Be Defended."*

6. Spillers, "All the Things You Could Be by Now," 379.

7. Agamben, "What Is the Contemporary?," 41.

8. Spillers, "All the Things You Could Be by Now," 378.

9. Sterne, "Sonic Imaginations," 3.

10. Agamben, "Philosophical Archaeology."

11. For "distribution of the sensible," see Rancière, *The Politics of Aesthetics*.

BIBLIOGRAPHY

Adorno, Theodor. "On Popular Music." In *Essays on Music*. Edited by Richard Leppert and translated by Susan H. Gillespie, 437–469. Berkeley: University of California Press, 2002.

Agamben, Giorgio. *Homo Sacer: Sovereign Power and Bare Life*. Stanford, CA: Stanford University Press, 1998.

———. "Philosophical Archaeology." *Law and Critique* 20, no. 3 (2009): 211–231.

———. "What Is the Contemporary?" In *What Is an Apparatus? And Other Essays*, 39–54. Stanford, CA: Stanford University Press, 2009.

Aparicio, Frances. *Listening to Salsa: Gender, Latin Music, and Puerto Rican Popular Culture*. Hanover, NH: Wesleyan University Press, 1998.

Auslander, Philip. *Liveness: Performance in a Mediatized Culture*. London: Routledge, 1999.

———. "Musical Personae." *TDR: The Drama Review* 50, no. 1 (2006): 100–119.

Austin, J. L. *How to Do Things with Words*. Cambridge, MA: Harvard University Press, 1975.

Babín, María Teresa. "The Inhabitants: Indians, Negroes, Jíbaros, and Creoles." In *The Puerto Rican's Spirit: Their History, Life, and Culture*, 27–66. New York: Collier, 1971.

Barthes, Roland. "Change the Object Itself: Mythology Today." In *Image, Music, Text*, 165–169. New York: Hill and Wang, 1977.

———. "The Grain of the Voice." In *Image-Music-Text*, 179–189. New York: Hill and Wang, 1977.

Bartra, Roger. *The Cage of Melancholy: Identity and Metamorphosis in the Mexican Character*. New Brunswick, NJ: Rutgers University Press, 1992.

Baudrillard, Jean. "Simulacra and Simulations." In *Selected Writings*, 166–184. Stanford, CA: Stanford University Press, 2001.

Benjamin, Walter. "Allegory and *Trauerspiel*." In *The Origin of German Tragic Drama*, 159–235. London: NLB, 1977.

———. "Little History of Photography." In *Selected Writings*, vol. 2, *1927–1934*, 507–530. Cambridge, MA: Belknap, 1999.

———. "The Work of Art in the Age of Its Technological Reproducibility: Third Version." In *Selected Writings*, vol. 4, 251–283. Cambridge, MA: Belknap, 1999.

Berlant, Lauren. *Cruel Optimism*. Durham, NC: Duke University Press, 2011.

—. *The Female Complaint: The Unfinished Business of Sentimentality in American Culture*. Durham, NC: Duke University Press, 2008.

—. "On the Case." *Critical Inquiry* 33, no. 4 (2007): 663–672.

Blanco, Tomás. "Elogio de la plena." In *Antología de ensayos*, edited by Florentino N. Torner, 97–106. Mexico City: Orión, 1953.

Bofill-Calero, Jaime O. "Improvisation in Jíbaro Music: A Structural Analysis." PhD diss., University of Arizona, 2013.

Boggs, Vernon. "Latin Ladies and Afro-Hispanic Music: On the Periphery but Not Forgotten." In *Salsiology: Afro-Cuban Music and the Evolution of Salsa in New York City*. New York: Greenwood, 1992.

Bourdieu, Pierre. *Distinction: A Social Critique of the Judgement of Taste*. Cambridge, MA: Harvard University Press, 2000.

Briggs, Laura. *Reproducing Empire: Race, Sex, Science, and U.S. Imperialism in Puerto Rico*. Berkeley: University of California Press, 2002.

Brooks, Daphne. "Afro-Sonic Feminist Praxis: Nina Simone and Adrienne Kennedy in High Fidelity." In *Black Performance Theory*, edited by Thomas F. DeFrantz and Anita González, 204–222. Durham, NC: Duke University Press, 2014.

Burgos, Julia de. *Desde la Escuela del Aire: Textos de radio teatro escritos por Julia de Burgos*. San Juan, PR: Ateneo Puertorriqueño, 1992.

Buscaglia-Salgado, José. *Undoing Empire: Race and Nation in the Mulatto Caribbean*. Minneapolis: University of Minnesota Press, 2003.

Canino, Marcelo. "Trovadores, improvisadores, versificadores y cantadores." In *La gran enciclopedia de Puerto Rico*, vol. 12: *Folklore*, 115. Madrid: Ediciones R, 1976.

Carpentier, Alejo. "Del folklorismo musical." In *Tientos y diferencias*, 41–56. Montevideo: Arca, 1967.

—. *La música en Cuba*. In *Obras completas XII*. Mexico City: Siglo XXI Editores, 1987.

Cavarero, Adriana. *For More Than One Voice: Toward a Philosophy of Vocal Expression*. Stanford, CA: Stanford University Press, 2005.

Chion, Michel. *The Voice in Cinema*. New York: Columbia University Press, 1999.

Colón Zayas, Eliseo. "Imagen discográfica e identidades: El caso de Lucecita Benítez." *Animus: Revista Interamericana de Comunicação Midiática* 11, no. 2 (2003): 88–103.

Connor, Steven. "Edison's Teeth: Touching Hearing." In *Hearing Cultures: Essays on Sound, Listening, and Modernity*, edited by Veit Erlmann, 153–172. Oxford: Berg, 2005.

Costa, Marithelma. "Ruth Fernández: Quien nunca entró por la puerta de atrás." *Resonancias: La Revista Puertorriqueña de Música* 2, no. 4 (2002): 26–33.

Dávila, Arlene M. *Sponsored Identities: Cultural Politics in Puerto Rico*. Philadelphia: Temple University Press, 1997.

Debord, Guy. *The Society of the Spectacle*. New York: Zone, 1995.

Deleuze, Gilles, and Félix Guattari. *Anti-Oedipus: Capitalism and Schizophrenia*. Minneapolis: University of Minneapolis Press, 1983.

———. *A Thousand Plateaus: Capitalism and Schizophrenia*. Minneapolis: University of Minneapolis Press, 1987.

Derrida, Jacques. *Voice and Phenomenon: Introduction to the Problem of the Sign in Husserl's Phenomenology*. Evanston, IL: Northwestern University Press, 2011.

Díaz, Carmen Graciela. *Huele a bomba: La paradójica esencia del periodismo de Avance*. San Juan, PR: Ediciones Puerto, 2014.

Díaz-Ayala, Cristóbal. *Música cubana: del areyto a la nueva trova*. Miami: Ediciones Universal, 1993.

Díaz-Quiñones, Arcadio. "Introducción." In *La guaracha del Macho Camacho*, by Luis Rafael Sánchez, 9–73. Madrid: Cátedra, 2000.

Dolar, Mladen. *A Voice and Nothing More*. Cambridge, MA: MIT Press, 2006.

Dudley, Donald R. *A History of Cynicism: From Diogenes to the 6th Century A.D.* New York: Mayo Press, 2008.

Edelman, Lee. *No Future: Queer Theory and the Death Drive*. Durham, NC: Duke University Press, 2004.

Eidsheim, Nina Sun. "Marian Anderson and 'Sonic Blackness' in American Opera." *American Quarterly* 63, no. 3 (2011): 641–671.

Escabí, Pedro C., and Elsa M. Escabí. *La décima: Estudio etnográfico de la cultura popular de Puerto Rico*. San Juan, PR: Editorial de la Universidad de Puerto Rico, 1976.

Evans, Dylan. *An Introductory Dictionary of Lacanian Psychoanalysis*. London: Routledge, 1996.

Felman, Shoshana. *The Scandal of the Speaking Body: Don Juan with J.L. Austin, or Seduction in Two Languages*. Stanford, CA: Stanford University Press, 2003.

Findlay, Eileen. *Imposing Decency: The Politics of Sexuality and Race in Puerto Rico, 1870–1920*. Durham, NC: Duke University Press, 1999.

Foucault, Michel. *Discipline and Punish: The Birth of the Prison*. New York: Vintage, 1995.

———. *Fearless Speech*. Los Angeles: Semiotext(e), 2001.

———. *The History of Sexuality*, vol. 1: *An Introduction*. New York: Vintage, 2012.

———. *The History of Sexuality*, vol. 3: *The Care of the Self*. New York: Vintage, 2012.

———. "Of Other Spaces." *Diacritics* 16, no. 1 (1986): 22–27.

———. "*Society Must Be Defended.*" *Lectures at the Collège de France, 1975–76*. Volume 3. New York: Picador, 2003.

Fox, Aaron A. *Real Country: Music and Language in Working-Class Culture*. Durham, NC: Duke University Press, 2004.

Freud, Sigmund. "The Archaic Features and Infantilism of Dreams." In *Introductory Lectures on Psychoanalysis*, 246–263. New York: Norton, 1966.

———. "Mourning and Melancholia." *The Standard Edition of the Complete Psychological Works of Sigmund Freud*, vol. 14 edited by James Strachey, 243–258. New York: Norton, 1959.

———. "Recommendations to Physicians Practicing Psycho-Analysis." In *The Freud Reader*, 356–363. New York: Norton, 1995.

García, Flavia, Susanne Marte, and Luis Rosario Albert. *WIPR-TV 50 años*. San Juan, PR: Corporación para la Difusión Pública, 2008.

Glasser, Ruth. *My Music Is My Flag: Puerto Rican Musicians and Their New York Communities, 1917–1940*. Berkeley: University of California Press, 1997.

Glissant, Édouard. *Caribbean Discourse: Selected Essays*. Charlottesville: University Press of Virginia, 1992.

Gramsci, Antonio. *Prison Notebooks*. New York: Columbia University Press, 2011.

Griffin, Farah Jasmine. *If You Can't Be Free, Be a Mystery: In Search of Billie Holiday*. New York: Free Press, 2001.

———. "When Malindy Sings: A Meditation on Black Woman's Vocality." In *Uptown Conversation: The New Jazz Studies*, edited by Robert G. O'Meally, Brent Hayes Edwards, and Farah Jasmine Griffin, 102–125. New York: Columbia University Press, 2004.

Gutiérrez, Laura G. *Performing Mexicanidad: Vendidas y Cabareteras on the Transnational Stage*. Austin: University of Texas Press, 2010.

Halberstam, Judith. *Gaga Feminism: Sex, Gender, and the End of Normal*. Boston: Beacon, 2012.

Hamilton, Marybeth. *In Search of the Blues*. New York: Basic Books, 2008.

Harney, Stefano, and Fred Moten. *The Undercommons: Fugitive Planning and Black Study*. Wivenhoe, UK: Minor Compositions, 2013.

Heidegger, Martin. *What Is Called Thinking?* New York: Perennial Library, 1968.

Hernández, Prisco. "Décima, Seis, and the Art of the Puerto Rican Trovador within the Modern Social Context." *Latin American Music Review/Revista de música latinoamericana* 14, no. 1 (1993): 20–51.

Hobsbawm, Eric. *The Age of Extremes: The Short Twentieth Century, 1914–1991*. London: Abacus, 1995.

Kahn, Douglas. "Art and Sound." In *Hearing History: A Reader*, edited by Mark M. Smith, 36–50. Athens: University of Georgia Press, 2004.

Koestenbaum, Wayne. *The Queen's Throat: Opera, Homosexuality, and the Mystery of Desire*. New York: Vintage, 1994.

Kun, Josh. *Audiotopia: Music, Race, and America*. Berkeley: University of California Press, 2005.

Lacan, Jacques. *Anxiety: The Seminar of Jacques Lacan, Book X*. Cambridge, MA: Polity, 2014.

———. *Encore: The Seminar of Jacques Lacan, Book XX: On Feminine Sexuality, the Limits of Love and Knowledge, 1972–1973*. New York: Norton, 1999.

————. *The Seminar of Jacques Lacan, Book I: Freud's Papers on Technique, 1953–1954.* New York: Norton, 1991.

————. *The Seminar of Jacques Lacan, Book VII: The Ethics of Psychoanalysis, 1959–1960.* New York: Norton, 1997.

————. *The Seminar of Jacques Lacan, Book XI: The Four Fundamental Concepts of Psychoanalysis.* New York: Norton, 1998.

————. "Seminar on 'The Purloined Letter.'" In *Écrits*, 11–48. New York: Norton, 2006.

————. "The Subversion of the Subject and the Dialectic of Desire in the Freudian Unconscious." In *Écrits*, 671–702. New York: Norton, 2006.

Laguerre, Enrique A., and Esther M. Melón. *El jíbaro de Puerto Rico: Símbolo y figura.* Sharon, CT: Troutman, 1968.

Lane, Jill. *Blackface Cuba, 1840–1895.* Philadelphia: University of Pennsylvania Press, 2005.

Lazo, Silvia Maria. "Three Facets of Pau Casals' Musical Legacy." PhD diss., University of Montana, 2013.

Lipsitz, George. *Footsteps in the Dark: The Hidden Histories of Popular Music.* Minneapolis: University of Minnesota Press, 2007.

Lluch Vélez, Amalia. *La décima culta en la literatura puertorriqueña.* San Juan, PR: Editorial de la Universidad de Puerto Rico, 1988.

López, Antonio M. *Unbecoming Blackness: The Diaspora Cultures of Afro-Cuban America.* New York: New York University Press, 2012.

López Cruz, Francisco. *La música folklórica de Puerto Rico.* Sharon, CT: Troutman, 1967.

————. *Método para la enseñanza del cuatro puertorriqueño.* San Juan, PR: F. López Cruz, 1980.

Malavet Vega, Pedro. "Música popular en Cuba y Puerto Rico: cinco siglos de intercambio." *La canción popular* 16 (2002): 108–147.

————. "Ruth Fernández." *La canción popular* 16 (2002): 4.

Manuel, Jeffrey T. "The Sound of the Plain White Folk? Creating Country Music's 'Social Origins.'" *Popular Music and Society* 31, no. 4 (2008): 417–431.

Manuel, Peter. *Caribbean Currents.* Philadelphia: Temple University Press, 1995.

Marsh Kennerley, Catherine. *Negociaciones culturales: Los intelectuales y el proyecto pedagógico del estado muñocista.* San Juan, PR: Ediciones Callejón, 2009.

Melamed, Jodi. *Represent and Destroy: Rationalizing Violence in the New Racial Capitalism.* Minneapolis: University of Minnesota Press, 2011.

Miller, Jacques-Alain. *Extimidad: Los cursos psicoanalíticos de Jacques-Alain Miller.* Buenos Aires: Paidós, 2000.

Molloy, Sylvia. "La flexión del género en el texto cultural latinoamericano." *Revista de crítica cultural* 21 (2000): 54–56.

Monod, David. "'Ev'rybody's Crazy 'Bout the Doggone Blues': Creating the Country Blues in the Early Twentieth Century." *Journal of Popular Music Studies* 19, no. 2 (2007): 179–214.

Monsiváis, Carlos. "Bolero: A History." In *Mexican Postcards*, 166–195. London: Verso, 1997.

———. "'Los que tenemos unas manos que no nos pertenecen': A propósito de lo queer y lo rarito." In *Que se abra esa puerta: Crónicas y ensayos sobre la diversidad sexual*, 49–75. Mexico City: Paidós Mexicana, 2010.

Moore, Robin. *Nationalizing Blackness: Afrocubanismo and Artistic Revolution in Havana, 1920–1940*. Pittsburgh: University of Pittsburgh Press, 1997.

Moten, Fred. "The Case of Blackness." *Criticism* 50, no. 2 (2008): 177–218.

Mowitt, John. "The Sound of Music in the Era of Its Electronic Reproducibility." In *The Sound Studies Reader*, edited by Jonathan Sterne, 213–224. New York: Routledge, 2012.

Muñoz, José Esteban. *Cruising Utopia: The Then and There of Queer Futurity*. New York: New York University Press, 2009.

Muñoz Santaella, María Luisa. *La música en Puerto Rico: Panorama histórico-cultural*. Sharon, CT: Troutman, 1966.

Nancy, Jean-Luc. *Being Singular Plural*. Stanford, CA: Stanford University Press, 2000.

———. *Listening*. New York: Fordham University Press, 2007.

Nazario Velasco, Rubén. *El paisaje y el poder: La tierra en el tiempo de Luis Muñoz Marín*. San Juan, PR: Ediciones Callejón, 2014.

Ngai, Sianne. *Ugly Feelings*. Cambridge, MA: Harvard University Press, 2005.

Ochoa Gautier, Ana María. *Aurality: Listening and Knowledge in Nineteenth-Century Colombia*. Durham, NC: Duke University Press, 2014.

———. "Disencounters between Music's Allure and the Expediency of Culture in Colombia." *Latin American Research Review* 48, Special Issue (2013): 12–29.

———. "Sonic Transculturation, Epistemologies of Purification, and the Aural Public Sphere." *Social Identities* 12, no. 6 (2006): 803–825.

Orovio, Helio. *Cuban Music from A to Z*. Durham, NC: Duke University Press, 2004.

Pabón, Carlos. *Nación postmortem: Ensayos sobre los tiempos de insoportable ambigüedad*. San Juan, PR: Ediciones Callejón, 2002.

Party, Daniel. "*Placer Culpable*: Shame and Nostalgia in the Chilean 1990s Balada Revival." *Latin American Music Review/Revista de Música Latinoamericana* 30, no. 1 (2009): 69–98.

Pedreira, Antonio S. "La actualidad del jíbaro." *Boletín de la Universidad de Puerto Rico* 6, no. 2 (1935): 16–19.

Pérez, Marvette. "La Negra de Ponce: Una entrevista con Ruth Fernández, 'El Alma de Puerto Rico Hecha Canción.'" *CENTRO Journal* 16, no. 1 (2004): 61–67.

Picó, Fernando. *Los gallos peleados*. Río Piedras, PR: Ediciones Huracán, 1983.

Quintero Rivera, Ángel. *Salsa, sabor y control: Sociología de la música "tropical."* Mexico City: Siglo Veintiuno Editores, 1998.

Randall, Annie J. *Dusty! Queen of the Postmods.* New York: Oxford University Press, 2009.

Rama, Ángel. *The Lettered City.* Durham, NC: Duke University Press, 1996.

Rancière, Jacques. *The Politics of Aesthetics: The Distribution of the Sensible.* London: Continuum, 2006.

Reina Pérez, Pedro. "Pablo Casals y la 'Operación Serenidad.'" In *Explorando la Operación Serenidad,* edited by Soraya Serra Collazo, 37–48. San Juan, PR: Fundación Luis Muñoz Marín, 2011.

Ríos Ávila, Rubén. *La raza cómica: Del sujeto en Puerto Rico.* San Juan, PR: Ediciones Callejón, 2002.

Rivero, Yeidy M. *Broadcasting Modernity: Cuban Commercial Television, 1950–1960.* Durham, NC: Duke University Press, 2015.

———. *Tuning Out Blackness: Race and Nation in the History of Puerto Rican Television.* Durham, NC: Duke University Press, 2005.

Rodríguez, Olavo Alén, and Ana Victoria Casanova Oliva. "Tras la huella de los músicos puertorriqueños en Cuba." In *La marcha de los jíbaros, 1898–1997: Cien años de música puertorriqueña por el mundo,* edited by Cristóbal Díaz-Ayala. San Juan, PR: Plaza Mayor, 1998.

Rodríguez-Santana, Ivette. "Conquests of Death: Disease, Health and Hygiene in the Formation of a Social Body (Puerto Rico, 1880–1929)." PhD diss., Yale University, 2005.

Roman, Kenneth. *The King of Madison Avenue: David Ogilvy and the Making of Modern Advertising.* New York: St. Martin's Griffin, 2010.

Romero Bravo, Alfredo. "Ruth Fernández: Una leyenda viviente de la música popular." *La canción popular* 18/19 (2004): 44–45.

Rosario Albert, Luis. "*Wonderful Island of Puerto Rico*: La radio y televisión educativas en Puerto Rico (1949–1958)." www.academia.edu.

Santiago, Javier. *Nueva ola portoricensis: La revolución musical que vivió Puerto Rico en la década del 60.* San Juan, PR: Editorial Del Patio, 1994.

Santiago-Díaz, Eleuterio. *Escritura afropuertorriqueña y modernidad.* Pittsburgh: Instituto Internacional de Literatura Iberoamericana, 2007.

Scott, James C. *Domination and the Arts of Resistance: Hidden Transcripts.* New Haven, CT: Yale University Press, 1990.

Serra Collazo, Soraya, ed. *Explorando la Operación Serenidad.* San Juan, PR: Fundación Luis Muñoz Marín, 2011.

Silverman, Kaja. *The Acoustic Mirror: The Female Voice in Psychoanalysis and Cinema.* Bloomington: Indiana University Press, 1988.

Smith, Jacob. *Vocal Tracks: Performance and Sound Media.* Berkeley: University of California Press, 2008.

Solís, Ted. "'You Shake Your Hips Too Much': Diasporic Values and Hawai'i Puerto Rican Dance Culture." *Ethnomusicology* 49, no. 1 (2005): 75–119.

Spillers, Hortense. "'All the Things You Could Be by Now, If Sigmund Freud's Wife Was Your Mother': Psychoanalysis and Race." In *Black, White, and in Color: Essays on American Literature and Culture*, 376–427. Chicago: University of Chicago Press, 2003.

Stavrakakis, Yannis. *Lacan and the Political.* New York: Routledge, 1999.

Sterne, Jonathan. "A Resonant Tomb." In *The Audible Past: Cultural Origins of Sound Reproduction*, 287–332. Durham, NC: Duke University Press, 2003.

———. "Sonic Imaginations." In *The Sound Studies Reader*, edited by Jonathan Sterne, 1–17. New York: Routledge, 2012.

———. "The Theology of Sound: A Critique of Orality." *Canadian Journal of Communication* 36 (2011): 207–225.

Szendy, Peter. *Listen: A History of Our Ears.* New York: Fordham University Press, 2007.

Thompson, Donald. "Film Music and Community Development in Rural Puerto Rico: The DIVEDCO Program (1948–91)." *Latin American Music Review* 26, no. 1 (2005): 102–114.

Thompson, Donald, and Francis Schwartz. *Concert Life in Puerto Rico, 1957–1992: Views and Reviews.* San Juan, PR: Editorial de la Universidad de Puerto Rico, 1998.

Tió Fernández, Teresa. *El cartel de Puerto Rico.* San Juan, PR: Editorial de la Universidad de Puerto Rico, 2003.

Trigo, Benigno. "Anemia, Witches and Vampires: Figures to Govern the Colony." In *Subjects of Crisis: Race and Gender as Disease in Latin America*, 69–89. Middletown, CT: Wesleyan University Press, 2000.

Varela, Mirta. *La televisión criolla: Desde sus inicios hasta la llegada del hombre a la luna, 1951–1969.* Buenos Aires: Edhasa, 2005.

Vargas, Deborah R. *Dissonant Divas in Chicana Music: The Limits of La Onda.* Minneapolis: University of Minnesota Press, 2012.

Vazquez, Alexandra T. *Listening in Detail: Performances of Cuban Music.* Durham, NC: Duke University Press, 2013.

Vega Santana, Rosaura. "Una canción llamada Sylvia." *La canción popular* 16: 3–16.

Venegas Lloveras, Guillermo. *Marzo dos: Una voz para los siglos.* San Juan, PR: N.p., 1991.

Vivoni Farage, Enrique, and Silvia Álvarez Curbelo. *Hispanofilia: Arquitectura y vida en Puerto Rico, 1900–1950.* San Juan, PR: Editorial de la Universidad de Puerto Rico, 1998.

Vogel, Shane. *The Scene of Harlem Cabaret: Race, Sexuality, Performance.* Chicago: University of Chicago Press, 2009.

Wald, Gayle. *Shout, Sister, Shout! The Untold Story of Rock-and-Roll Trailblazer Sister Rosetta Tharpe.* Boston: Beacon, 2007.

Weheliye, Alexander G. *Phonographies: Grooves in Sonic Afro-Modernity.* Durham, NC: Duke University Press, 2005.

Zenón Cruz, Isabelo. *Narciso descubre su trasero: El negro en la cultura puertorriqueña.* Humacao, PR: Editorial Furidi, 1974.

Žižek, Slavoj. "The Undergrowth of Enjoyment: How Popular Culture Can Serve as an Introduction to Lacan." In *The Žižek Reader*, 11–36. Oxford: Blackwell, 1999.

INDEX

Benítez (*continued*)
music criticism of, 210–12; New York performances by, 177–80, 265n68; queerness and, 180, 183, 184, 198, 215, 221, 223, 226; surveillance of, 186–87, 208–16; thinking voice of, 172–80; voice, description of, 194

Berlant, Lauren, 15, 234n12

Best Foreign Artist of Cuba, Silva named as, 35

Billboard magazine, 151

Bing, Rudolf, 68, 84, 241n6

biopolitics: in *jíbaro* music, 127–32, 227–28; of voice, 4–5

bios (Agamben), 133, 141

blackness: as acousmatic, 73, 82, 91, 229; in Afro-Caribbean music and poetry, 73–84; Benítez's embrace of, 186–99, 202–16; commercialization of, 90; cultural marginalization in Puerto Rico of, 125; and exoticism, 75; Fernández's identification with, 89–101, 105–20; as normative, 101; as sonic or auditory, 73, 83–84, 108; in the *tango-congo*, 54, 73

Blanco, Tomás, 73, 95

blues music, racist marginalization of, 129, 252n24

Boggs, Vernon, 241n10

bohemia: in Benítez's music, 223; and the city of Caguas, 157; Fernández and double nature of, 80–81; Reyes, and deviant behavior associated with, 124, 140–41; Reyes, and persona of, 51–53

Bohemia (magazine), 37, 87

Bohemia libre puertoriqueña (magazine), 45, 63

Bola (crystal ball), in Silva's performances, 59–63

Bola de Nieve (Ignacio Villa), 89

bolero, 6; by Fernández, 77–78, 94; Lucecita and, 6, 182–83, 219; Monsiváis on, 239n65; Reyes's performances of, 122, 145, 249n3; Silva as bolero songwriter, 26, 51–52, 53, 63, 66; Silva's marginalization in, 19

bomba, 50, 53; Fernández and, 81, 94, 95, 98, 109, 111; the national-popular and, 125

Books for the People, 136

Boria, Juan, 83

Borinquen canta (television show), 167

Boscana, Lucy, 122

bozal, 82

Brack, Ray, 151

Brau, Salvador, 126

Brisas navideñas (album), 145–51, 167

Brooks, Daphne, 205, 208, 262n34

Brown, Roy, 214, 265n67

bugalú, 55, 98, 132; in Silva's work, 57–59, 114, 132

bugarrón, in Silva's work, 57

Buscaglia-Salgado, José, 254n33

Buscando estrellas (radio show), 177

Bustamante, Bienvenido, 98

Cabán Vale, Antonio "El Topo," 199

cabareteras, in Mexican films, 24

Cabral, Facundo, 195, 212

Caguas, Puerto Rico, 157

Camero, Cándido, 187

"Camina como Chencha" (song, 1961), 39–42

"Camina como Chencha" (song, live performance, 1970s), 65–66

"Camina como Chencha la gambá" (song, 1946), 37, 38, 39, 73

"Camino abandonado" (song), 194–95

"Campanitas de cristal" (song), 122, 249n3

canciones cortavenas, 223–24

Grever, María, 19
Griffin, Farah Jasmine, 115, 233n5
guajiro, 254n33
guaracha, 235n3, 238n49; Silva's affinity
for, 16–20, 24–25, 38
Guillot, Olga, 21, 45–46, 183

Hamilton, Marybeth, 252n24
Hawai'i, Puerto Rican music in, 252n26
Heidegger, Martin, 8, 210, 227, 259n2
"Hello Dolly" (song), 173
Henderson, Mae, 205
Herger, Alfred D., 176–77, 179–80,
184–85, 259n8, 261n19
"Hermano dame tu mano" (song), 199.
See also "Traigo un pueblo en mi voz"
Hernández, Rafael, 19–20, 25, 28, 30,
48–49, 64–65, 77, 99, 114, 149, 168, 223,
226, 228, 249n3
Hernández Colón, Rafael, 116, 182
Hit Parade of Puerto Rico, 181
Hudo, Nana, 200

Instituto de Cultura Puertorriqueña
(Institute for Puerto Rican Culture),
10, 102, 226, 246n73
"I Only Want to Be With You" (song),
173

"jalda arriba" (Muñoz Marín), politics
of, 128
Jalda arriba (PPD anthem), 128, 251n20
"Janitizio" (Revueltas), 98
jíbara, representation of, 132–34
jíbaro, 9, 97, 115, 126, 128, 254n33
jíbaro music: by Benitez, 220; commercial recordings of, 145; in *controversias*, 154–57; gendered discourse on,
139–44; jukebox sales of, 151; as Puerto
Rican national symbol, 126–32

Johnson, Robert, 129
José José (Mexican pop idol), 182
Julio Roqué Orchestra, 19
"Júrame" (song), 19

Kitt, Eartha, 21
Kun, Josh, 233n6

"La Borinqueña" (Puerto Rican national
anthem), 9–10
"La borrachita" (song), 77
La Calandria. *See* Reyes, Ernestina
"La Calandria: An unforgettable sufferer" (Torres Torres), 123–24, 158
La Calandria canta . . . (album), 151–54
La Calandria, "en salsa" (album), 168–70
*La Calandria Wishes You a Merry Christ-
mas* (album), 168
Lacan, Jacques: ethics, 12, 64; extimacy,
34, 72, 133, 238n54; "full emptiness,"
in Silva's work, 37, 40, 63; gap, 238n42;
letter, 34, 71, 108, 238n38; linguisterie,
82–83; part-object, 8, 45, 66, 234n13,
238n38; "policy of the ostrich," 71; real,
60; signifierness, 34, 36, 41, 237n37;
sinthome, 66; Thing, 227, 267n3
La correspondencia (radio program), 122
La Escuela del Aire (radio program), 127
"La finquita de La Calandria" (song), 155
La hora del volante (radio program), 121,
123
"La infortunada" (song), 158, 162–67, 170
"La jíbara se va" (song), 148–49
La Lupe, 5, 21, 53, 218
Lamarque, Libertad, 5, 87, 91–92
"Lamento borincano" (song), 114, 115
"Lamento de un boricua" (song), 76–77,
115
La Montaña Canta (radio program), 157
Landestoy, Rafael "Bullumba," 111

Orovio, Helio, 88–89
Orquesta Sinfónica de Puerto Rico
    (Puerto Rico Symphony Orchestra),
    102
Ortiz, Carmen, 122–23, 141, 144, 158
Ortiz, José Ángel, "El Jíbaro de Yauco,"
    141–42
Ortiz, Mario, 168–69
Ortiz Piñero, Francisco, 136
Osorio, Ramón, "Moncho," 157, 257n60
"Oubao Moin" (song), 214–15

Pabón, Carlos, 215
Palés Matos, Luis, 73
Pan-Americanism, 91; Fernández, musi-
    cal representation of, 98–101
Pan-Latino aesthetic: in Fernández,
    Lewisohn concert, 98; in jíbaro music,
    134; in U.S. music industry, 23–24
parlando (speech-song), 12; Silva's use of,
    27–28, 30, 54, 57–58, 228
Parra, Violeta, 6
parrhesia (Foucault), 12, 204, 240n75,
    263n49
Partido Popular Democrático (PPD). See
    Popular Democratic Party
Partido Socialista Puertorriqueño (PSP),
    199–200
Party, Daniel, 217
pava, 97, 115,134, 145, 152, 167
Pavone, Rita, 183
Pedreira, Antonio S., 126, 132, 251n15
Peña, Lito, 98, 109, 119–20
Pérez, Martha, 98, 147
Pérez, Marvette, 68, 103, 106
Pérez, Perla, 147–48
Pérez Glass, Mercedes, 151
Pérez Prado Orchestra, 37
Picó, Fernando, 133
pie forzado, 123

"Piénsalo bien" (song), 77
Playboy magazine, Latino protests
    against, 17
plena, 50; Blanco's characterization of,
    73, 95; Fernández and, 81–84, 94, 95,
    109, 111; the national-popular and, 125
poesía afroantillana (Afro-Antillean
    poetry), 72, 82–84, 93–94
politics: in Benítez's music, 199–216;
    Fernández and, 13, 70–71, 101–13,
    114–18
Ponce, Puerto Rico, music culture of, 75,
    80–81, 93, 91, 114, 116, 243n30
Ponce Massacre, 67
"Po Po Po" (song), 82–84
Popular Democratic Party (Puerto Rico):
    anthem of, 128, 251n20; Fernández
    and, 70–72, 91–92, 114–20, 227;
    governmentality and, 44; origin nar-
    rative of Puerto Rican culture and,
    129, 254n36; pava symbol used by, 97,
    134; political marketing and, 117–18,
    244n53; race policies of, 71, 77, 101,
    254n35; Reyes and, 121, 137–44
popular music: Adorno opinion of,
    242n27; Casals opinion of, 247n75;
    changed Puerto Rican sound-
    scape of, 180; DIVEDCO films and,
    255n38; Fernández and debates over
    twentieth-century role of, 93–100;
    ELA (Estado Libre Asociado) project
    and, 10, 44, 80, 90; evolution of com-
    mercialized jíbaro music and, 128–32;
    gender and accounts of, 5, 7,18, 21, 141;
    grid of identity as, 116; Latin Ameri-
    can women in, 2–5; thought in, 14
"Por algo será" (song), 35–37
Pozo, Chano, 32, 237n31
"Preciosa" (song), 49
Puente, Tito, 53